Disinformation

Disinformation

The Nature of Facts and Lies in the Post-Truth Era

Donald A. Barclay

WITHDRAWN

ROWMAN & LITTLEFIELD
Lanham • Boulder • New York • London

Published by Rowman & Littlefield
A wholly owned subsidiary of The Rowman & Littlefield Publishing Group, Inc.
4501 Forbes Boulevard, Suite 200, Lanham, Maryland 20706
www.rowman.com

86-90 Paul Street, London EC2A 4NE

British Library Cataloguing in Publication Information Available

Library of Congress Cataloging-in-Publication Data
Names: Barclay, Donald A., author.
Title: Disinformation : the nature of facts and lies in the post-truth era / Donald A. Barclay.
Description: Lanham : Rowman & Littlefield, [2021] | Includes bibliographical references and index.
Identifiers: LCCN 2021037908 (print) | LCCN 2021037909 (ebook) | ISBN 9781538144084 (cloth) | ISBN 9781538144091 (ebook)
Subjects: LCSH: Information technology--Moral and ethical aspects. | Disinformation. | Truthfulness and falsehood.
Classification: LCC ZA3073 .B37 2021 (print) | LCC ZA3073 (ebook) | DDC 303.48/33--dc23/eng/20220103
LC record available at https://lccn.loc.gov/2021037908
LC ebook record available at https://lccn.loc.gov/2021037909

∞™ The paper used in this publication meets the minimum requirements of American National Standard for Information Sciences—Permanence of Paper for Printed Library Materials, ANSI/NISO Z39.48-1992.

With love to Caroline, Tess, Emily, and Alexandra.
And with the hope that, wherever they may be,
Rich and Roscoe are there together.

Contents

Acknowledgments

So many people to thank. Let's start with Charles Harmon and Erinn Slanina of Rowman & Littlefield, who keep me always honest and always on task. Professor Jeffrey Yoshimi of the University of California, Merced, who was unbelievably gracious and helpful as I was writing the chapter on philosophy (though everything that may be off the mark in that chapter is entirely my own fault and must not in any way be attributed to Jeff). I of course need to thank friends who quite voluntarily agreed to read draft chapters, an act which I always find immensely encouraging during the long slog of writing a book: Bruce Miller, Phillip Kreck, Claudia Lange, Steve Corbett, Tom Morgan, and Jan Wilbur Morgan.

Finally, thank you to Caroline for putting up with my COVID book and for all those stimulating early morning conversations about the latest chapter as we walked Olive on Bear Creek. I could not have done it without both your love and your tolerance for my writing hobby.

Preface

"There are years that ask questions and years that answer."

          –Zora Neale Hurston, *Their Eyes Were Watching God*[1]

IS TRUTH DEAD?

The starkly composed cover of *Time Magazine* for April 8, 1966, consisted of a jet-black background on which a bold red font asked a shocking question: "Is God Dead?" Intentionally provocative, and soon to become iconic, this cover generated a powerful reaction, including thirty-five hundred letters to the editor, more than for any other issue of *Time* in its history.[2] Almost every letter was an expression of outrage.

Just over a half century later, the April 3, 2017, cover of *Time Magazine* employed the exact same colors, font, and layout used on the April 8, 1966, cover to ask a different provocative question: "Is Truth Dead?"

As might be expected, the 2017 reaction to *Time*'s question was over-whelmingly digital—no need for paper, envelopes, stamps, or the approval of an editor to get your opinion out there for others to (possibly) see. There may have been, in 2017, far more than thirty-five hundred written responses to the "Is Truth Dead?" issue of *Time*, but those responses were droplets lost in the ocean of words that is the digital discourse. In the twenty-first century, a born-analog newsmagazine does not generate the buzz it did back in a time when reading meant ink-on-paper, most people in the United States had a choice of no more than three television channels, and the internet was a vague idea of something that could possibly someday become a reality. In whatever way you measure it, the reaction to the 2017 cover was muted compared to the reaction to the 1966 cover, and as a catalyst for generating a cultural uproar the "Is Truth Dead?" issue of *Time* does not hold a candle to that of the "Is God Dead?" issue. It may be that people have simply grown that much harder to shock over the last fifty years. Or maybe the question "Is Truth-Dead?" did not shock—or even surprise—anyone in the year 2017. By the time the "Is Truth Dead?" cover appeared, Oxford Languages had already selected *post-truth* as the Word of the Year for 2016.[3]

Cultural uproar or not, "Is truth dead?" is a valid question in a time when phrases like "alternative facts" are uttered with straight faces, science is dismissed as nothing more than someone else's politically motivated opinion, and it has become positively yawn worthy to see public figures shrugging off *prima facie* evidence of their own wrongdoing as "fake news." On the other hand, it is possible that the present day is not so different from the past. Considering that lies, deception, and propaganda have been around for millennia, it may be the case that our sophisticated technology has simply made it possible for the average person to be exposed to far more lies, deceptions, and propaganda than at any time in the past. When it comes to the reporting of news by journalistic (and pseudo-journalistic) sources, we may be experiencing a return to an unapologetically nonobjective news media following a fairly short-lived period in which objective journalism has been the expectation (at least in those countries where media is not under direct government control). It was not until the 1920s that "modern analytical procedures and fairness" became the norm for journalism,[4] as before that time essentially all sources of news reflected one partisan point of view or another, making no pretense at being objective in their reportage of news and events. A return to that older model may be inevitable in a world in which journalism has been so consistently savaged in pursuit of political and financial goals that the entire concept of objective journalism has come to be regarded as, at best, a failed experiment or, at worst, a joke. There is also the growing recognition that the most profitable sources of news and opinion—whether giant cable news networks or lone YouTube political commentators—are highly partisan and frequently strident. In an unaired interview conducted in 2019, Dutch historian Rutger Bregman accused a popular cable news personality of being a "millionaire funded by billionaires."[5] While the accusation infuriated the program's host, from an entirely cynical, money-driven perspective, it is a fair question to ask how many aspiring journalists, pundits, and online celebrities would choose to go broke reporting the objective truth—or at least something as close the objective truth as imperfect human beings can get—for the benefit of the few when it is possible to get rich being unobjectively partisan to the delight of the millions.

It was the furor over fake news that arose during the U.S. elections of 2016 that inspired me to write *Fake News, Propaganda, and Plain Old Lies: How to Find Trustworthy Information in the Digital Age*, a book that was published in mid-2018. In *Fake News, Propaganda, and Plain Old Lies*, I tried to take an objective (at least as close as I could get to objective) approach to evaluating the credibility of information. In the opening chapter of that book, I related the story of a young man who walked into Comet Pizza in Washington, DC, while carrying a rifle. Operating entirely on uncredible information, the young man had come in search of a child sex ring allegedly run by Hilary Clinton and other leaders of the U.S. Democratic Party. The would-be hero ended up firing three harmless shots before being arrested and taken to jail. That all seems like a very long time ago.

I signed the contract for the book you are reading now in December 2019. While I was writing it, a few noteworthy events unfolded right before the eyes of the world, events that make the Comet Pizza fiasco look like a bit of slapstick comedy. The first noteworthy event was the COVID-19 pandemic and the massive reaction against credible information it set off. A virus—a *submicroscopic infectious agent*—was politicized almost from the moment it was discovered, as was every bit of the scientific information that was shared about the, I repeat, *submicroscopic infectious agent*. Even as I write this, in June 2021, there remains a significant movement to deny the safety and effectiveness of COVID-19 vaccines despite the overwhelming evidence that the vaccines are not only safe, but also are even more effective than public health experts had predicted. The title of a multiauthor opinion piece published in the December 2020 issue of the *Journal of the Association for Information Science and Technology* sums up the situation most precisely: "Global Health Crises Are Also Information Crises."[6] (For the record, I caught the COVID-19 virus in December 2020, was sick at home for three weeks, and consider myself to have gotten off easy. I got vaccinated as soon as I was eligible.)

The second noteworthy event to unfold while I was writing this book was the takeover of the U.S. Capitol Building by several hundred people who believed, without any credible evidence to support their belief, that voter fraud had stolen the election from Donald Trump. That last sentence may sound political, but I would like to repeat the key words it contains: *without any credible evidence*. Is it possible that the election was stolen? Anything is possible. Is there any credible evidence that it was stolen? None has emerged so far. Could such evidence emerge in the future? Again, anything is possible. However, the standard of "anything is possible" is a very low bar indeed. Is it possible that ten years from now everyone who got a COVID-19 vaccine will develop Tourette syndrome? Sure. It is *possible*. But it is just as possible that everyone who got the COVID-19 vaccine will live in perfect health to well beyond the age of one hundred years. The point is that *possible* is not the same as *certain*. It is not even the same as *probable*. Making a decision or, especially, taking an action based on credible evidence is wisdom; doing either of those things based on nothing more than your gut feelings and the fact that your feelings rise to meet the extremely low bar of "anything is possible" may be the ultimate expression of unchecked egotism. One of the unintended consequences of the fast, cheap, and good communications brought about by digital technology is that all this technology has somehow facilitated a too-loving embrace of the *possible* in the popular imagination. It is fun to speculate on what is possible: *"Since it is* possible *that I could win the Powerball Lottery, this is what I would do with my $450 million."* The entire genre of science fiction is based on speculation about what is *possible*, and science fiction can certainly be a lot of fun. But making crucially important decisions based on mere speculation, on the facile truism that "anything is possible," is guaranteed to ultimately produce consequences that are the opposite of fun.

A third significant event took place as I was writing this book, though it was one that did not make any headlines. Someone who I and my family loved and enjoyed being around took his own life. Though this person had struggled for much of his life with depression, the final straw may have been the oppressive emotional weight of the various conspiracy theories and politically motivated disinformation to which he had become vulnerable as he spiraled ever deeper into depression and despair. That he took his own life on January 20, 2021—Inauguration Day in the United States—was not entirely coincidental. Though I would never say that he died of fake news, I am convinced the emotional turmoil generated by the relentless clatter of the post-truth culture was a contributing factor in his death. This single death, though unnoted by most of the world, brought home to me on a personal level something I already knew on an intellectual level: that the abuse and misuse of information in the pursuit of power, profit, and celebrity can have truly devastating consequences, that all the word games and mind games of the post-truth culture are not harmless fun and must not be treated as a source of carefree entertainment for bored people with nothing better to do. In the Information Age, information can become a tool that humanity uses to improve the quality of life for everyone and everything on the planet, or it can become a weapon with which humanity will eventually destroy itself.

DEFINING A FEW TERMS

I struggled with a phrase to frame the concept of life in a world where truth, at worst, no longer matters or, at best, plays a sorely diminished role in human decision making. The phrase *post-truth world* seemed like an overstatement in that it may make the current zeitgeist seem like a natural, rather than a human-created, phenomenon. I considered *post-truth climate*, but that carries echoes of the phrase *climate change*, which could be a distraction for some readers. I finally settled on *post-truth culture* on the grounds that, while not a perfect phrase, it places some necessary emphasis on the human element of what we are seeing. Yes, the post-truth culture has been made possible by digital technology, but it is really our human responses to digital technology that have led to the turmoils we are now experiencing. It is important to always remember that the problems of the post-truth culture are problems that we humans created and so are in our collective power to solve.

I have already used the phrase *digital discourse* and will use it again throughout this book. Digital discourse is not a phrase I created out of whole cloth but which, I believe, I am using in a way that is new. Within the covers of this book, when I refer to the digital discourse, I am lumping together all forms of communication that contribute to the post-truth culture. I include as part of the digital discourse not only the obvious candidates—Facebook, YouTube, Twitter, Instagram, TikTok, and the like—but also such heritage analog media as film, television, radio, photography, newspapers, magazines, and books. Even though some of those media still exist, and actually thrive, in their analog forms, each simultaneously coexists in one or more digital formats. The digital discourse is not, however, just about technology. It is also about the people who participate in it, including such familiar types as the boomers of Facebook, the cool kids of Insta and TikTok, and all the assorted academics, politicians, journalists, celebrities, influencers, and streamers—anybody, in fact, who is making themselves heard or seen in the post-truth culture.

ORGANIZATION AND PURPOSE

In writing *Fake News, Propaganda, and Plain Old Lies*, I took a mostly practical, how-to approach to the topic, imagining it as a book that might be used in a high school or college classroom or picked up by a nonstudent adult seeking to get a better handle on evaluating the credibility of information. The present book takes a higher-level, maybe even philosophical, approach by considering how human and technological forces have combined to create the post-truth culture.

- Chapter 1 starts out at an ambitiously high level by surveying major philosophical understandings of the basic concepts of truth itself and then specifically considering how the twentieth-century philosophies of existentialism and postmodernism are influencing the post-truth culture.

The final part of the chapter turns more practical by looking at how philosophers construct logical arguments and how the philosopher's method differs from the way most arguments unfold in the digital discourse.

- Chapter 2 considers how human cognition shapes, and in some ways limits, our ability to process information. This chapter describes a number of the most common cognitive biases and recounts the work of Amos Tversky and Daniel Kahneman in establishing a mathematical connection among cognitive bias, probability, and heuristics. The chapter ends with discussions of the ways in which the human brain is predisposed to harbor cognitive biases and why our brains can remain stubbornly immune to the influence of facts.

- Chapter 3 turns from the human to the technological as it considers how the history of digital technology—including the creation, structure, and early utopian visions of cyberspace—helped lay the groundwork for the conflict that marks the digital discourse and the post-truth culture.

- Chapter 4 attempts to knit together the human foci of chapters 1 and 2 with the technological focus of chapter 3 by looking at how digital technology may be reshaping human cognition. In particular, this chapter considers the ways in which digital technology has pushed the world beyond the Gutenberg Parenthesis into a new age of secondary orality in which the importance of established, recorded facts has been diminished.

- Chapter 5 explores the history of propaganda and its present-day role in the post-truth culture. One goal of this chapter is to describe the principal techniques of propaganda so that readers will be aware when such techniques are being employed. A second goal of this chapter is to suggest ways of dealing with messages that are mixtures of persuasion and propaganda so that the useful and credible content of such messages— assuming there is any—can be separated from what is propagandistic and deceptive.

- Chapter 6 considers the many, sometimes subtle, ways in which the economics of cyberspace and the treatment of information as (increasingly) valuable property influence the creation, distribution, and availability of information. This chapter considers how the concept of intellectual property impacts the creation of, and access to, information (especially access to scholarly information) as well as reviewing the economic foundations of cyberspace.

- Chapter 7 focuses in on the post-truth culture's obsession with conspiracy theories, explaining how conspiracy theories manage to gain footholds in the popular imagination and offering practical tips on identifying them and resisting their allure.

- Chapter 8 ties together a number of the earlier themes of the book by looking at the powerful influence of popular culture—as amplified by digital technology—on the post-truth culture.

When I say that this book takes a philosophical approach, what I really mean is that I hope it helps anyone who reads it think more carefully about the contexts in which information is created, shared, understood, and reacted to; that this book will help readers to be more awake to the idea that that post-truth culture is subject to a variety of influences—historical, technological, economic, and psychological—that are not always obvious and are too often left out of overly simplistic discussions about the digital discourse. This book does not offer clear-cut solutions to the problems we face in a time when facts and truth are easily shoved aside in favor of feelings and biases. It does not offer easily identified villains to blame nor heroes to whom we can turn. In a time when superhero movies routinely do business in the billions of dollars, few of our most pressing problems can be solved by heroes, super or otherwise. In his brilliant, if sadly too-forgotten, comic strip, *Pogo*, the great Walt Kelly (1913–1973) wrote the immortal line, "We have met the enemy and he is us." While the pessimistic reading of this quotation is that we have nobody but ourselves to blame, there is a shred of optimism in the idea that, as the creators of the problem, we possess the power to solve it. In the case of the post-truth culture, we just need to (carefully) think our way out of it. I believe we can think our way out, though I cannot say for certain that we will.

NOTES

1. Zora Neal Hurston, *Their Eyes Were Watching God: A Novel* (New York: Negro Universities Press, 1969), 38.
2. Robert T. Elson, Curtis Prendergast, and Geoffrey Colvin, *Time Inc.: The Intimate History of a Publishing Enterprise*, first edition (New York: Atheneum, 1968), 112.
3. Oxford Languages, "Word of the Year 2016," *Oxford Languages*, accessed March 24, 2020, https://languages.oup.com/word-of-the-year/2016/.
4. Michael Schudson, "The Objectivity Norm in American Journalism*," *Journalism* 2, no. 2 (August 2001): 161.
5. Allyson Chiu, "'Millionaire Funded by Billionaires': Bregman's Fox Clash Goes Viral," *The Sydney Morning Herald*, February 21, 2019, https://www.smh.com.au/world/north-america/millionaire-funded-by-billionaires-bregman-s-fox-clash-goes-viral-20190222-p50zh8.html.
6. Bo Xie, et al., "Global Health Crises Are Also Information Crises: A Call to Action," *Journal of the Association for Information Science and Technology* 71, no. 12 (December 2020): 1419–23.

BIBLIOGRAPHY

Chiu, Allyson. "'Millionaire Funded by Billionaires': Bregman's Fox Clash Goes Viral." *The Sydney Morning Herald*. February 21, 2019. https://www.smh.com.au/world/north-america/millionaire-funded-by-billionaires-bregman-s-fox-clash-goes -viral-20190222-p50zh8.html.

Elson, Robert T., Curtis Prendergast, and Geoffrey Colvin. *Time Inc.; The Intimate History of a Publishing Enterprise*, first edition. New York: Atheneum, 1968.

Hurston, Zora Neal. *Their Eyes Were Watching God: A Novel*. New York: Negro Universities Press, 1969.

Oxford Languages. "Word of the Year 2016." *Oxford Languages*. Accessed March 24, 2020. https://languages.oup.com/word-of-the-year/2016/.

Schudson, Michael. "The Objectivity Norm in American Journalism*." *Journalism* 2, no. 2 (August 2001): 149–70.

Xie, Bo, Daqing He, Tim Mercer, Youfa Wang, Dan Wu, Kenneth R. Fleischmann, Yan Zhang, et al. "Global Health Crises Are Also Information Crises: A Call to Action." *Journal of the Association for Information Science and Technology* 71, no. 12 (December 2020): 1419–23.

1

The Meaning of Truth in the Post-Truth Culture

"To say of what is that it is, or of what is not that it is not, is true."[1]

–Aristotle (385–323 BCE)

A popular sentiment often heard coming from the mouths of politicians, pundits, and the like goes something like this: *"The world needs more welders than philosophers."*

I can agree with that. There are not a lot of jobs to be had down at the old philosophy factory, while it takes armies of welders to create new goods and maintain the existing infrastructure of the physical world we inhabit. What I can't agree with is a variation on the theme that goes: *"The world needs welders* more *than it needs philosophers."*

The world needs philosophers just as much as it needs welders (though, admittedly, far fewer of the former than of the latter). One reason the world needs philosophers is that philosophical ideas and philosophical ways of thinking help us better understand our world and our place in it. More to the point of the struggle to make sense of the monsoons of information to which we are exposed every day, philosophy challenges us to examine ideas and conventions that we might otherwise accept without question. In the famous phrase attributed to the Greek philosopher Socrates (c. 470–399 BCE) by his student Plato (423–347 BCE), "The unexamined life is not worth living."[2]

More specifically, philosophy challenges us to:

- Think carefully about the essence of truth itself and how we can really know anything with certainty.

- Meaningfully question and examine our own beliefs and the underlying assumptions on which they (often precariously) rest.
- Be more consistent in our beliefs.
- Thoughtfully weigh the validity of the ideas, opinions, and ethics of others without losing our own identity in the process.
- Construct arguments in ways that are as enlightening to us as they are to those with whom we disagree.
- Use logic to support our arguments and recognize when others, as well as ourselves, employ faulty logic.

For anyone who has spent much time in the crossfire of ideas, accusations, facts, lies, data, pseudo-data, boasts, and threats that have become the hallmarks of early twenty-first-century's digital discourse, the value of all of the above philosophy-based survival skills should be apparent. The unexamined social media post is, after all, not worth the paper on which it is not printed.

Textbox 1.1
Philosophical Resources

In this chapter, the focus is on what philosophy can reveal to us about the nature of the post-truth culture and how philosophy *might* help us survive the times in which we live without surrendering our sanity or identity. If you are interested in expanding your knowledge of philosophy, a few of your options (short of the best option: enrolling in an in-person philosophy course or two) include:

- Taking an online introductory course in philosophy. Two cost-free examples are:
  - Hank Green's *Crash Course in Philosophy*.[3] This breezy and entertaining course requires seven hours to complete.
  - Coursera's "Introduction to Philosophy."[4] Developed by faculty at the University of Edinburgh, this course requires fifteen hours to complete and is structured more like a traditional college introductory course than Green's less formal *Crash Course*.
- Reading a philosophy textbook that provides a general introduction to the subject. The ideal textbook will be reasonably current and not too specialized in its focus. For anyone who is new to philosophy, a textbook that surveys philosophy across the board is going to be more useful than one that deals exclusively with, say, "the Philosophy of Education" or "the Philosophy of Religion." For two examples, among many, see:
  - Eugene Kelly's *The Basics of Western Philosophy*[5]
  - Richard H. Popkin and Avrum Stroll's *Philosophy Made Simple*[6]

- Accessing online reference works focused on philosophy can also be a useful learning strategy. Some excellent examples include:
  - *Stanford Encyclopedia of Philosophy*[7]
  - *Internet Encyclopedia of Philosophy*[8]
  - "The Basics of Philosophy: A Huge Subject Broken down into Manageable Chunks"[9]

WHAT IS TRUTH?

"You keep using that word. I do not think it means what you think it means."

–Inigo Montoya, *The Princess Bride* (1987)

It is impossible to think about post-truth without first asking, "What is truth?" On the surface, this seems like a simple enough question. Isn't truth either yes or no? Black or white? One or zero? Fact or fiction? Many ancient philosophers, including Plato, insisted that truth (and reality) must be eternal and unchanging. Shouldn't that level of certainty be the standard for truth today? One of the common angry rants encountered in the digital discourse is the demand for media that reports only "facts and truth" without any opinion getting in the way. If only achieving such a goal were as simple as the complainers would have it. It is not simple. The concept of truth is, in fact, so complex that in navigating the chaos of our daily lives we often simplify the chore of sorting the true from the false by resorting to any number of familiar and convenient proofs.

I know a thing is true because . . .
. . . I saw it with my own eyes.
. . . my uncle was there and told me all about it.
. . . I've been doing this for a long time, and, believe me, I know.
. . . that's what I was taught.
. . . it's just common sense.
. . . that's the way it has always been.
. . . I read it somewhere.
. . . I saw it on screen.
. . . it was in the news.
. . . a parent just knows.
. . . it *feels* true.
. . . if it wasn't true, I don't know that I could go on living.
. . . it is the Holy Word of God.

If asked, a philosopher would say that establishing truth is not so simple an undertaking and none of these proofs stand up to rigorous scrutiny. This is not to say that any statement employing one of these proofs could not turn out to be, in the end, true; rather, it is that familiar and convenient proofs such as those listed here are insufficient to establish the truth of anything. (Though exactly that type of convenient, overly simplistic, insufficient proof tends to dominate the digital discourse.) Phenomena such as our senses, intuitions, past experiences, reportage, or the testimony of others do not establish truth to the degree that the rigorous discipline of philosophy demands. The philosopher's discipline is so rigorous, in fact, that the profession has grappled with questions surrounding the concept of truth for well over two millennia without coming up with a perfect answer to the question, *"How do we know a thing is true?"* Historically, whenever a philosopher has made any assertion regarding the essential nature of truth, it has served as an open invitation for other philosophers to challenge that assertion. (Challenging each other's assertions is kind of what philosophers do.) Regarding attempts to generate a simple understanding of truth, philosopher Donald Davidson argues that simple formulas to define truth, of which there are many, all fail to hold up when confronted with counterexamples. Writes Davidson, "We should apply this obvious observation to the concept of truth: we cannot hope to underpin it with something more transparent or easier to grasp."[10] While the professional philosopher's relentless challenging of assertions about the nature of truth does not allow for easy answers, the fact is that if everyone employed the tough mental discipline philosophers employ in their thinking, the post-truth culture might be less of a mess than it currently is.

EPISTEMOLOGY

Although it encompasses a vast and complex field of study, at its most basic level *epistemology* can be defined as the study of knowledge. Philosophers have, for centuries, asked the epistemological questions, "What can we know?" and "How do we know what we know?" In the arena of the digital discourse, if you come across a fact, scientific finding, or statement, it is not a foolish question to ask, "How does anyone know if any of this is true or not true?" While the field of epistemology has produced many theories of how humans gain knowledge and determine what is true or not true, for the purposes of weathering the post-truth culture, we can focus on two main epistemological approaches: *rationalism* and *empiricism*.

RATIONALISM

Closely associated with the philosophers Plato, Rene Descartes (1596–1650), and Immanuel Kant (1724–1804), rationalism is based on the idea that we acquire knowledge solely through the process of reason rather than via the perceptions of our senses. The experience of Descartes, who is widely considered to be the father of modern philosophy, provides an excellent lens through which to examine the basic principles of rationalism. A brilliant mathematician and ground-breaking scientific investigator, Descartes was a key figure of the Enlightenment, the European intellectual and philosophical movement that brought sweeping changes to the way people thought about the world and humanity's place in it. In contemplating how it was possible to know anything with certainty, Descartes concluded for a short time that his senses were incapable of proving the existence of anything, including his own existence. If we perceive the world through our senses, Descartes wondered, and if our sensuous perceptions are then interpreted by our minds, how can we be assured that our senses, our minds, or both are not deceiving us? What if the thing we believe to be the physical world is an illusion, a dream, or a cruel practical joke played on us by an evil demon? This philosophical crisis grew so severe that Descartes came to doubt the reality of his own existence and, at one point, seriously questioned whether he had a physical body. Descartes eventually overcame his crisis by mentally stripping away everything he had acquired through knowledge and experience until the only thing left was his mind. Concluding from this that his ability to think was proof of his existence, Descartes famously declared *"Cogito, ergo sum"* ("I think, therefore I am"). From his new starting point, Descartes rebuilt the reality of his world to, in the end, conclude that God, as the creator of all eternal truths, would not toy with humanity by creating a reality that could not be perceived through the senses. For Descartes, information obtained through the senses can be trusted only after the acuity of the senses had been proven through a process of rational thought.

EMPIRICISM

Closely associated with Scottish philosopher David Hume (1711–1776) and foundational to modern scientific thinking, empiricism is the view that human knowledge comes initially through perception (as when a lab scientist conducts and observes an experiment) and is expanded by logical inferences (as when that same scientist draws conclusions from the results of an experiment). As science and scientific ways of thinking became more prominent, empiricism became the dominant strain of epistemology. For example, in the year 1925 British philosopher G.E. Moore's "A Defence of Common Sense," makes the case for an empirically based understanding of the world. Moore supports his position though such statements as:

> There exists at present a living human body, which is *my* body.
> . . . [my body was] much smaller when it was born, and for some time after-wards, than it is now.
> . . . there have, at every moment since [my body's] birth, been large numbers of other living human bodies . . . and many of these bodies have already died and ceased to exist.[11]

To argue that such commonplaces are real might seem so obvious as to be a waste of breath for a half-baked college freshman, much less one of the leading philosophers of the early twentieth century. However, Moore's position represents a radical departure from the more metaphysical strands of philosophy to which Moore himself had been exposed while a student at Cambridge. Moore's position is the exact opposite of Rene Descartes' doubts about the existence of his own physical body and the need to prove the acuity of the senses through rationalism. In rejecting philosophical thinking that he saw as too esoteric to apply to the ordinary experiences of human life, the empirically minded Moore became one of the foundational figures of Analytical Philosophy, a school of thought that would influence British and American philosophy for much of the twentieth century and into the present day. While it is an oversimplification to say that proponents of Analytical Philosophy believe that seeing (or touching or tasting or smelling) is believing, that statement roughly gets at their central thesis.

SOCIAL EPISTEMOLOGY

The epistemology of both Descartes and Moore can be described as *individual epistemology*—one person seeks to determine what is true, to determine facts without reference to the experience of others. In contrast, *social epistemology*, which came into being as a field of study in the mid-twentieth century, considers how an individual can determine what is true with the help of others. In one sense, social epistemology articulates with scientific thinking in that scientists rely on each other—the scientific community—to establish truth through such processes as peer review and replication studies. In a different sense, social epistemology touches on how truths are created in a digital world where the ideas, opinions, and voices of others can be highly influential. The ways in which the influence of friends and family, experts, and collective group beliefs (as seen in the echo chamber phenomenon) shape thinking and knowledge are examples of questions with which philosophers engage using the techniques and methodologies of social epistemology.

EPISTEMOLOGICAL QUESTIONS IN THE POST-TRUTH CULTURE

As extreme as Descartes' doubts about the ability of his senses to perceive the world may seem, there is scientific evidence that our basic perception of reality is not as accurate as we believe. Experiments conducted by neuroscientists show that human consciousness lags eighty milliseconds in the past.[12] What we perceive with our eyes as real time is, in fact, an illusion created by our brains to compensate for the (very short) lag between the microsecond when our eyes take in visual information and the microsecond our brains require to process that information. In effect, we are always living in the (extremely recent) past even though we perceive what we are seeing as the present. Without realizing it, we have all been time traveling since the day we were born.

An eighty-millisecond lag is not enough to impact the physical world in which (philosophical crises aside) we live our daily lives. After all, skilled batters can hit fastballs traveling at one hundred miles per hour, and even average drivers can negotiate traffic at freeway speeds without leaving trails of destruction in their wakes. What can, and occasionally does, impact life in the physical world is becoming so uncertain of how we know anything at all that, like Descartes, we spiral into the deepest levels of doubt regarding the reality of existence. Our own as well as that of others. Philosophically, it is not a silly question to ask how we know anything—important or insignificant, abstract or concrete—with any certainty. How do we *really* know there ever was such a place as ancient Athens? An individual named David Hume? A language called English that is spoken and mutually understood by approximately 1.5 billion people around the world? How do we know that our being and existence are real? In popular culture, the anxiety produced by such questions is seen played out in films like *Blade Runner* (1982), *The Matrix* (1999), and *The Truman Show* (1998). But anxieties of this sort are not just the stuff of movies. In 2012, a scientific journal article entitled "The 'Truman Show' Delusion: Psychosis in the Global Village" reported on five patients who believed that their daily lives were being filmed to be broadcast as entertainment for the public.[13]

To reach the point of completely doubting the reality of not only your own life but also the lives and others—and, especially, to believe that other people are so unreal as to lack thought, emotion, and agency—opens up the possibility of becoming incapable of feeling empathy for any other living creature.

At its worst, such thinking moves into the dark territories of psychopaths and war criminals. An example of how, in the post-truth culture, our trust in the fundamental reality of other persons can be undermined is illustrated by the problem presented by tweets and other digital communications that purport to be from human beings but which are actually generated by computer algorithms. In such a climate of doubt, it becomes convenient to dismiss any communication that contradicts our beliefs as machine-generated propaganda. While it is good to be wary, mistakenly dismissing a human-generated communication as the work of a machine has the effect of dismissing the reality of the person who created it.

In the post-truth culture, two common, yet contradictory, ways in which anxiety over the epistemological challenges of knowing what is real/true and unreal/false are manifested in, first, the hard-core nihilist's rejection of any and all information presented as truth and, second, the gullible conspiracy buff's willingness to reject the most credible of information while eagerly embracing that which is least credible. For if we cannot say with absolute certainty how we know what we know, if we cannot pin down *the truth* and know that our belief in it is justified, how are we supposed to believe in anything? And if no truth can be proven to us to with absolute certainty, is not then every truth (no matter how fatuous) equal? How do we know for certain that we, like the androids in *Blade Runner*, are not living with implanted memories that cause us to believe we were born and had childhoods when we, in fact, emerged from some factory in adult form? How do we know, really, that the batter we see hitting a blazing fastball is not a mass hallucination? How do I, as a writer, know that words printed on this page mean (even approximately) the same thing to every English speaker who reads them? For anyone living under a lowering cloud of epistemological doubt, talk of such things as "alternative facts" starts making way too much sense. And if reality is all lies and illusions, why not pick the lies and illusions that best suit your mood and most conform to your existing biases? Isn't that what seeking your bliss is all about?

On at least one level, philosophers address the fundamental epistemological question of how we know what is true or not true as a way of insulating humanity (and themselves) from the emotional chaos that ensues when philosophical doubt loosens an individual's sometimes tenuous grip on reality. Experiencing a total lack of confidence in the concepts of reality and truth is like being lost in rowboat in the middle of a dark ocean with no GPS, compass, or stars to steer by. Any direction in which you point your prow seems as good as another, though some directions lead to land and safety while others lead even further out to sea and ruin. The undermining of reality, whether an intentional or unintentional consequence of the digital discourse, may in part explain how the post-truth culture came to exist in the first place. Intentionally instilling epistemological doubt by undermining confidence in the nature of reality is a technique that can be, and has been, used to influence the thinking of others and, in the worst cases, to lead others out to sea under the guise of pointing them to shore. The act of gaslighting someone as a prank is a relatively lightweight example of undermining an individual's grasp on reality. In his essay "I Quit," science-fiction author and activist Cory Doctorow considers the more serious case of manufacturing doubt for propagandistic purposes, "The pandemic revealed the high price of epistemological chaos, of replacing informed debate with cynical doubt. Argue with an anti-vaxer and you'll soon realize that you don't merely disagree on what's true—you disagree on whether there is such a thing as truth, and, if there is, how it can be known."[14] Most extreme are the notorious totalitarian re-education programs that rely on convincing those who fall into their clutches that all previous ways of thinking were not merely wrong, but so completely based on untruths as to be the opposite of truth. The goal of such re-education programs is not merely to impose a new, officially approved version of the truth, but to reset the dial on the way truth is perceived, to disrupt the basic understanding of how anyone knows anything to the point that the individual's essential perception of reality has been transformed.

Convincing anyone that the entirety of reality as they know it is a figment—*"Everything you know is wrong!"*—is a tall order. Even those regimes that employ isolation, starvation, sleep deprivation, and other physically coercive techniques as part of their re-education programs do not achieve complete transformations of every individual. Among psychologists who study mind control, the idea that people can be completely brainwashed is at best controversial and at worst considered the product of either political paranoia or hack writers looking for a convenient plot device. On the other hand, instilling enough doubt in the nature of reality to persuade another person to seriously question, and possibly disavow, some significant part of what they have always accepted as true is a more achievable outcome. "*I used to completely believe* This One Thing. *But now that I've been exposed to the real truth, I believe* This Other Thing *that turns out to be the exact opposite of what I once believed*," is a common enough claim among some of the loudest partisans shouting in the echo canyons of the digital discourse. For partisans, a radical turned hardcore-conservative or a hardcore-conservative turned radical comes off as more credible than those whose political views have been more or less consistent throughout their lives.

For a simple example of how doubt in the nature of reality is instilled, suppose I set out to convince you of the benefits of my amazing, all-organic, all-natural wonder supplement by undermining your confidence in scientific medicine. To achieve this outcome, I might ask such questions as:

- How can you prove that everything you've ever been told about so-called scientific medicine is not a carefully manufactured lie promoted by the elites of business, education, and the government?
- What proof is there that the medical establishment, including physicians and Big Pharma, are not involved in a conspiracy to hide the truth about natural remedies so that the medical-industrial complex can turn huge profits from unnatural medicines and invasive medical procedures that actually make people sicker?
- How can you trust the so-called results of clinical studies when they are created by same crooked physicians who are part of, and profiteering from, the conspiracy against natural remedies? Were you present to witness that the studies were done properly? Do you even know enough about science to tell if you are being misled?
- If scientific medicine is so great, why do so many people die in hospitals or overdose on prescription medicines?

If my points seem convincing, it is because there is always an element of truth, no matter how tenuous, to any questions directed toward anything that falls short of perfection, including the imperfect (if quite remarkably successful) human endeavor that is modern scientific medicine. Also, note that my list of questions does not provide one bit of proof that my amazing wonder supplement actually works. I do not need to provide affirmative proof if I make my case entirely by undermining your confidence in whatever it is I am trying to turn you against. It can be difficult to resist when skillfully assaulted with a broadside of philosophical doubt. The best defense is to recognize when such tactics are being used and to remember that any *"How can you really know . . .?"* statement also applies to the person asking the question. For example, one perfectly reasonable response to a question such as, *"How do you really know the Earth is a sphere?"* is the question, *"How do you know it is not?"* It may also help to remember that philosophers have been asking, *"How can you really know?"* for centuries without coming up with an answer that satisfies everyone all the time.

CONTINENTAL PHILOSOPHY IN THE POST-TRUTH CULTURE

While it is an oversimplification, it is reasonably correct to divide present-day philosophers into one of two schools: Analytical Philosophy and Continental

Philosophy. *Analytical Philosophy* originated largely in Great Britain and North America and traces its roots back to such philosophers as Ludwig Wittgenstein (1889–1951), Bertrand Russell (1872–1970), and G.E. Moore. The foundations of Analytical Philosophy are math and logic, its approaches and methods are more closely aligned to the sciences than to humanistic studies, and the philosophers of this school tend analyze problems outside of any historical context. Continental Philosophy, on the other hand, originated largely in continental Europe and traces its roots back to such philosophers as Georg Wilhelm Friedrich Hegel (1770–1831), Friedrich Nietzsche (1844–1900), and Martin Heidegger (1889–1976). Continental philosophers tend to reject the objectivity/authority of the natural sciences and to take an approach that considers how factors like time, language, history, and culture shape human understanding and knowledge. Continental Philosophy encompasses a number of subfields, of which two resonate strongly in the post-truth culture: existentialism and postmodernism.

Existentialism

Existentialism is a school of philosophical thought closely associated with French philosopher Jean Paul Sartre (1905–1980) and the philosophers and writers in his circle. While existentialism's roots extend back to such philosophers as Friedrich Nietzsche, Soren Kierkegaard (1813–1855), and even Aristotle, existentialism in its current form emerged from the ashes and disillusionment of the Second World War. The central tenet of existentialism is that human beings are not born with any predetermined purpose (as reflected in Sartre's existentialist credo "existence precedes essence"[15]) and so are free to make choices that shape the course and meaning of their lives. The latter idea is reflected in Sartre's assertion, "Man is condemned to be free,"[16] a concept he found to be both liberating and terrifying. For Sartre and his fellow existentialists, the futility of life in a meaningless and indifferent universe can be transcended only by making choices that are authentic to one's genuine self.[17] Existentialism values honesty, bravery, individuality, and taking responsibility for one's actions and choices while being opposed to acts of "bad faith" in which a person somewhat automatically follows a path set down by others (peers, parents, teachers, governments, clerics) without considering alternatives. If the values of existentialism sound a lot like the personal codes of countless heroes of film and fiction, it is because the "existentialist hero" has become a stock character in mass entertainment, readily recognizable to millions who have never so much as considered opening a book of philosophy. Pop culture examples of existentialist heroes include most superheroes (Batman is the exemplar), the various hardboiled detectives of *film noir*, cowboys (of both the horse-riding and spaceship-flying variety), bikers, loners, iconoclasts, flinty antiheroes, and every disgusted-but-righteous cop who has resigned from the force by ritualistically thumping down his badge on the chief's desk.

Whether it is cause or effect, the existentialist hero is just one part of an ongoing cultural trend that has seen the individual elevated to a level of importance that would be inconceivable to people from more self-effacing cultures and times. In the digital discourse, you are less likely to hear someone positively described as "modest," "quiet," or "self-effacing" than you are to hear them positively described as "outrageous," "in your face," or "unapologetic." While it may seem like nothing more than speculation to claim that social media has brought out the self-absorbed narcissist in millions of individuals, there is evidence supporting such a claim. A 2018 meta-analysis of sixty-two studies involving a total of 13,430 subjects found a positive relationship between grandiose narcissism ("the extraverted, grandiose and callous form of narcissism") and each of the following indices:

a. time spent on social media,
b. frequency of status updates/tweets on social media,
c. number of friends/followers on social media, and
d. frequency of posting pictures of self or selfies on social media.[18]

Social scientists Jean M. Twenge and Keith W. Campbell have gone so far as to declare that we are currently living through a "narcissism epidemic," pointing to such indicators as surveys finding that "51% of 18-to-25-year-olds said that 'being famous' was an important goal of their generation" and that nearly one-third of American high school students indicate "they expected to be famous someday."[19] Survey results aside, anyone looking for evidence of narcissistic hyper-individualism in the post-truth culture need look no further than such familiar types as the smack-talking self-promotor who lives to bad-mouth their (real or imaginary) competition, the before-it-was-cool hipster scrambling to remain always in front of whatever is trending, and the social-media unicorn hustling to monetize their self-declared uniqueness.

Viewed through the lens of genuine existentialism (rather than the knock-off, popular-culture version), the many versions of narcissism on display in the digital discourse can be seen as having badly missed the original philosophical point. For an existentialist, the consumerist, advertising-based economic foundation of social media and popular entertainment all but precludes authentic behavior. When everyone with a social media account seemingly has some kind of money-making hustle going on,[20] the possibility of authenticity flies out the window. Such crass commercialism would certainly appall

Sartre, an anticapitalist who considered the amassing of possessions to be antithetical to the pursuit of genuine freedom. Surveying social media in particular, an existentialist would consider the following narcissistic behaviors to be acts of bad faith:

- Measuring your worth as an individual by the number of likes and followers accumulated. The freedom of the individual to make choices is negated when those choices are made with an eye on how others will respond to them.
- Commercializing the qualities that make you (allegedly) unique for the purposes of convincing as many people as possible to emulate (and ultimately consume) your uniqueness. In June of 2021, Googling the phrase "how to be unique" (with quotation marks) returned "about 13,700,000 results," including a long string of YouTube videos providing tips on how to be unique.
- Signifying your individuality through the goods you possess. Whether those goods be unicycles, assault rifles, essential oils, or monster trucks, for an existentialist the absurdity lies in the notion of creating an individual identity through the ownership of products that anyone with enough money can purchase.

"Us loners got to stick together."

–Niki, *Spacehunter: Adventures in the Forbidden Zone* (1983)

It is a stretch to say that existentialism is solely and entirely responsible for the existence of online influencers, reality-show stars, sovereign citizens, or millions of wannabe YouTube and TikTok stars. It is not a stretch, however, to say that the influence of existentialism, however diluted and divergent from its founders' intentions, echoes in the post-truth culture. To put it in political terms, the fingerprints of existentialism can be seen in conservative/libertarian appeals to promote individual freedom as well as in liberal/New Age appeals to embrace the unique specialness of each person.

Postmodernism

Postmodernism is a late-twentieth-century philosophical movement encompassing art, architecture, literary criticism, and philosophy. If you have ever read literary criticism that includes such jargon words as *hermeneutic, poioumena, subaltern,* or *intertextuality* you have encountered postmodernism (aka poststructuralism[21]) firsthand. Developed, for the most part, by French philosophers and literary theorists, postmodernism emerged after the end of the Second World War (though somewhat later than existentialism), coming to prominence in the mid-1970s. The word *postmodernism* is derived from the movement's rejection of modernist ideas about the perpetual progress of humanity through such mechanisms as technology, science, and education. While postmodernism is varied and difficult to put into a box, its outstanding characteristic is its rejection of universal absolutes regarding knowledge, truth, and beauty as well as its replacement of traditional concepts of authority with the idea that authority can come from anywhere and anyone. Or, possibly, from everyone. In his influential essay "The Death of the Author," postmodernist literary critic Roland Barthes (1915–1980) argues against the idea of the author as creative genius and the work of the author as an artifact of unique self-expression. For Barthes, the credit for any writing belongs less to any one individual author and more to the influence of multiple cultural sources. Barthes writes, "The text is a tissue of quotations drawn from the innumerable centres of culture."[22] Expanding on this idea, postmodernism tends to frame everything from literature to architecture to music to human individuality as socially constructed and relative. In the extreme, postmodernism rejects all forms of rational and scientific thinking as the products of cultural bias and political ideology, even to the point of denouncing as forms of oppression such acts as educating others or asserting a statement of fact. (The well-known lyrics of Pink Floyd's "Another Brick in the Wall" are an expression of this aspect of postmodernism.) In his slim but brilliant book *True to Life: Why Truth Matters*, American philosopher Michael Lynch succinctly describes this aspect of postmodernist thinking as "the attitude that objective truth is an illusion and 'truth' is just another name for power."[23] In the post-truth culture, postmodernism is sometimes manifested in the stereotype of the social justice warrior who is quick to identify the forces of racism, sexism, and oppression at work in everything from popular entertainment to everyday language to politics.

While the spirit of postmodernism is liberating in the sense that it rejects passively accepting anything as great or right or beautiful simply because some authority (recognized or self-appointed) has declared it to be so, such thinking can open the door to the kind of anti-intellectualism in which one source of authority is deemed as good as any other, regardless of facts or evidence. While postmodernism is not entirely to blame for the kinds of "balanced" debates in which a person who knows nothing about the subject in question is given equal credence (and screen time) with someone who has studied and researched the subject for decades, some of the blame lies there.

Over the years postmodernist thinking has been, and continues to be, a target of conservative critics, notably Allan Bloom in *The Closing of the American Mind*[24] and Lynne Cheney in *Telling the Truth*,[25] who see the relativism of postmodernism as a rejection of truths established through a centuries-long cultural tradition. The conservative antipathy for postmodernist ideas is not surprising given that the originators of postmodernism—including Barthes, Michel Foucault (1926–1984), Jean-François Lyotard (1924–1998), and Jacques Derrida (1930–2004)—were on the left politically. In addition, many conservatives see postmodernism as antithetical to the artistic and cultural traditions which they consider to be the cornerstones of Western civilization. To such critics, Michael Lynch offers the caution that their sense of cultural superiority "confuses caring about truth with caring about what you believe is certain."[26] Despite this long-standing antipathy, in recent years, some conservatives have adopted the arguments of postmodernism to further such antiscience agendas as creationism and climate-change denial. American philosopher Lee McIntyre makes the case that "there is today such a thing as 'right-wing postmodernism' that uses doubts about truth, objectivity, and power to assert that *all* truth claims are politicized."[27] There is no doubt that the leftist French thinkers whose work shaped postmodernism would be shocked to know that their philosophy is serving the purposes of the conservatism against which they stood in opposition.

In the post-truth culture, both existentialism and postmodernism have produced results that stray quite far from the ideas and ideals on which each was founded. Perhaps the takeaway is that the post-truth culture makes possible the popularization of philosophical concepts from which most of the complexity and nuance has been stripped, transforming what originated as sophisticated ways of thinking about the world into undemanding lifestyle brands that are as easy to acquire and flaunt as anything that can be ordered online for next-day delivery.

ETHICS IN THE POST-TRUTH CULTURE

As a branch of philosophy, Ethics is concerned with such questions as:

What is the definition of right conduct?
How should people act?
How does one live a life that is worth living?

Philosophical systems of ethics have existed for millennia, with such examples as Hedonism, Stoicism, and Humanism having originated in Ancient Greece. Over the centuries, philosophers have proposed far more fields and subfields of ethics than can be covered in this chapter. For example, the field of Normative Ethics, which attempts to develop rules or norms for human action, encompasses many diverse subfields, including Utilitarianism, which defines as right those actions that do the most good for the largest number of people, and Divine Command Theory, which contends that actions are only right if God has decreed them. The field of Applied Ethics, which attempts to apply theoretical ideas about ethics to the real world, includes such subfields as Medical Ethics, Data Ethics, and Business Ethics, whereas the field of Meta Ethics broadly considers questions of how we define right or moral behavior.

Time out. Is there a difference between ethics and morality? Not really. The terms are used interchangeably for the most part. Contemporary philosophers have, to a considerable extent, moved away from morals, or at least the idea of trying to determine any kind of universal rules regarding morals. (It is not so much a case of philosophy having abandoned morality, but morality having abandoned philosophy.) Nonetheless, there are today philosophers actively working on moral questions, such as those working in the subfield of moral epistemology who attempt to answer the question, *"How is moral knowledge possible?"*

Even though ethical questions are at the root of all the big controversies and partisan bickering that characterize the post-truth culture, memorizing every philosophical approach to ethics is not all that helpful. People who express their opinions for the consumption of strangers don't wear t-shirts announcing the school of philosophy from which their ethics originate and, quite likely, could not name the philosophical source of their ethics if asked. Not to mention that an individual's ethics can be such a mash-up of influences that there is no identifiable source from which they originated. What is helpful, if difficult and often humbling, is to think about where our own ethics come from and how consistent, or not, we are in applying them. It is also helpful to acknowledge that other people, including those with whom we disagree, may, by their own standards, be behaving quite ethically even though the foundation on which their ethics are built is at odds with our own ethical bedrock. For example,

- If the managers of a shareholder-owned company can increase shareholder profits by permanently laying off fifty employees, that is the ethical thing to do by the standards of business ethics; even more, not laying off those employees would be *unethical* by the standards of business ethics. For obvious reasons, the laid-off employees and their families would view the managers' behavior as anything but ethical.
- Person A supports strong gun control. Person B believes that individuals have an inalienable right to own firearms. Assume both are operating from an identical ethical principle: Violent crime is a social ill that must

be stopped. Even though their chosen solutions produce conflict, both believe that their chosen solution will fulfill the same ethical goal by, in the language of utilitarian ethics, doing the greatest good for the greatest number of people.

- Most people would agree that lying is, as a general rule, unethical. But, at the same time, most agree that there are times when lying could be seen as ethical. For example, parents routinely lie in order to comfort their children. Telling a worried toddler, *"Nothing bad can happen to you. I will always be here to protect you,"* is a lie, but few would consider it unethical. For a more extreme example, is it ethical to lie to prevent a murder? Most people would say such a lie is ethical because the act of lying is a far less serious and damaging than the act of murder. But what if someone lies to a woman to prevent her from obtaining an abortion? Mostly likely, your evaluation of the ethicality of such a lie depends more on your stance on the ethics of abortion than on the ethics of lying.

ARGUING LIKE A PHILOSOPHER

What do you picture when you think of a philosopher? A bearded, toga-wearing resident of Ancient Greece? A pipe-smoking ivory-tower intellectual who is totally disconnected from the reality of daily life? In whatever way you picture philosophers, the fact is that their highly disciplined ways of thinking have practical applications for anyone trying to make sense of the post-truth culture. Nowhere is this more apparent than in the field of logic, which includes the study of arguments.

Everyone who has spent time online knows what an argument is: An argument is a competitive contest in which two or more people (and occasionally bots) strive to rack up the most likes by coming off as the cleverest or most authoritative or simply the loudest voice in the conflict. Facts, which may or may not be true, are thrown about. Aspersions are cast on a person's lack of sexual experiences (for males) or large number of sexual experiences (for females). Someone's mother is compared to an impossibly large object. F-bombs may or may not be dropped (but probably are). Philosophers mean something very different when they use the word *argument*—and the world would be a better place if the rest of us emulated philosophers when we choose to engage in arguments.

An argument is called for when asked (by others or yourself), *"Why do you believe this conclusion is true?"* To argue in the manner of a philosopher you need to create one or more true *statements* (sentences which can be either true or false) that lead to a logical conclusion.

The following are examples of statements:

Though it is based on actual historical events and the lives of real people, *Hamilton: An America Musical* is a creative work of fiction.

It is too hot to walk the dog this afternoon.

I got a *B* on my physics final.

The following, on the other hand, are examples of nonstatements because they cannot be either true or false:

Did the historical King George the Third ever use the phrase "that little guy" to describe U.S. President John Adams?
(This is a question, not a statement.)

"Do not walk the dog this afternoon."
(This is a command, not a statement.)

What a relief!
(This is an exclamation, not a statement.)

A series of statements do not necessarily make an argument. Someone ranting on social media can make dozens of statements (whether true or false) without formulating anything approaching an argument. Organized logically, though, statements can be used to formulate two principal types of arguments: deductive arguments and inductive arguments.

To formulate a *deductive argument*, you need at least one statement that serves as a *premise* and another that serves as *a conclusion*. A premise is a type of statement that guarantees (i.e., assures the validity of) a subsequent conclusion. Both premises and conclusions must be statements and therefore must be either true or false. The following is an example of a two-statement deductive argument:

First Premise: The air temperature is over ninety degrees Fahrenheit.

Conclusion: It is too hot to walk the dog.

Even when premise and conclusion are combined in a single sentence the result is still a deductive argument:

First Premise: Because the air temperature is over ninety degrees Fahrenheit,

and Conclusion: it is too hot to walk the dog.

Deductive arguments often consist of more than one premise:

First Premise: The sun is shining, and the air temperature is ninety degrees Fahrenheit.

Second Premise: Those conditions mean the temperature of the pavement could be as high as 135 degrees Fahrenheit.

Third Premise: Pavement at that temperature will burn a dog's paws.

Conclusion: It is too hot to walk the dog.

A deductive argument is considered *valid* if the premises guarantee the conclusion:

First Premise: Jane Austen, the British novelist, was seventeen feet tall.

Second Premise: Jane Austen weighed over nine hundred pounds.

Conclusion: Jane Austen was too big to ride a horse.

This deductive argument is valid because the premises guarantee the conclusion. However, because the premises are false, this is an example of an *unsound* deductive argument. To be *sound*, a deductive argument must be valid *and* its premises must all be true.

First Premise: Aretha Franklin was an American musician and civil rights activist.

Second Premise: There are eighty-nine albums of Aretha Franklin's music.

Third Premise: Fifteen of Aretha Franklin's albums have been certified gold, three have been certified platinum, and one has been certified double platinum.

Conclusion: Aretha Franklin was a successful recording artist.

Although the exact definition of "successful recording artist" is open to some level of interpretation, a reasonable person would agree that the premises guarantee the conclusion and, as a result, this is a valid deductive argument. In addition, if each of these premises is true (some fact checking would be required to determine that with confidence), then this deductive argument is both valid *and* sound.

When you encounter a deductive argument, beware of conclusions that are not actually guaranteed by the premises that proceed them. For example:

First Premise: The First Amendment to the U.S. Constitution says, "Congress shall make no law . . . abridging the freedom of speech, or of the press."

Second Premise: Doug is a citizen of the United States.

Conclusion: The Constitution gives Doug the right to say or write any-
                   thing he wants.

That this conclusion is not guaranteed by the premises can be demonstrated
by the use of *counterexamples*. Such as:

- The First Amendment does not give Doug the right to falsely shout, *"The
  passenger next to me has a bomb!"* while flying on a commercial airliner.
- The First Amendment does not give Doug the right to commit libel,
  slander, or perjury.

The important point to be aware of here is that even if someone makes the
case that the premises of their argument are true, as they are in the freedom
of speech example, this alone does not guarantee the conclusion reached from
those premises. While ensuring that the premises of an argument are true is an
important part of thinking critically about an argument, equally important is
trying to think of counterexamples that show the conclusion does not follow
from its (true) premises.

To formulate an *inductive argument*, the premises must make the conclusion *probable* rather than guaranteeing it. Well-formulated inductive
arguments are said to be *inductively strong*, which means their conclusions
are *likely* to be true rather than being unqualifiedly true. The following is
example of a typical inductive argument:

First Premise: The wind was blowing hard all night long.

Second Premise: A number of limbs from the tree by the parking lot were lying
                  on the pavement first thing this morning.

Conclusion: The wind blew the limbs off the tree.

While we do not know for certain that the wind was responsible, the conclusion is so likely that this argument can be considered inductively strong.
    This next example presents a much weaker inductive argument:

First Premise: On Tuesday, over three hundred dollars went missing from
                  the store's cash register.

Second Premise: Kevin was working the cash register on Tuesday.

Third Premise: On Wednesday, Kevin, who is always broke, purchased a
                  new gaming console.

Conclusion: Kevin stole the money from the cash register.

Because this argument is inductive, the conclusion is probabilistic. It suggests that Kevin stole the money, but it does not guarantee that he did. If Kevin went to trial, the prosecutor would likely argue that the three premises (each of which is true) establish Kevin's guilt beyond reasonable doubt. But if you were on the jury and there was no additional evidence against Kevin, could you say with moral certainty that he was guilty beyond a reasonable doubt? Both inside and outside of courtrooms, advocates will often act as if the probabilistic conclusions of inductive arguments carry the same weight of certainty as a sound deductive argument when, under critical examination, they do not. The difference between something being *probably* true and simply true is significant.

One of the things you are not allowed to do when presenting a philosophical argument is to fall back on *logical fallacies*. For example, a statement such as "Anyone who doesn't like 'Stairway to Heaven' is the kind of mouth-breathing idiot who listens to the Black Eyed Peas"

is an example of an "ad hominem" logical fallacy in which the argument is based on insults rather than valid premises.

For another example of a fallacy, a statement such as "My grandfather says 'Stairway to Heaven' is the greatest song of the twentieth century, and he should know because he's been rocking out since the sixties" is an example of the "argument from authority" logical fallacy. Your grandfather, of course, has the right to an opinion, and his opinion may be based on a deep knowledge of rock music, but just because he says something is true does not make it true. There are dozens of logical fallacies and becoming familiar with them will not only help you construct better arguments (by avoiding fallacies, not by employing them in your arguments), it will also help you recognize when others are using fallacies to prop up their arguments. (Warning: Shameless self-promotion ahead.) I devote a chapter to logical fallacies in my previous book, *Fake News, Propaganda and Plain Old Lies*,[28] making it one source you can turn to if you want to learn about fallacies. Alternatively, the Writing Center of the University of North Carolina at Chapel Hill provides a helpful online guide to logical fallacies,[29] and the online *Stanford Encyclopedia of Philosophy* includes a lengthy and detailed article on fallacies.[30]

THE PHILOSOPHY OF RELIGION AND THE POST-TRUTH CULTURE

While most people do not, and possibly cannot, identify the school of ethics that most closely matches their own code of ethics, many people are able, and are often more than willing, to identify their religious orientation, whether that be Southern Baptist, Sunni Islam, or no religion at all. What light, then, can the Philosophy of Religion shed on what is one of the most divisive points of contention in the post-truth culture, not to mention most of human history?

First off, it is important to understand that the purpose of the Philosophy of Religion is not to prove or disprove whether God (or any other Supreme Being) exists. Nor is its purpose to determine whether one religion is better than another. Instead of analyzing doctrinal differences among religious sects, the Philosophy of Religion primarily strives to create a framework which allows both believers and nonbelievers to think mindfully about what they believe and to fully understand and consider the reasons why they choose to believe what they believe (and reject that which they do not). A second purpose of the Philosophy of Religion is to demonstrate how religious belief connects to, yet stands apart from, such social concepts as morality, law, politics, and science. These purposes are, of course, the exact opposite of much of what passes for religious debate in the digital discourse. Religious differences have, in both past and present, spurred wars of the sort that involve sharp implements, explosives, and guns. In the post-truth culture, religious disagreements rarely spur much more than wars of words that rage on endlessly despite the fact that all the clever memes and sick burns under Heaven or Hell are unlikely to shift anyone's religious convictions or alter their opinions on whether there is, or is not, a God. Unlike many proselytizers of the digital discourse, philosophers of religion have never attempted to resolve all religious disagreements once and for all. With those limitations on the table, the basic concepts of the Philosophy of Religion can nonetheless help us better understand the intractable nature of religious disagreements and how those disagreements complicate anything like a universal understanding of truth.

Philosophers of religion use the term *fideism* to describe religious belief based on faith or revelation without the need for any empirical proof, and it is true that faith and revelation are foundational to religious beliefs across the board. For many believers, the idea that existence of God could be proven by empirical evidence is irrelevant and, quite possibly, offensive. The concept of fideism is depicted in the Broadway musical comedy *The Book of Mormon* when the young missionaries sing lyrics stating that, because they are Mormons, they "just believe" in the doctrine of their faith and the existence of God. While the writer of those lyrics may be mocking the concept of fideism, a devout Mormon would not find it at all odd to "just believe." Nor would billions of devout believers from other faiths. And, from a metaphysical perspective, just believing makes as much sense as not believing. The seventeenth-century philosopher Blaise Pascal (1623–1662) illuminated this line of thinking when he developed what has become known as "Pascal's

Wager." Having faith in God is the safe bet, Pascal argues, because if God does exist you get the reward of eternal life, while, if God does not exist, you have lost little or nothing for having believed.

There are, of course, degrees among believers. While it is rare to encounter believers who completely reject reason and empirical evidence on the grounds that all aspects of life should be based exclusively on faith and revealed truth, there are many people of faith who believe that empirical evidence of the existence of God is found in such phenomena as prayer, miracles, the beauty of the natural world, scientific knowledge, and other tangible phenomena. Then there are others who believe that faith applies to religion and philosophy while accepting the role of reason and empirical evidence in other aspects of life. For example, a scientist could be a practicing Christian who accepts as scientific fact the same theory of evolution through natural selection that some other practicing Christians might totally reject as anti-Biblical. Such a scientist would likely agree with the poet Emily Dickinson, who wrote:

"Faith" is a fine invention
For Gentlemen who *see!*
But Microscopes are prudent
In an Emergency![31]

In addition to fideists who accept the existence of a higher power (to one degree or another) on faith, the belief spectrum ranges wide. There are Deists who see God as a noninterfering creator subject to the same natural laws as humans. Agnostics who are unsure to skeptical about the existence of God. Atheists who absolutely reject faith-based belief and the existence of God. And you can add to those enough variations on the theme to inspire countless books, articles, blogs, and YouTube videos. This is not to say that fideists are anything like a united block—a fact evidenced by the planet's multiple religions and billions of faithful, some of whom have been, at various times throughout history (and in the present day), infamously bad at peacefully coexisting with each other. As long as people define truth in terms of fideistic (faith-based) belief, and as long as there exist multiple faiths, there will never be agreement on the basic definition of truth. A Buddhist monk, a Catholic priest, and an atheist may walk into a bar,[32] but no matter how hilarious the resulting punchline may be, their concepts of truth are never going to align. What the Philosophy of Religion shows us is that, while our response to the vast array of religious beliefs must fall somewhere from, on the one hand, a broadminded acceptance of all truths to, on the other hand, a dogmatic insistence that there can be one, and only one, truth, only we can determine where on this spectrum of acceptance/rejection our response falls.

ETHICS, RELIGION, AND THE CHALLENGE OF TOLERANCE

Whether our disagreements with others are based on ethical and/or religious principles, we are all left with deciding among (1) what we see as understandable differences reasonable people can accept and (2) what we see as intolerable differences that lie beyond the pale. While it is easy to say, in theory, that you are accepting of all religious faiths, that is not so easy in real life. For example, imagine a religion that claims for its believers the right to assault and rob random strangers as part of a divinely ordained ritual. Rejecting that religious belief as unacceptable is a pretty easy call for most people. Less easy would be the case of an Evangelical Christian whose religion dictates that marriage can only be between one man and one woman. Should such a person be accepting of a religion or code of ethics that approves of same-sex marriage or would such acceptance constitute a sin in itself? Conversely, should an agnostic lesbian be accepting of a religion that condemns same-sex relationships as sinful? And when a religious belief or ethical point of view is perceived as entirely unacceptable, what is the proper course of action? Silent disapproval? Speaking out against beliefs that offend you? Taking up arms against the infidels? The slope can get slippery in hurry.

By challenging us to think more clearly about our own core beliefs, the Philosophy of Religion and the formal study of Ethics can help us think more clearly about why others may think differently than us, though neither the Philosophy of Religion nor Ethics provides anything like clear guidelines on when the merely *different* becomes the *intolerable*. In the fictional universe of *Star Trek*, there is a rule called the Prime Directive which forbids Starfleet from interfering in the normal development of any society. However, as played out multiple times on screen and page, Starfleet officers seem to have little hesitation in violating the Prime Directive if they feel their doing so has been justified by one ethical loophole or another. The cultural arrogance required for space travelers to make such judgments about interfering in alien cultures is beyond imagination when, in real life, people who share the same planet, country, and language cannot agree when being different has crossed some invisible line to become being intolerable.

One thing that may help us earthbound humans maintain perspective is remembering that the ethical and religious disagreements that generate the most heat today were not always hot-button issues, and disagreements that once divided people into (literal) armed camps have faded into insignificance over time. In sixteenth-century Europe, being opposed to the baptism of infants could get you burned at the stake (a real flame-war situation), while, in the twenty-first century, infant baptism is not something you are likely to see people getting red in the face about on cable television or YouTube.

Nineteenth-century American Christians didn't much concern themselves with abortion or same-sex marriage because their attentions were consumed by such divisive issues as slavery and, following the Civil War, temperance. In a complete reversal, some twenty-first-century Christians are troubled by what they see as a secular-humanist "War on Christmas," whereas their Puritan spiritual forerunners straight-up outlawed Christmas celebrations on the grounds they were pagan and idolatrous. Perhaps the takeaway is that nonstop news cycles and always-on social media tend to get us so wrapped up in the alleged urgency of every cause *de jour* that we fail to step back and consider the long-term, big-picture significance of whatever it is that is being presented to us as so demanding of our immediate attention and action. Philosophy challenges us to take the broader view and to question assumptions about truth, first principles, and knowledge that partisans would rather we accept without hesitation, much less careful consideration.

THE ELUSIVE NATURE OF TRUTH

A skilled competitive debate team could convincingly argue in favor of, say, a communist system of economics, without anyone knowing whether they actually believe what they are advocating. A competent defense attorney may convince a jury of the innocence of a client whom the attorney knows to be absolutely guilty. Truth, it turns out, cannot be determined by even the most persuasive of arguments, the cleverest of one-liners, or the pointiest of PowerPoint presentations. Nor can it be determined (entirely or, in some cases, at all) through such means as popular votes, official pronouncements, or appeals to common sense. Over two millennia of philosophy shows that truth, though not completely abstract, is not easily captured for permanent display under glass. Maybe what people are discovering in the post-truth culture is that the opening up of so many channels of communication to so many voices has made the work of unpacking the truth far harder than it has ever been in the human past. Philosophers have always known that even coming close to the truth requires clear and careful thinking, and if that is the only lesson we learn from philosophy, it will serve us well as we negotiate the storms and squalls of the post-truth culture.

NOTES

1. Aristotle, *Aristotle's Metaphysics*, translated by W. D. Ross, two volumes (Oxford: Clarendon Press, 1924), 284.

2. "Plato, Apology, Section 38a," accessed February 28, 2020, http://www.per-seus.tufts.edu/hopper/text?doc=Perseus:text:1999.01.0170:text=Apol.:section=38a& highlight=unexamined.

3. *Crash Course Philosophy Preview*, accessed February 18, 2020, https://www.youtube.com/watch?v=BNYJQaZUDrI.

4. "Introduction to Philosophy," *Coursera*, accessed February 18, 2020, https://www.coursera.org/learn/philosophy.

5. Eugene Kelly, *The Basics of Western Philosophy* (Westport, CT: Greenwood Press, 2004).

6. Richard H. Popkin and Avrum Stroll, *Philosophy Made Simple*, second edition, revised (New York: Three Rivers Press, 1993).

7. *Stanford Encyclopedia of Philosophy*, accessed March 12, 2020, https://plato.stanford.edu/index.html.

8. James Fieser and Bradley Dowden, eds., *Internet Encyclopedia of Philosophy*, accessed July 21, 2020, https://www.iep.utm.edu/.

9. "The Basics of Philosophy: A Huge Subject Broken Down into Manageable Chunks," accessed March 12, 2020, https://www.philosophybasics.com/.

10. Donald Davidson, "The Folly of Trying to Define Truth," *The Journal of Philosophy* 93, no. 6 (1996): 265.

11. G.E. Moore, "A Defence of Common Sense," in *Contemporary British Philosophy: Personal Statements*, edited by John H. Muirhead and James Ward (London: G. Allen and Unwin, Ltd., 1925), 192–93.

12. George Musser, "Time on the Brain: How You Are Always Living in the Past, and Other Quirks of Perception," *Scientific American Blog Network*, accessed January 26, 2020, https://blogs.scientificamerican.com/observations/time-on-the-brain -how-you-are-always-living-in-the-past-and-other-quirks-of-perception/.

13. Joel Gold and Ian Gold, "The 'Truman Show' Delusion: Psychosis in the Global Village," *Cognitive Neuropsychiatry* 17, no. 6 (November 2012): 455–72.

14. Cory Doctorow, "I Quit," *Medium*, June 4, 2021, https://doctorow.medium .com/i-quit-9ae7b6010c99.

15. Jean-Paul Sartre, *Existentialism Is a Humanism: (L'Existentialisme Est Un Humanisme)*, edited by John Kulka, translated by Carol Macomber (New Haven: Yale University Press, 2007), 20.

16. Sartre, 29.

17. For an engaging counterargument to the idea that free choices are truly free or that we know as much as we think we do about what is, or is not, good for us, see Kent Greenfield's *The Myth of Choice* (New Haven: Yale University Press, 2011).

18. Jessica L. McCain and W. Keith Campbell, "Narcissism and Social Media Use: A Meta-Analytic Review," *Psychology of Popular Media Culture* 7, no. 3 (July 2018): 318–21.

19. Jean M. Twenge and W. Keith Campbell, *The Narcissism Epidemic: Living in the Age of Entitlement*, 1st Free Press hardcover edition (New York: Free Press, 2009).

20. Thanks to my Amazon author's page, personal website, and Facebook presence—each of which I established for the purpose of selling my books—I am as guilty as the next digital hustler.

21. A philosopher might argue that, instead of the term *postmodernism*, the more correct term for what we are talking about here is *poststructuralism*. While postmodernism and poststructuralism are not the same thing, they are closely related and often spoken of in the same breath. I choose to use the term *postmodernism* simply because it is the more familiar of the two.

22. Roland Barthes, "The Death of the Author," in *Image, Music, Text: Roland Barthes*, translated by Stephen Heath (London: Fontana Press, 1977), 142–48.

23. Michael P. Lynch, *True to Life: Why Truth Matters* (Cambridge, MA: MIT Press, 2004), 2.

24. Allan Bloom, *The Closing of the American Mind*, first Touchstone edition (New York: Simon and Schuster, 1988).

25. Lynne V. Cheney, *Telling the Truth: Why Our Culture and Our Country Have Stopped Making Sense, and What We Can Do about It* (New York: Simon & Schuster, 1995).

26. Lynch, 3.

27. Lee McIntyre, *Post-Truth* (Cambridge, MA: MIT Press, 2018), 133.

28. Donald A. Barclay, *Fake News, Propaganda, and Plain Old Lies: How to Find Trustworthy Information in the Digital Age* (Lanham, MD: Rowman & Littlefield, 2018).

29. "Fallacies," *The Writing Center*, accessed February 28, 2020, https://writing-center.unc.edu/tips-and-tools/fallacies/.

30. Hans Hansen, "Fallacies," in *The Stanford Encyclopedia of Philosophy*, edited by Edward N. Zalta, Metaphysics Research Lab, Stanford University, 2019, https://plato.stanford.edu/archives/fall2019/entries/fallacies/.

31. Emily Dickinson, *The Poems of Emily Dickinson (Poems 1-526)*, Variorum edition (Cambridge, MA: Belknap Press of Harvard University Press, 1998), 134.

32. The Imam and the Mormon stake president don't walk into the bar in the first place because their religions ban the drinking of alcohol altogether.

BIBLIOGRAPHY

Aristotle. *Aristotle's Metaphysics*, translated by W.D. Ross, two volumes (Oxford: Clarendon Press, 1924).

Barclay, Donald A. *Fake News, Propaganda, and Plain Old Lies: How to Find Trustworthy Information in the Digital Age* (Lanham, MD: Rowman & Littlefield, 2018).

Barthes, Roland. "The Death of the Author," in *Image, Music, Text: Roland Barthes*, translated by Stephen Heath (London: Fontana Press, 1977), 142–48.

Bloom, Allan. *The Closing of the American Mind*, first Touchstone edition (New York: Simon and Schuster, 1988).

Cheney, Lynne V. *Telling the Truth: Why Our Culture and Our Country Have Stopped Making Sense, and What We Can Do about It* (New York: Simon & Schuster, 1995).

Crash Course Philosophy Preview, accessed February 18, 2020, https://www.youtube.com/watch?v=BNYJQaZUDrI.

Davidson, Donald. "The Folly of Trying to Define Truth," *The Journal of Philosophy* 93, no. 6 (1996): 263–78.

Dickinson, Emily. *The Poems of Emily Dickinson (Poems 1-526)*, Variorum edition (Cambridge, MA: Belknap Press of Harvard University Press, 1998).

Doctorow, Cory. "I Quit." *Medium*, June 4, 2021. https://doctorow.medium.com/i-quit-9ae7b6010c99.

"Fallacies," *The Writing Center*, accessed February 28, 2020, https://writingcenter.unc.edu/tips-and-tools/fallacies/.

Fieser, James, and Bradley Dowden, eds. *Internet Encyclopedia of Philosophy*, accessed July 21, 2020, https://www.iep.utm.edu/.

Gold, Joel, and Ian Gold. "The 'Truman Show' Delusion: Psychosis in the Global Village," *Cognitive Neuropsychiatry* 17, no. 6 (November 2012): 455–72.

Hansen, Hans. "Fallacies," in *The Stanford Encyclopedia of Philosophy*, edited by Edward N. Zalta, Metaphysics Research Lab, Stanford University, 2019, https://plato.stanford.edu/archives/fall2019/entries/fallacies/.

"Introduction to Philosophy," *Coursera*, accessed February 18, 2020, https://www.coursera.org/learn/philosophy.

Kelly, Eugene. *The Basics of Western Philosophy* (Westport, CT: Greenwood Press, 2004).

Lynch, Michael P. *True to Life: Why Truth Matters* (Cambridge, MA: MIT Press, 2004).

McIntyre, Lee. *Post-Truth* (Cambridge, MA: MIT Press, 2018).

Moore, G.E. "A Defence of Common Sense," in *Contemporary British Philosophy: Personal Statements*, edited by John H. Muirhead and James Ward (London: G. Allen and Unwin, Ltd., 1925), 192–233.

Musser, George. "Time on the Brain: How You Are Always Living in the Past, and Other Quirks of Perception," *Scientific American Blog Network*, accessed January 26, 2020, https://blogs.scientificamerican.com/observations/time-on-the-brain-how-you-are-always-living-in-the-past-and-other-quirks-of-perception/.

Plato. "Apology, Section 38a," accessed February 28, 2020, http://www.perseus.tufts.edu/hopper/text?doc=Perseus:text:1999.01.0170:text=Apol.:section=38a&highlight=unexamined.

Popkin, Richard H., and Avrum Stroll. *Philosophy Made Simple*, second edition, revised (New York: Three Rivers Press, 1993).

Sartre, Jean-Paul. *Existentialism Is a Humanism: (L'Existentialisme Est Un Humanisme)*, edited by John Kulka, translated by Carol Macomber (New Haven: Yale University Press, 2007).

Stanford Encyclopedia of Philosophy, accessed March 12, 2020, https://plato.stanford.edu/index.html.

"The Basics of Philosophy: A Huge Subject Broken down into Manageable Chunks," accessed March 12, 2020, https://www.philosophybasics.com/.

Twenge, Jean M., and W. Keith. Campbell. *The Narcissism Epidemic: Living in the Age of Entitlement*, first Free Press hardcover edition (New York: Free Press, 2009), http://catdir.loc.gov/catdir/enhancements/fy0906/2008044705-s.html.

2

The Science of the Mind and the Post-Truth Culture

My wife and I routinely walk our dog, Olive (her real name), along a creek near our house. While walking, we often see and say hello to a pair of friends, Lisa and Pam (not their real names). Lisa is petite, while Pam is tall and slender. One foggy Saturday morning, my wife and I saw the familiar sight of petite Lisa and tall Pam coming toward us, both of them bundled up in winter jackets and knit caps. It was not until the pair was nearly within arm's length of us that we realized Lisa was not walking with Pam but was, instead, accompanied by a tall, slender man whom we had never before seen. After they had passed us, my wife and I shared a similar thought: If the tall person we saw in the distance had suddenly attacked Lisa and run off in the opposite direction, we both would have sworn under oath that Pam was the guilty party. (Yes, we watch far too much true-crime television at our house.) While our error in identifying Lisa's walking partner that morning did not put an innocent person behind bars for twenty years, the incident serves as a classic example of how mistaken identity occurs. Working on preexisting assumptions—petite Lisa and tall Pam always walk the creek together—our minds filled in the details without benefit of fact. What is more, if the tall stranger had actually attacked Lisa, the two of us no doubt would have reinforced each other's confidence that we had, in fact, seen what our brains told us we had seen: Pam attacking Lisa. We would have made the mistake of establishing truth by consensus instead of by the actual evidence. While what transpired as we walked the creek may sound a lot like the philosophical uncertainty over the nature of reality discussed in chapter 1, it is not. My wife and I took in and processed the exact same set of visual cues. We agreed on what we saw, and neither of us was suffering a philosophical crisis over the nature of reality à la Rene Descartes. The root of our misinterpretation of reality was not philosophical in nature. It was psychological.

A number of psychological forces influence how our brains process and react to information in all its forms. What makes the forces problematic is that they are not only powerful but are also capable of exerting their influence without our being aware of it. The first part of this chapter will describe the workings of the strongest and most common of these psychological forces with the goal of illuminating how they influence human processing of, and reaction to, information; in addition, the conclusion of this chapter will consider how the nature of the human mind severely limits the swaying of hearts and changing of minds with the relative weak tools of facts and persuasion.

THE PSYCHOLOGY OF WHAT WE SEE AND REMEMBER

Textbox 2.1
Selective Attention Test

Here is an experiment you can try for yourself. Before reading the text that appears below this box, visit http://simonslab.com/videos.html. Once there, watch the video labeled "Selective Attention Test" and (as instructed) count the number of times the players wearing white shirts pass the basketball. Good luck coming up with the correct number of passes.

Spoiler alert. Did you watch the video discussed in Textbox 2.1? (If not, you should before you read any further.) This video was created as a component of an experiment conducted in 1999 by psychologists Daniel J. Simons and Christopher F. Chabris. What their experiment found is that 50 percent of the people who watch the video for the first time fail to see an obvious anomaly.[1] (I fell into that oblivious 50 percent, much to my own amazement.) What is most interesting is that this and similar experiments show the world is not neatly divided up between people who always notice anomalies like the one seen in the video and people who do not. Everybody is capable of failing to see something obvious at one time or another.[2] The results of Simons and Chabris' experiment are just one part of a large body of scientific evidence demonstrating that our vision is not the reliable instrument we assume it to be. While the video used in the experiment is as amusing as is it revealing, decades of research conducted by psychologist Elizabeth Loftus demonstrate that, in the courtroom, the unreliability of eyewitness testimony is no joke.[3] Over the years, Loftus' initial findings that unreliable eyewitness testimony regularly leads to miscarriages of justice have been disturbingly well supported by subsequent DNA-backed exonerations of persons found guilty chiefly or solely on the basis of eyewitness testimony.

Just as humans do not always see with perfect acuity, human hearing is similarly susceptible to errors. For example, among air-traffic controllers the problem of mishearing the responses of pilots (known in the profession as "hearback errors") has been described by researchers as a "well-known phenomenon."[4] If a group of professionals with as much motivation to pay close attention as air-traffic controllers can mishear, it is not surprising that such errors also occur among the general public. In daily life, almost everyone has experienced the embarrassment of responding inappropriately after mishearing someone else's words. A humorous example of the human tendency to mishear takes the form of mondegreens—the misunderstanding of a word or phrase of a song lyric compounded by the substitution of often out-of-context words or phrases in place of the correct lyrics. A well-known example of a mondegreen is mishearing the Jimi Hendrix lyric "'scuse me, while I touch the sky" as "'scuse me, while I kiss this guy."

Compounding the problem of unreliable senses is the fact that what humans believe they remember turns out to be similarly unreliable. The fallibility of human memory is so universally accepted among scientists who study the subject that an essential reference work for the field of psychology flatly states: "Whatever else memory may be, it is not a tape recorder that has recorded all the sights, sounds, experiences, and so on that we might remember under appropriate circumstances."[5] Factors such as stress, age, health, motivation, and suggestion can influence memory. Most notorious is the well-documented ability of trained persuaders to invoke entirely false "recovered memories" from their victims.[6] For a chilling example of how a false memory can be implanted, take a few minutes to watch the video clip from the "Memory Hackers" episode of the Public Broadcasting Service's nonfiction television series *Nova* in which psychologist Julia Shaw persuades a test subject to remember a traumatic event that never actually happened:[7] https://www.drjuliashaw.com/research.

Less chilling, but just as telling, are the many examples of failures of collective memory in which thousands of people misremember the same event or fact. Popular culture provides some well-known examples of this phenomenon:

- In the film *Casablanca*, Humphrey Bogart never says, "Play it again, Sam."
- In the original *Star Trek* television series, Captain Kirk never says, "Beam me up, Scotty."
- In the *Star Wars* films, Darth Vader never says, "Luke, I am your father."

Strangely enough, a surprising number of people cling so strongly to collective false memories that they refuse to admit their error even when confronted with irrefutable evidence that their memories are faulty; instead, they attribute the inconsistency between their memory and the thing remembered to various conspiracy theories, some involving parallel or alternate universes. Such collective-memory conspiracy theories fall under the heading of the "Mandela Effect," so called because thousands of people have (or claim to have) a memory of Nelson Mandela dying in prison when, in fact, he was freed from prison in 1990 and went on to be elected president of South Africa. Another example of a popular Mandela Effect conspiracy theory involves the widespread belief that the popular children's book series *The Berenstain Bears* was originally titled *The Berenstein Bears* and that the series was, for whatever reason, retitled with a new spelling.[8]

The fact that the reliability of both eyewitness evidence and memory fall very far short of perfection creates some serious problems for everyone living in the post-truth culture. If we cannot rely on the most basics tools of human perception, does that open the door for an alternative-facts free-for-all? If enough people cling to the notion that *The Berenstain Bears* was originally titled *The Berenstein Bears*, does that then become the reality in spite of the fact that some 260 million copies of books dating back to the 1960s are printed with the name spelled as *Berenstain*? Let's hope not. If anything, the psychological evidence surrounding the unreliability of what people see and hear coupled with known fallibility of human memory should teach us to be extremely wary of assigning too much credibility to what individuals say they saw and heard or what they remember—even when the person in question is someone we trust and the things they say nicely conform to our view of world. On the other hand, while being wary of the credibility of eyewitness accounts and memories is prudent, it does not give us a license to dismiss out of hand the entirety of all eyewitness accounts and remembered events. People may not be perfect tape recorders, but they are capable of seeing and remembering at least some significant part of their experiences.

What we, as receivers of information, must do is balance all the evidence. If a nonagenarian veteran of D-Day claims he saw President Franklin Delano Roosevelt running along Omaha Beach waving a sword to urge the troops forward, we need to weigh that (obviously questionable) memory against the solid evidence that Roosevelt was in the United States on D-Day and, even if he had not been, was incapable of walking unaided, much less running down a beach waving a sword. Conversely, if a number of people at a demonstration say they were protesting peacefully when they were set-upon by counterprotestors *and* their claims are backed up by additional evidence, their testimony cannot simply be dismissed out of hand because we happen to side with the counterprotestors. When it comes to eyewitness accounts and memory, we need to be careful that we do not fall into the trap of selectively giving credence to the testimonies and recollections (our own as well as those of others) that make us feel justified and consistent in our worldview while dismissing as fabrications all testimonies and recollections that have the opposite effect on us.

COGNITIVE DISSONANCE

The human desire for justification and consistency has, in fact, everything to do with cognitive dissonance—the mental stress we feel when we encounter information, ideas, or behaviors that conflict with our most fundamental beliefs, ideals, or values. Cognitive psychologists use the phrase *magnitude of dissonance* to describe the amount of cognitive dissonance a person experiences when trying to internally reconcile conflicting ideas. The human need to keep the magnitude of dissonance at an acceptable level explains why you rarely, if ever, encounter someone who can casually and honestly describe themselves as, say, "a Buddhist, pro-gun, anti-war, pro-life, anti-whale, pro-same-sex marriage, Evangelical Christian Communist." The emotional discomfort caused by corralling such a grab bag of conflicting beliefs into a single mind would overwhelm anyone with a functioning grip on reality. That the digital discourse is subjected to endless arguments and acrimony over what information to believe or not believe is, in part, driven by the human need to manage cognitive dissonance. The psychological burden of accepting certain information as true simply creates too much cognitive dissonance for anyone to bear.

People try to avoid feelings of cognitive dissonance because those feelings are never good. If you ever try to honestly reconcile all the logical inconsistencies floating around in your mind, you will most likely end up feeling like a hypocrite. Imagine trying to reconcile the following:

How can I consider myself an environmentalist even though I drive a gas-guzzling SUV every day?

How can I consider myself an honest person when I work for a company that profits from convincing senior citizens to put their money in risky investments?

While nobody likes feeling a hypocrite (though almost all of us are, to some extent, hypocrites), having your hypocrisy exposed on the battlefields of the digital discourse can be a near-fatal liability, giving, as it does, your opposition the opportunity to stick in the knife and twist:

Hypocrite! You call yourself an environmentalist but look at your giant SUV.

Hypocrite! On Sunday you throw a few bucks in the collection plate but during the week you steal the life savings of old folks.

Whether it is to avoid the external affront of being called a hypocrite or a first-class case of internal angst, people go to great lengths to turn down the dial on cognitive dissonance. At the most fundamental level, in order to reduce the magnitude of dissonance and achieve cognitive balance people must either change their behaviors (what they do) or change their cognition (what they think). For example:

Changing behavior:

"I was worried about my drinking, so I completely gave up alcohol."

Changing cognition:

"I always thought drinking was a personal choice that I made of my own free will, but now I realize I was powerfully influenced by peer pressure and advertising."

The problem, of course, is that changing behaviors and cognition are some of the hardest things a human being can do. Just consider how much time, effort, and money people put into quitting smoking or how difficult it is to change deeply ingrained likes or dislikes. An alternative, and generally less challenging, approach is to lessen the magnitude of dissonance through the justification of behaviors or cognitions. For example:

"I will continue to drink alcohol, but only on the weekend."

"I will continue to drink alcohol, but only beer and wine. No hard stuff."

"I will continue to drink alcohol unless it begins to interfere with my job performance."

Another way for people to balance the magnitude of dissonance that is rife in the post-truth culture is for individuals to stack the deck of evidence in such a way that their behaviors and thinking feel consistent and justified. This may be achieved by paying attention only to information that supports entrenched behaviors and thoughts while ignoring or rejecting all contradictory evidence. Selective attention comes into play when, for example, conspiracy theorists focus on some minute detail that supports their theory:

"The direction of the flames in this one photograph prove that the explosion was the result of pre-set charges in World Trade Center South Tower. There were no planes at all."

Such selective attention must ignore, of course, the fact that thousands of people witnessed a jetliner crashing into the South Tower while millions more saw live video of the crash on television.

A related tactic is refusing to accept evidence that runs contrary to your entrenched beliefs unless it can meet some impossibly high standard of proof:

> *"I will not accept that HIV causes AIDS until there is a clinical trial in which healthy people develop AIDS after being injected with HIV."*

The reason there has never been (and never will be) such a clinical trial is, of course, that injecting healthy people with HIV would be mind-bogglingly unethical and completely illegal. (Besides which, there is no need for any such clinical trial. The scientific evidence long ago established the fact that HIV causes AIDS.)

People will also trivialize facts to achieve balance. A smoker might dismiss the overwhelming evidence demonstrating the link between smoking and lung cancer by arguing that some people smoke their entire lives without ever getting lung cancer.

The well-documented psychological concept of *motivated reasoning* explains many of these justifications by considering how the pursuit of cognitive balance can shape our reasoning. Put simply, motivated reasoning explains why people tend to arrive at whatever conclusions they wanted to arrive at in the first place.[9] Suppose, for example, a team of highly ethical engineers have been given the task of designing a two-mile-long suspension bridge. Because these engineers are deeply committed to both safety and their professional reputations, their reasoning is driven by *accuracy goals*. Which is to say, these engineers, invested as they are in doing their jobs correctly, are unwilling to fall into the trap of motivated reasoning; instead, they give serious thought to all the evidence they uncover as they research their project, including evidence that points out potential flaws in their designs or calls for design changes that will drive up the cost of the project. On the other hand, consider the decisions that led to the disaster involving the space shuttle *Challenger* in 1986. Despite strong warnings that the cold weather predicted for the day of the launch could cause the shuttle's o-rings to fail catastrophically, the managers in charge of the project approved going ahead with the launch as scheduled. By engaging in motivated reasoning and allowing themselves to be driven by *directional goals* instead of accuracy goals, the managers built a case that ignored the engineering evidence and created a seemingly rational justification for the outcome—launch on schedule—the managers desired in the first place.

Those who engage in motivated reasoning can seem convincing because they are not necessarily making up facts out of thin air; rather, they weave together selected facts (while ignoring contradictory facts) to create a ratio-nale that feels logical and free from the discomfort of cognitive dissonance. Often, the politicians, pundits, and social media megaphones who engage in motivated reasoning brag of the impeccability of their logic and the sound-ness of their arguments even though they are motivated far more by direc-tional goals than by accuracy goals. Anyone who starts out with the idea of proving a predetermined conclusion is likely engaging in motivated reasoning and is more likely to produce a rationalization rather than a truly reasoned argument.

COGNITIVE BIAS

Of all the psychological forces shaping the post-truth culture, cognitive biases are perhaps the most powerful and prevalent. Defined as "cases in which human cognition reliably produces representations that are systematically dis-torted compared to some aspect of objective reality,"[10] cognitive biases are not one-time mistaken interpretations of objective reality, as when you look in the sky and mistake a distant helicopter for an airplane (or, on a foggy morning, mistake a tall, slender man for a tall, slender woman). Instead, cognitive biases are the source of persistent and repeated distortions of objective reality. The challenge presented when our cognitive biases (and we all have them) come into play is that it is extremely difficult for us to recognize when we are oper-ating under their influence. Take, for example, the cognitive bias known as *anchoring*, which manifests as a tendency to instinctively place more impor-tance on the first information learned about a topic while placing less impor-tance on information encountered later (even if that later information is highly credible). Say that someone who is especially prone to anchoring initially learned that Cuban revolutionary (and t-shirt icon) Ernesto "Che" Guevara was a brilliant and courageous leader who helped the Cuban people overthrow the violent and repressive Bautista Regime; it would then be extremely diffi-cult, if not impossible, for this person to accept subsequent information show-ing Guevara to have frequently acted with violence and cruelty. And because cognitive biases operate invisibly, those who consider Guevara to have been one of the great villains of the twentieth century (as many people do) are likely to dismiss the admirer of Che as stupid, stubborn, evil, or brainwashed rather than as someone operating under the influence of anchoring—a compelling, difficult-to-overcome cognitive bias. Cognitive biases, of which anchoring is only one example, comprise a powerful influence in the digital discourse and help explain why arguments over the credibility of contradictory information and the definition of objective reality can become so heated.

There are more cognitive biases than can be considered in this chapter. While the number varies from source to source, social scientists have identified close to two hundred cognitive biases, with newly identified biases being added to the list from time to time. (Of all the lists of cognitive biases, perhaps the most visually interesting takes the form of a graphic found on the website *The Visual Capitalist*.[11]) The following partial list highlights the cognitive biases that most often surface in the endless arguments being aired out in the digital discourse.

Authority bias is the tendency to believe information is more credible because it comes from an authority figure *regardless of the content of the information.* An example of this would be giving credence to a Nobel Prize–winning economist's opinion on the safety of GMO foods even though that distinguished economist has no real expertise in food safety.

Availability cascade is a cognitive bias that leads people to accept the credibility of a collective belief the more often it is repeated. For example, the more often unverified information—such as a rumor, propaganda, a meme, false advertising, or a conspiracy theory—is repeated, the more likely people are to accept that it is partly or completely true.[12] The theory that President John F. Kennedy was assassinated as the result of a conspiracy has been repeated so many times that, according to a poll conducted in 2017, 61 percent of those polled believe that Lee Harvey Oswald did not act alone.[13] (Is it possible that Kennedy was the victim of a conspiracy? Perhaps. The point here is that many who believe in Kennedy assassination conspiracies do so as a result of repetition—the availability cascade—rather than from any thorough and impartial consideration of the all the evidence.)

Backfire effect describes the behavior of clinging more tightly to existing beliefs when confronted with contradictory evidence. An example would be a person who believes they have developed a foolproof system for winning the lottery committing even more strongly to the validity of their system in spite of repeatedly failing to win the lottery. A related bias, *conservatism in belief revision*, is the tendency to not sufficiently revise beliefs when presented with contradictory information. Both of these biases are related to the cognitive bias known as either *irrational escalation* or *escalation of commitment*, which can be thought of as the tendency to stick to your guns despite mounting evidence that you are wrong.

Bias blind spot is the conviction that we ourselves are not biased while others are. This bias is seen when adherents of rival factions—in realms ranging from sports to politics to religion—accuse those on the other side of the rivalry of being biased while failing to acknowledge their own biases. *"After all, not only are we fans of the State U. Armadillos completely impartial in our judgments of those cheaters at Tech State, all those Tech fans are totally biased against our beloved 'Dillos."*

Confirmation bias describes the nearly universal tendency to seek out, interpret, and remember information that supports what we already believe while avoiding or dismissing information that challenges our existing beliefs. If someone strongly believes that people of Northern European descent are biologically superior to people of all other races, confirmation bias drives them to seek out and accept only evidence that supports their view while avoiding and dismissing the large body of evidence that contradicts it.

Textbox 2.2
A Tale of Confirmation Bias

In the State of Idaho, most vehicle license plates include county designator codes. Ada County, which is home to the state's capital and largest city, Boise, has the designator 1/A. One of Ada County's neighboring counties, Canyon County, has the designator 2/C. When I was a teenager and young adult living in Boise, it was widely believed among the residents of Boise that drivers of cars with 2/C plates constituted a menace on the roadways. There may have been a grain of truth to that belief. Canyon County was largely rural with a much smaller population than Boise, and so it is possible that drivers from Canyon County made a few more than their share of mistakes while navigating the unfamiliar streets of what was, by the modest standards of Idaho, a megacity. I am more inclined to think, though, that Boiseans' dim view of Canyon County drivers was the result of cognitive bias. When a car with 2/C plates did anything that might be considered bad driving, it registered in our 1/A brains as confirmation of a theory we had all heard many times. If, on the other hand, a car with 1/A plates exhibited bad driving, we might think the driver was an idiot, but we did not attribute the behavior to the driver being from Ada County. Also, cognitive bias had us mentally tallying up incidents of bad driving on the part of 2/C drivers while not keeping track of the times their driving was just fine. The fact that Boiseans reveled in exchanging stories of inferior Canyon County driving only served to reinforce this confirmation bias.

Declinism is the belief that society is getting progressively worse and that the past was better than it actually was. A recent example of declinism is the widespread labeling of Millennials as an entitled generation spoiled by soft parenting and social coddling. These accusations were given credence even though the Baby Boomers who (for the most part) level these charges against

Millennials were themselves, in their youth, similarly scorned by their elders as selfish, spoiled, and ungrateful.

The Dunning-Krueger effect describes a tendency for inexperienced persons to overestimate their ability at something they have never done. For example, someone who has never run a small business might think doing so is easy until they try it themselves and learn that it is much harder than it looks from the outside.

False consensus effect occurs when someone overestimates the extent to which others agree with their thinking. This can be seen in echo chamber social media groups in which similarly minded people reinforce shared ideas. If you were to spend all your time online among those who believe (or claim to believe) that the Earth is flat, you might come away thinking that belief in a flat Earth is far more prevalent than it actually is.

False uniqueness bias is the tendency for people to see themselves as more unique and individualistic than they really are. *"Call me weird, but I really love ice cream and cookies."*

Fundamental attribution error occurs when we attribute our own behaviors and actions to the situation while attributing the behaviors and actions of others to their personalities. *"I was denied my goal of complete financial independence by age forty due to a terrible economy and a system that is rigged against people like me. You, on the other hand, failed to achieve your financial goals because you didn't work hard and made bad choices."* The cognitive bias *ultimate attribution error* is similar except that the attribution is to an entire group of people instead of individuals within it.

Hostile attribution bias attributes hostility to the behavior of others—and characterizes them as the enemy—even when their actions do not exhibit hostility. An example of this would be characterizing those who accept that the Earth is around 4.6 billion years old as acting out of hostility toward those who believe in Young Earth Creationism rather than out of acceptance of the scientific evidence. *"The opposition is out to get us,"* implies something very different from, *"Those other people think differently than we do."*

Humor effect recognizes that people are better able to remember things they find amusing. Teachers often use humor as a way to make important points memorable to students, as do entertainment-oriented political pundits and social media comedians (both professional and would-be). The competition to come up with the funniest putdowns of "those idiots on the other side" can be fierce, and the sharing of humorous burns in social media echo chambers is common. Condensing a complex social or political issue down to fit in a tweet or on a bumper sticker may create a memorable zinger, but such cleverness does nothing to promote critical thinking about the truthfulness, or lack thereof, of any ideas thus expressed.

Illusory correlation (not to be confused with the logical fallacy of mistaking correlation with causation) is a bias resulting from the tendency of rare or highly unusual events or behaviors to remain memorable and for people to connect what is memorable with certain groups in a stereotypical way. For example, although relatively few Italian Americans have any connection to organized crime, the outrageous, and thus memorable, actions of Italian American criminals (as much in fiction as in real life) has led to the stereotyping of Italian Americans as Mafiosi.

Illusory truth effect is a cognitive bias that favors the acceptance of easily comprehended (and therefore easily repeatable) explanations of events over more complex, and usually more accurate, explanations. It is easier for some to believe, for example, the easily understood (though erroneous) explanation that ancient space aliens built the Mayan pyramids than to process the complex history of the rise of the Mayan civilization, its remarkable achievements, and its eventual decline.

Ingroup bias is the tendency to favor those who are more like ourselves (the ingroup) over those who are less like ourselves (the outgroup). This can take such obvious forms as blatant racism and xenophobia or the less obvious form of implicit bias.

Textbox 2.3
Implicit Bias

Implicit bias describes the phenomenon of harboring a bias without consciously realizing it. An example of implicit bias could take the form of an office supervisor (whether male or female) claiming to be in favor of equal treatment of men and women while nonetheless consistently rating male employees higher than female employees with no conscious awareness of doing so. Such an example of implicit bias is different from the explicit bias of someone who is openly against equal treatment of women in the workplace (even though, in the end, the results of both kinds of bias are equally harmful). The Harvard-based Project Implicit offers a number of free online tests that anyone can take to see if they harbor implicit biases and, if so, how strong those biases may be.[14]

Just-world hypothesis is the belief that life's playing fields are naturally level and anyone who fails to succeed is to blame for their failure while anyone who succeeds did so entirely as a result of their superior intelligence, character, and effort. While it is rather common for those who have succeeded to subscribe to the just-world hypothesis, they are in some ways the persons least-qualified to judge the levelness of the playing field. The closely related *self-serving bias* positions people to take personal credit for their successes while downplaying their responsibility for their failures.

Naïve realism biases a person to believe in a simple, absolute objective reality that is perceived in exactly the same way by everyone and to characterize anyone who sees the world in any other way as irrational or a liar. When someone says that an idea or way of behaving is "just common sense," they may be exhibiting the influence of naïve realism.

Puritanical bias is the tendency to hold individuals personally responsible for any shortcoming without regard to outside forces. Someone operating under this bias might dismiss the owners of failed mom-and-pop shops as bad businesspeople without considering how the huge competitive advantages held by the big-box chain stores and online retailers put small shops out of business in the first place.

Reactance is a cognitive bias that inspires people to do the opposite of what others want them to do, typically in the name of preserving personal freedom. Reactance may explain why people sometimes reject social programs that would increase their incomes or otherwise improve the quality of their lives.

Reactive devaluation is the tendency to reject an idea because it comes from an adversary. This is seen in highly partisan politics where the goal is more about making the other side look bad than doing what is best for all concerned. Hypothetical examples would be liberals rejecting a beneficial environmental bill because it originated with conservatives or conservatives rejecting a bill that would sustainably promote small businesses because it originated with liberals.

Salience bias causes people to focus on matters that are more outstanding or carry greater emotional weight than on equally important, but less striking, matters. For example, people may focus more on the number of children killed with firearms than they do on children drowned in backyard swimming pools even though children die more far frequently in backyard drownings than in incidents involving firearms. Salience bias is related to the tendency for bad news to overpower good news to such an extent that people focus on, and remember, bad news more than good.[15] A similar cognitive bias, the *von Restorff effect*, results in any stimulus that is distinct from other stimuli standing out and becoming memorable. People are more likely to notice and remember the tallest tree in a forest rather than a tree of average height.

Subjective validation is the belief that information that is personally meaningful must be true. Horoscopes leverage this bias by making general statements that apply to anyone—*"Today you will learn something new about a person who is close to you"*—and then allowing the influenced reader to make the specific connection. A somewhat different example of this bias would be someone who owns a motorcycle unquestionably accepting as true a statement such as, *"People who own motorcycles are the kindest, bravest, warmest, most wonderful human beings on Earth."*

System justification is the tendency to prefer things remain the way they are rather than accept economic, social, or political changes. As might be expected, this bias is more common among those holding positions of privilege, power, and influence than among those who are less satisfied with the status quo.

Third-person effect is a hypothetical (yet to be scientifically tested) cognitive bias founded on the idea that people tend to see themselves as largely immune to the influence of mass media and popular culture while seeing others, especially their adversaries, as gullible dupes who believe everything they read or hear. Admittedly, one of the reasons anyone is talking about fake news and post-truth (and reading books like this one) is the possibly exaggerated fear that millions of people accept without question every blatant lie and bit of nonsense that comes to their attention.

Trait ascription bias is the tendency to view oneself as a fully rounded and intelligent being while viewing the others as one-dimensional robots who behave in entirely predictable ways. Trait ascription bias is in play when people view their adversaries as unthinking Pavlovian dogs, automatically and predictably responding to their master's bell (or, to use a currently popular phrase, "dog whistle"). The popularity of zombie movies may, in fact, reflect a fictional playing out of this cognitive bias—if only dealing with real-life adversaries were as easy and guilt free as mowing down mindless, lock-step hordes of the living dead.

PROBABILITY AS THE SCIENTIFIC BASIS OF COGNITIVE BIAS

Suppose that someone, possibly you, were to ask, *"Are cognitive biases based on real science or are they just pulled out of thin air?"* That is a fair enough question. The answer is that the concept of systematic human cognitive bias developed from foundational scientific research conducted in the early 1970s by psychologists Amos Tversky (1937–1996) and Daniel Kahneman (1934–).[16] (Kahneman would eventually go on to win the Nobel Prize for Economics.) Highly mathematical in their approach, Tversky and Kahneman developed the scientific foundations of cognitive bias after repeated observations of the unreliability of nearly everyone's intuitive reasoning when confronted with even fairly simple calculations of probability. One simple test that Tversky and Kahneman cite in their influential article, "Judgment under Uncertainty: Heuristics and Biases,"[17] involves surveying subjects about the gambler's fallacy, a concept which can be expressed as: *"If the roulette ball has landed on black six times in a row, red is now 'due' so I should bet on red.*" While the gambler's fallacy is absurd when you consider that a previous random outcome (ball lands on black) has no possible influence on a subsequent random outcome (ball lands on red), intuitive thinking nonetheless causes many people to accept the gambler's fallacy as a rational proposition. A more complex test employed by Tversky and Kahneman was to ask undergraduate students to rate the likelihood of the ratio of girl/boy births (which normally occur at a ratio of 50 percent girls to 50 percent boys) exceeding 60 percent boys in a single day in a large versus a small maternity ward. Most students rated the likelihood to be the same in both locations. However, an outcome of 60 percent boys in a single day is statistically more likely in a small maternity ward than in a large one because the larger sample of babies in the larger maternity ward is less likely to stray from the 50 percent norm than is the smaller sample in the smaller maternity ward. Think about it this way. Suppose two teammates on a collegiate women's soccer team eventually go on to give birth to two children each, all four of whom are boys. Hardly a remarkable outcome. Suppose, instead, that thirty teammates from a single collegiate women's soccer team go on to give birth to two children each, all sixty of whom are boys. Such a probability-defying outcome would become a believe-it-or-not news story. Tversky and Kahneman find that people's intuitive thinking about probabilities is flawed because the "fundamental notion of statistics is evidently not part of people's repertoire of intuitions."[18]

A more recent example of how our intuitive reasoning can mislead us was used by Kahneman during a talk delivered at the headquarters of Google in 2011. Shortly after a terrorist attack, international travelers were asked:

A. How much would you pay for insurance that provides one hundred thousand dollars in case of death for any cause?
B. How much would you pay for insurance that provides one hundred thousand dollars in case of death in a terror incident?

According to Kahneman, more people were willing to pay (and pay more) for Policy B than for Policy A even though, from a statistical perspective, that is an entirely absurd things to do.[19] Death due to any cause is far more statistically likely than death by terrorism; what is more, because Policy A covers "death for any cause," it would also pay off in the event of death by terrorism. Tversky and Kahneman theorize that, rather than carefully thinking through probabilities, human beings (including many who are trained in statistics and probability) often employ a kind of intuitive-based short cut called a *heuristic* in their decision-making processes. People routinely and frequently resort to heuristics, which are the foundation of cognitive biases, because the time and effort involved in gathering all the information and calculating all the probabilities for every decision is simply overwhelming. While Tversky and Kahneman admit that heuristics are quite useful, they also warn that heuristics sometimes "lead to severe and systematic errors."[20]

Tversky and Kahneman point out that people use heuristics not only to make decisions about probabilities, but also use "representative heuristics" to make other important decisions, including decisions regarding other human beings. Going back to the creek near my house, on our walks my wife and I sometimes see and say hello to a tall gentleman with a handsomely weathered face and somewhat long, graying hair. My wife and I have (jokingly) concluded that this man must be a former rock musician who has, for whatever unlikely reason, retired to our small, out-of-the-way town. Our use of a representative heuristic in this case is rather harmless because (1) we do not truly believe that this gentleman is a former rock musician and (2) even if we did, our interactions with him are so brief and infrequent that our uninformed assumptions have zero impact on his life or the way in which we treat him. On the other hand, representative heuristics can have profound consequences when they lead to such conclusions as *"Every dark-skinned man is a potential threat who should be treated with suspicion"* or *"Any job candidate who stutters while speaking is unintelligent."* Discouragingly enough, there is a wealth of evidence-based empirical data demonstrating that potentially harmful representative heuristics are prevalent and work their influence without our being aware. For just one example, in an experiment in which test subjects were shown body types of both black and white males, black male bodies with prominent musculature were consistently rated as more threatening and of lower social status than white male bodies displaying identical musculature.[21]

An example of representative heuristics at work in the digital discourse can be seen in memes consisting of photographs of people who are neither celebrities nor public figures. When such memes become popular in social media, commenters who have no context beyond what is depicted in a single photograph often make impossibly far-reaching, entirely intuitive assumptions about the beliefs, behaviors, and motivations of the subjects of the photographs. A well-known example of this is a widely shared photograph depicting a young white woman wearing her light-colored hair in dreadlocks.[22] Her neo-hippie appearance is furthered by wire-rimmed glasses, a brightly colored shirt, and a floppy, multicolored knit cap. This woman's image has appeared in dozens of memes in which she is presented as the embodiment of the stereotypical college-aged social justice warrior. Based solely on her appearance in one photograph, she is routinely vilified for being spoiled, hypocritical, naïve, anti-Christian, anti-male, anticapitalist, judgmental, easily offended, and worse. Maybe the woman in the photograph is all these things. Her appearance certainly does not fit any popular stereotypes of College Republicans or devout Southern Baptists. However, it is likely that neither the meme-makers who use her image as a social media punching bag nor those enjoy seeing her mocked have any fact-based knowledge of her actual beliefs, behaviors, or motivations.

Automobiles provide another common example of how quick we are to employ representational heuristics:

"Everyone who drives a hybrid is a pretentious, deluded tree hugger who thinks she is single-handedly saving the planet."

"Everyone who drives a big pick-up truck is a gun-owning buffoon who sees his truck as proof of his toxic masculinity."

Or maybe the hybrid driver is merely trying to save money by owning a small, efficient car. And maybe the guy drives a big truck because his work requires him to haul bulky materials and equipment.

Did you notice that I made the driver of the hybrid female and the driver of the truck male? Representative heuristics in action. And you might be thinking, *"Yeah, but most of the time the generalizations about drivers of hybrids and big trucks are closer to the stereotype than not."* Even if that is a true statement, *most* of the time is not *all* of the time. And if you think most of the time is good enough, think about you feel when someone assumes something untrue about you based on your race, sex, appearance, clothing, political views, possessions, hobbies, entertainment preferences, and the like. Why can't a conservative be a vegan or liberal be an avid hunter? In the digital discourse, the aspersions cast on people for something as trivial as liking or not liking pineapple on pizza go miles beyond anything you could rationally hypothesize about a person's behavior or motivations based on nothing more than a pizza topping.

COGNITIVE BIASES AND THE HARDWIRED HUMAN BRAIN

Some cognitive scientists have questioned Tversky and Kahneman's use of probability-based assessments to measure the accuracy (or lack thereof) of intuitive reasoning. Their counterargument holds that because probability is such an abstract and, for many people, artificial concept, probability-based measures underestimate the accuracy of the average (and above-average) person's intuition. In contrast, assessing intuitive reasoning via problems presented in less-abstract forms than mathematical probabilities—for example, frequencies visualized in a bar graph—demonstrates that the human ability to make reasonably accurate intuitive assessments is, overall, quite sufficient.[23]

Rather than viewing heuristics and cognitive biases as examples of lazy or undisciplined thinking, many scientists who study the brain conceive of them as, instead, examples of processing shortcuts hardwired into the human brain through natural selection. Adam Gazzaley, a neurologist whose research includes studies of how the human brain manages attention and deals with distraction, considers how the ability to closely focus attention would have been crucial to the survival of early humans in a world filled with predators. When, for example, an early human glimpsed a pattern or smelled an odor that might indicate the presence of a predator, the human's neural activity, which is modulated by the prefrontal cortex, would be entirely focused on that pattern or smell to the exclusion of everything else.[24] In this highly focused, heightened state of alert, the slightest hint that a predator was present would have sent an early human scurrying to safety. Such a flight reaction is, in fact, an example of a cognitive bias known as *agent detection*. Even if the early human had been mistaken and no predator was present, instinctively responding to the cognitive bias of agent detection would have paid off for the simple reason that the small loss of time and energy expended in seeking safety was trivial when compared to the much greater loss of being killed and eaten while taking the time to gather additional information in order to make a more accurate calculation of the probability that a predator was lurking nearby. From the perspective of evolutionary psychology, a cognitive bias such as agent detection—which would have directly contributed to survival on the savanna of one hundred thousand years ago—is not "a design *flaw*—it is a design *feature*."[25] The problem for modern humans is that the environment under which our human ancestors evolved and their brains developed, which is known as the "environment of evolutional adaptiveness," is very different from the world we now inhabit, a world where cognitive biases that served useful purposes in harsh ancient environments now manifest themselves as flaws and where relying on heuristics can, to repeat the words of Tversky and Kahneman, "lead to severe and systematic errors." The modern world is an environment where it is extremely rare for our most important, most life-changing decisions to take place at the speed of a leaping tiger. More to the point, it is an environment where relying on heuristic shortcuts that are not much more than gut instincts will *not* positively impact the fitness of decisions such as where to most profitably invest money for retirement, which candidate is best suited to hold office, the long-term impacts of burning fossil fuels, or whether immunization is a better survival strategy than not immunizing.

It is important to point out that scientific findings showing that we are under the influence of cognitive bias do not mean that human beings are incapable of reasoning. Reason is, after all, an adaptation for living in complex human societies. Nor do the scientific findings mean that humans lack agency to such an extent that we are forever locked into behaviors that were hardwired into our brains long before such modern innovations as agriculture or permanent human settlements existed. For example, despite the fact that the size of the human brain suggests the ideally sized human social network numbers about 150 members,[26] many people function in much larger social networks and, obviously, humans are capable of living among populations that are many orders of magnitude larger than 150 individuals. Similarly, the fact that being suspicious of outsiders was a successful evolutionary design feature at a time when any outsider had the potential to bring violence or a previously unknown disease to your tiny band of humans does not mean that modern people are condemned by biology to live lives dominated by xenophobic fears. Just as humans are subject to cognitive forces that lead to the stigmatization of outsiders, they are also subject to cognitive forces that lead humans to cooperate for mutual benefit.[27]

IS THE HUMAN MIND IMMUNE TO FACTS?

The focus of this chapter thus far has been to point out the strong psychological forces hindering (though, by no means, entirely blocking) the ability of humans to objectively process and interpret information. Notably:

- Human senses and memory are less accurate and more susceptible to error than is generally understood.
- Human information processing is powerfully influenced by cognitive biases which, having developed under the harsh conditions of humanity's prehistoric past, do not lend themselves to solving the kinds of problems typically faced in the modern world.

Making the situation even more challenging is the fact that, very often, these combined psychological forces exert their influence without our being aware. No wonder, then, that one of the most troubling questions of the post-truth culture has become, *"Why don't facts have the power to change the way people think?"* Or that it has become routine to see the publication of articles with titles like, "Humans Are Hardwired to Dismiss Facts That Don't Fit Their Worldview,"[28] and full-length books such as *Denying to the Grave: Why We Ignore the Facts That Will Save Us.*[29]

Discouragingly enough, there is a significant amount of research-based evidence backing up the gloomy conclusion that our feelings, intuitions, and cognitive biases often triumph over facts. For example, a major meta-study found that non-scientists' attitudes toward climate change—*Is climate change really happening? If so, is it being caused by human activity?*—are determined more by existing political beliefs than by scientific evidence, with conservatives less likely to support taking action on climate change and liberals more likely to support such action.[30] Along the same lines, a number of studies have shown that identification with a political party has more influence than facts on how individuals stand on the issues.[31] And, no, the triumph of preexisting beliefs, attitudes, and group affiliations over facts is not some new phenomenon born of digital social media. A widely cited study conducted in the pre-social-media year of 1979 found that strongly held beliefs persist even when the evidence supporting them is discredited and additional evidence countering those strongly held beliefs is introduced.[32]

Even more daunting is the scientific evidence that the preexisting beliefs and attitudes determining our receptivity to facts are themselves more determined by biology than by the rational exercise of informed free choice. A few selected examples from the research include the following:

- Using magnetic resonance imaging technology, neuroscientists were able to observe and quantify test subjects' mental resistance when presented with facts conflicting with their political beliefs. As a result of their experiments, the researchers concluded that the negative emotions produced by challenging evidence were so disturbing that subjects resorted to "discounting its source, forming counterarguments, socially validating their original attitude, or selectively avoiding the new information."[33]
- Not only is challenging evidence disturbing to us, but experimental evidence also shows that humans actually experience pleasure, in the form of a "rush of dopamine," when they process information that confirms their existing beliefs.[34]
- A study of twins in Australia and the United States found that political views are inheritable to so great an extent that genetics are about twice as influential on political views as external influences.[35]
- Two recent independent neuroimaging studies found that satisfaction with the existing status quo and "reluctance to participate in social protest aimed at changing the status quo" are strongly linked to the size of the amygdala, an almond-shaped region of the brain involved in the experiencing of emotions.[36]

With the human brain seemingly hardwired to resort to cognitive shortcuts, reject information that conflicts with existing worldviews, and take pleasure in information that reinforces those same worldviews, it is not surprising that efforts to change another person's mind through facts and persuasion so often end in acrimony and failure. Does this mean, then, that the answer is to simply give up? No. It still matters that people speak up for their beliefs even when those who hear their words are not inclined to be receptive. People benefit from being reminded from time to time that not everyone sees the world the same way they do. And it still matters when members of a community of belief show support for each other's shared values. These things remain true despite the danger that both speaking up and reinforcing community values will, in some cases, result in the spread of less-then-credible information, echo chamber fearmongering, and hate speech; sadly, those are the inevitable evils that go hand in hand with the virtues of free expression. That said, anyone who would try to change the hearts and minds of others by challenging their core beliefs and strongly held opinions must remember that everyone they try to reach is operating under the influence of psychological forces of which they are not necessarily aware and do not necessarily control.

Instead of getting angry at those with whom we disagree or rejecting out of hand information that flies in the face of our beliefs, we are better off considering what psychological forces may be in play. First, accepting that someone who has dug in their mental heels on an issue—be it taxation, the existence (or not) of God, or the legalization of recreational drugs—is very unlikely to be swayed by a recitation of facts. As a straight-up practical strategy, understanding that facts by themselves are unlikely to change a core belief at least saves you the trouble of fruitlessly firing off a broadside of facts at those with whom you disagree. Second, recognizing when someone (yourself included) may be acting under the influence of a cognitive bias is a skill worth developing. While recognizing a cognitive bias is in play may not provide a clear path forward for influencing someone else's thinking, it can at least hint at strongpoints to avoid. If that person who despises millennials seems to be influenced by the cognitive bias of *declinism*, you are unlikely to get far by arguing that the past was just as bad as the present day. If that outspoken critic of capitalism who insists he is a one-of-kind original is operating under the influence of *false uniqueness bias*, trying to shake his conviction by pointing out that he is neither the first not the only person to criticize capitalism is not going to make much of an inroad.

To be clear, becoming aware of the psychological forces driving the opinions of others does not prohibit us from having lines that we will not cross. *"I do not care what cognitive biases are driving someone to spread racist hatred, I am not having a bit of it."* Nor should awareness and empathy prohibit us from evaluating the credibility of information and rejecting that which is clearly false. *"I really do understand where you are coming from but, for real, the Earth is not flat."* At the same time, responding with a full-frontal assault on the opinions, values, and group identities of those with whom we disagree is unlikely to change anyone's mind and will, more likely, trigger an automatic rejection of facts and opinions that challenge strongly held beliefs and opinions. Consider this. While listening to or reading arguments that fly in the face of the ideals you most value, have you ever thought, *"This is torture"*? Well, according to the research cited previously, it is. And because nobody likes being tortured, instead of assaulting someone with painful facts and pointed arguments it may be the wiser course to take a more nuanced approach. For example, a conservative might listen to an argument that puts forward the economic benefits of sustainable environmental stewardship where a pro-environmentalism argument based on an appeal to the beauty of the natural world would get nowhere. Similarly, a liberal who opposes firearms ownership might be more open to the idea that millions of gun owners safely enjoy shooting sports than the argument that you need a firearm on your person at all times to protect yourself from lurking criminals or to fight-off shadowy Deep State operatives.

Which is not to say that the soft approach is going to be entirely effective. However nuanced and honey-coated they may be, facts and arguments of any sort are unlikely to overcome the psychological forces and brain wiring that have shaped one person to be a resolute climate change denier or another to loudly advocate for the repeal of the Second Amendment. Effective or not, backing off the urge to charge sabers out into every battle of ideas may at least help bring some small measure civility to the digital discourse. To some extent, the moral imperative to never back down, to never shy from an argument has been normalized by pundits and media stars whose incomes depend on heightened polarization and creating conflict. Such persons have no desire to actually change anyone's mind because their economic interests depend on turmoil, on turning the dial up to eleven for even the most trivial of differences and keeping the war of words at maximum volume for as long as possible. Puff-chested media tough talkers and clench-fisted cultural warriors who never back down from a fight may provide audiences and followers with the kind of entertainment that boosts ratings and increases clicks, but puff-chested tough talk and clenched-fisted telling it like it is do nothing to resolve differences or unite divided people. While some may deride anything less than a total-war, confrontational approach as weakness, the scientific evidence says that anyone who thinks they will win anyone over by beating them over the head with facts (true or not) and high-octane arguments is bound to fail. The psychological forces in play are too strong and too deeply ingrained in the human mind to be easily routed by litanies of facts or onslaughts cleverly framed arguments.

NOTES

1. Christopher F. Chabris and Daniel J. Simons, *The Invisible Gorilla: And Other Ways Our Intuitions Deceive Us* (New York: Crown, 2010), 5–8.

2. *The Invisible Gorilla (Featuring Daniel Simons)–Regional EMMY Winning Video*, accessed June 16, 2020, https://www.youtube.com/watch?v=UtKt8YF7dgQ.

3. Elizabeth F. Loftus, *Eyewitness Testimony* (Cambridge, MA: Harvard University Press, 1979).

4. Steven T. Shorrock, "Errors of Perception in Air Traffic Control," *Safety Science* 45, no. 8 (October 2007): 899.

5. Raymond J. Corsini, Anne Anastasi, and Mary J. Allen, *Encyclopedia of Psychology*, second edition, volume 2 (New York: Wiley, 1994), 382.

6. Charles J. Brainerd and Valerie F. Reyna, *The Science of False Memory*, Oxford Psychology Series 38 (New York: Oxford University Press, 2005).

7. Julia Shaw, "Psychological Scientist," *Dr Julia Shaw*, accessed June 22, 2020, https://www.drjuliashaw.com/research.

8. Aaron French, "The Mandela Effect and New Memory," *Correspondences* 6, no. 2 (2018): 208–10.

9. Ziva Kunda, "The Case for Motivated Reasoning," *Psychological Bulletin* 108, no. 3 (1990): 480–98.

10. Martie G. Haselton, Daniel Nettle, and Damian R. Murray, "The Evolution of Cognitive Bias," in *Handbook of Evolutionary Psychology*, edited by David M. Buss, second edition (Newark, NJ: John Wiley & Sons, Inc., 2015), 968.

11. Jeff Desjardins, "Every Single Cognitive Bias in One Infographic," *The Visual Capitalist*, September 25, 2017, https://www.visualcapitalist.com/every-single-cognitive-bias/.

12. Nicholas DiFonzo, Jason W. Beckstead, Noah Stupak, and Kate Walders, "Validity Judgments of Rumors Heard Multiple Times: The Shape of the Truth Effect," *Social Influence* 11, no. 1 (January 2, 2016): 22–39.

13. Harry Enten, "Most People Believe In JFK Conspiracy Theories," *FiveThirtyEight*, October 23, 2017, https://fivethirtyeight.com/features/the-one-thing-in-politics-most-americans-believe-in-jfk-conspiracies/.

14. "Project Implicit," accessed May 26, 2020, https://implicit.harvard.edu/implicit/index.jsp.

15. Roy F. Baumeister, Ellen Bratslavsky, Catrin Finkenauer, and Kathleen D. Vohs, "Bad Is Stronger Than Good," *Review of General Psychology* 5, no. 4 (December 2001): 323–70.

16. Amos Tversky and Daniel Kahneman, "Belief in the Law of Small Numbers," *Psychological Bulletin* 76, no. 2 (1971): 105–10

17. Amos Tversky and Daniel Kahneman, "Judgment under Uncertainty: Heuristics and Biases," *Science* 185, no. 4157 (September 27, 1974): 1125.

18. Tversky and Kahneman, 1125.

19. Daniel Kahneman, *Daniel Kahneman: "Thinking, Fast and Slow"* | *Talks at Google–YouTube* (Mountain View, California, 2011), https://www.youtube.com/watch?v=CjVQJdIrDJ0.

20. Tversky and Kahneman, 1124.

21. Colin Holbrook, Daniel M.T. Fessler, and Carlos David Navarrete, "Looming Large in Others' Eyes: Racial Stereotypes Illuminate Dual Adaptations for Representing Threat versus Prestige as Physical Size," *Evolution and Human Behavior* 37, no. 1 (January 2016): 67–78.

22. "College Liberal," *Know Your Meme*, accessed May 10, 2020, https://know yourmeme.com/memes/college-liberal.

23. Gerd Gigerenzer, "Ecological Intelligence: An Adaptation for Frequencies," in *The Evolution of Mind*, edited by Denise Dellarosa Cummins and Collin Allen (New York: Oxford University Press, 1998), 9–29.

24. Adam Gazzaley and Larry D. Rosen, *The Distracted Mind: Ancient Brains in a High-Tech World* (Cambridge, MA: MIT Press, 2016), 54.

25. Martie G. Haselton, Daniel Nettle, and Damian R Murray, "The Evolution of Cognitive Bias," in *Handbook of Evolutionary Psychology*, edited by David M. Buss, second edition (Newark, NJ: John Wiley & Sons, Inc., 2015), 968.

26. R.I.M. Dunbar, "Coevolution of Neocortical Size, Group Size and Language in Humans," *Behavioral and Brain Sciences* 16, no. 4 (December 1993): 681–94.

27. Robert Kurzban and Mark R. Leary, "Evolutionary Origins of Stigmatization: The Functions of Social Exclusion.," *Psychological Bulletin* 127, no. 2 (2001): 187–208.

28. Adrian Bardon, "Humans Are Hardwired to Dismiss Facts That Don't Fit Their Worldview," *The Conversation*, January 31, 2020, http://theconversation.com/humans-are-hardwired-to-dismiss-facts-that-dont-fit-their-worldview-127168.

29. Sara E. Gorman and Jack M. Gorman, *Denying to the Grave: Why We Ignore the Facts That Will Save Us* (New York: Oxford University Press, 2016).

30. Toby Bolsen, James N. Druckman, and Fay Lomax Cook, "Citizens', Scientists', and Policy Advisors' Beliefs about Global Warming," *The ANNALS of the American Academy of Political and Social Science* 658, no. 1 (March 2015): 286.

31. Michael Bang Petersen, Martin Skov, Søren Serritzlew, and Thomas Ramsøy, "Motivated Reasoning and Political Parties: Evidence for Increased Processing in the Face of Party Cues," *Political Behavior* 35, no. 4 (December 2013): 831–54.

32. Charles G. Lord, Lee Ross, and Mark R. Lepper, "Biased Assimilation and Attitude Polarization: The Effects of Prior Theories on Subsequently Considered Evidence," *Journal of Personality and Social Psychology* 37, no. 11 (1979): 2098–109.

33. Jonas T. Kaplan, Sarah I. Gimbel, and Sam Harris, "Neural Correlates of Maintaining One's Political Beliefs in the Face of Counterevidence," *Scientific Reports* 6, no. 1 (December 2016): 39589: 1.

34. Elizabeth Kolbert, "That's What You Think: Why Reason and Evidence Won't Change Our Minds," *The New Yorker*, February 27, 2017, 66.

35. John R. Alford, Carolyn L. Funk, and John R. Hibbing, "Are Political Orientations Genetically Transmitted?" *American Political Science Review* 99, no. 2 (May 2005): 153–67.

36. H. Hannah Nam, John T. Jost, Lisa Kaggen, Daniel Campbell-Meiklejohn, and Jay J. Van Bavel, "Amygdala Structure and the Tendency to Regard the Social System as Legitimate and Desirable," *Nature Human Behaviour* 2, no. 2 (February 2018): 133–38.

BIBLIOGRAPHY

Alford, John R., Carolyn L. Funk, and John R. Hibbing. "Are Political Orientations Genetically Transmitted?" *American Political Science Review* 99, no. 2 (May 2005): 153–67.

Bardon, Adrian. "Humans Are Hardwired to Dismiss Facts That Don't Fit Their Worldview." *The Conversation*, January 31, 2020, http://theconversation.com/humans-are-hardwired-to-dismiss-facts-that-dont-fit-their-worldview-127168.

Baumeister, Roy F., Ellen Bratslavsky, Catrin Finkenauer, and Kathleen D. Vohs. "Bad Is Stronger Than Good." *Review of General Psychology* 5, no. 4 (December 2001): 323–70.

Bolsen, Toby, James N. Druckman, and Fay Lomax Cook. "Citizens', Scientists', and Policy Advisors' Beliefs about Global Warming." *The ANNALS of the American Academy of Political and Social Science* 658, no. 1 (March 2015): 271–95.

Brainerd, Charles J., and Valerie F. Reyna. *The Science of False Memory.* Oxford Psychology Series 38. New York: Oxford University Press, 2005.

Chabris, Christopher F., and Daniel J. Simons. *The Invisible Gorilla: And Other Ways Our Intuitions Deceive Us.* New York: Crown, 2010.

"College Liberal." *Know Your Meme.* Accessed May 10, 2020, https://knowyourmeme.com/memes/college-liberal.

Corsini, Raymond J., Anne Anastasi, and Mary J. Allen. *Encyclopedia of Psychology.* Second edition, volume 2. New York: Wiley, 1994.

Desjardins, Jeff. "Every Single Cognitive Bias in One Infographic." *The Visual Capitalist*, September 25, 2017, https://www.visualcapitalist.com/every-single-cognitive-bias/.

DiFonzo, Nicholas, Jason W. Beckstead, Noah Stupak, and Kate Walders. "Validity Judgments of Rumors Heard Multiple Times: The Shape of the Truth Effect." *Social Influence* 11, no. 1 (January 2, 2016): 22–39.

Dunbar, R.I.M. "Coevolution of Neocortical Size, Group Size and Language in Humans." *Behavioral and Brain Sciences* 16, no. 4 (December 1993): 681–94.

Enten, Harry. "Most People Believe in JFK Conspiracy Theories." *FiveThirtyEight*, October 23, 2017, https://fivethirtyeight.com/features/the-one-thing-in-politics-most-americans-believe-in-jfk-conspiracies/.

French, Aaron. "The Mandela Effect and New Memory." *Correspondences* 6, no. 2 (2018): 201–33.

Gazzaley, Adam, and Larry D. Rosen. *The Distracted Mind: Ancient Brains in a High-Tech World.* Cambridge, MA: MIT Press, 2016.

Gigerenzer, Gerd. "Ecological Intelligence: An Adaptation for Frequencies." In *The Evolution of Mind*, edited by Denise Dellarosa Cummins and Collin Allen, 9–29. New York: Oxford University Press, 1998.

Gorman, Sara E., and Jack M. Gorman. *Denying to the Grave: Why We Ignore the Facts That Will Save Us*. New York: Oxford University Press, 2016.

Haselton, Martie G., Daniel Nettle, and Damian R. Murray. "The Evolution of Cognitive Bias." In *Handbook of Evolutionary Psychology*, edited by David M. Buss, second edition, 968–87. Newark, NJ: John Wiley & Sons, Inc., 2015.

Holbrook, Colin, Daniel M.T. Fessler, and Carlos David Navarrete. "Looming Large in Others' Eyes: Racial Stereotypes Illuminate Dual Adaptations for Representing Threat versus Prestige as Physical Size." *Evolution and Human Behavior* 37, no. 1 (January 2016): 67–78.

Kahneman, Daniel. *Daniel Kahneman: "Thinking, Fast and Slow" | Talks at Google—YouTube*. Mountain View, California, 2011, https://www.youtube.com/watch?v=CjVQJdIrDJ0.

Kaplan, Jonas T., Sarah I. Gimbel, and Sam Harris. "Neural Correlates of Maintaining One's Political Beliefs in the Face of Counterevidence." *Scientific Reports* 6, no. 1 (December 2016): 39589.

Kolbert, Elizabeth. "That's What You Think: Why Reason and Evidence Won't Change Our Minds." *The New Yorker*, February 27, 2017.

Kunda, Ziva. "The Case for Motivated Reasoning." *Psychological Bulletin* 108, no. 3 (1990): 480–98.

Kurzban, Robert, and Mark R. Leary. "Evolutionary Origins of Stigmatization: The Functions of Social Exclusion." *Psychological Bulletin* 127, no. 2 (2001): 187–208.

Loftus, Elizabeth F. *Eyewitness Testimony*. Cambridge, MA: Harvard University Press, 1979.

Lord, Charles G., Lee Ross, and Mark R. Lepper. "Biased Assimilation and Attitude Polarization: The Effects of Prior Theories on Subsequently Considered Evidence." *Journal of Personality and Social Psychology* 37, no. 11 (1979): 2098–109.

Nam, H. Hannah, John T. Jost, Lisa Kaggen, Daniel Campbell-Meiklejohn, and Jay J. Van Bavel. "Amygdala Structure and the Tendency to Regard the Social System as Legitimate and Desirable." *Nature Human Behaviour* 2, no. 2 (February 2018): 133–38.

Petersen, Michael Bang, Martin Skov, Søren Serritzlew, and Thomas Ramsøy. "Motivated Reasoning and Political Parties: Evidence for Increased Processing in the Face of Party Cues." *Political Behavior* 35, no. 4 (December 2013): 831–54.

"Project Implicit." Accessed May 26, 2020, https://implicit.harvard.edu/implicit/index.jsp.

Shaw, Julia. "Psychological Scientist." *Dr Julia Shaw*. Accessed June 22, 2020, https://www.drjuliashaw.com/research.

Shorrock, Steven T. "Errors of Perception in Air Traffic Control." *Safety Science* 45, no. 8 (October 2007): 890–904.

The Invisible Gorilla (Featuring Daniel Simons)–Regional EMMY Winning Video. Accessed June 16, 2020, https://www.youtube.com/watch?v=UtKt8YF7dgQ.

Tversky, Amos, and Daniel Kahneman. "Belief in the Law of Small Numbers." *Psychological Bulletin* 76, no. 2 (1971): 105–10.

Tversky, Amos, and Daniel Kahneman. "Judgment under Uncertainty: Heuristics and Biases." *Science* 185, no. 4157 (September 27, 1974): 1124–31.

3

Digital Utopias Lost

How the Conflicting Dreams from the Dawn of Cyberspace Diverged

When those of us who find ourselves subject to the storms and squalls of the post-truth culture think about the words we use to describe the cultures and communities of cyberspace—a virtual landscape which encompasses all of the internet, including social media—words like "utopian," "harmonious," and "tolerant" do not spring readily to mind. For many, cyberspace is anything but. Such pessimism was not always, however, the dominant attitude. In the formative years of what would become cyberspace, there was a strongly optimistic sense that a networked digital world could, and would, be a better world than the analog one humanity had inhabited for the previous two hundred thousand years. Underlying these rosy early visions of a cyberutopia, however, were irreconcilable structural and philosophical differences that, looking back, point in the direction of the divisive post-truth culture of the early twenty-first century. Understanding how and why the initial optimism about a networked world turned into world weariness and polarization holds lessons that can help us better understand how and why the post-truth culture became what it is.

AS *WE* ONCE THOUGHT

In July 1945, the *Atlantic Monthly* published "As We May Think," an article by the distinguished inventor and engineer Vannevar Bush (1890–1974).[1] The ostensible focus of "As We May Think" is the "memex," a theoretical device Bush conceived of as a tool that scientists and, eventually, scholars in other fields of study would use not only to record and share their own ideas and findings but also to access information created by other scholars. Although the article did not exactly predict digital technology, anyone reading "As We May Think" in the twenty-first century will see in Bush's description of the memex a foreshadowing of desktop computers, hypertext, the internet, and online encyclopedias. "As We May Think" was clearly ahead of its time.

Bush himself, on the other hand, was in many ways thoroughly a man of his time. For the duration of the Second World War, Bush served as head of the U.S. Office of Scientific Research and Development, the government office in charge of all research and development for the U.S. military during the war. Among many its responsibilities, the U.S. Office of Scientific Research and Development oversaw the Manhattan Project, with Bush himself personally witnessing the test of the first atomic bomb at the Trinity Site in New Mexico. By the time "As We May Think" appeared in print, Germany had already surrendered, while the Empire of Japan would follow suit within a month— compelled to do so in part by the new technology Bush had played a role in developing. As an American scientist and technologist, Bush was proud of the role that he and his colleagues had played in winning the Second World War. He was equally proud of the role of science and technology in steadily improving the overall quality of life by providing humanity (or at least the more-privileged part of humanity) with increased wealth, greater comfort, and longer and healthier lives. And Bush was optimistic that even greater scientific and technological achievements would follow the imminent end of the war.

On one level, when Bush titled his essay "As We May Think," he included all of humanity in his *We*. In his view, everyone stood to benefit from advances in science and technology. On another level, though, Bush was not speaking to all of humanity; instead, he was speaking to a rather elite group of his highly educated colleagues: the mostly white, male, and Anglo-American scientists and engineers who shared Bush's values, can-do attitude, and optimistic confidence that they, as an elite group, held the keys to solving humanity's most vexing problems. At the time Bush was writing "As We May Think," he and his fellow scientists and engineers had good reasons to feel confident about themselves and their work. Their genius and ingenuity had contributed immensely to the winning of the war, though it would be a few weeks after the publication of "As We May Think" before the bulk of humanity would learn exactly to what extent, and through what fearsome means, Bush's scientific and engineering elite had sealed victory for the Allies. Regardless of what the bombing of Hiroshima and Nagasaki implied for the future of humanity, the end of the Second World War and the years following it were a time when Bush and other "men of science" were almost universally respected, deferred to, and lauded. It was a time when being included among Bush's elite *We* was to be in a position of considerable prestige and privilege.

It is not an overstatement to say that "As We May Think" cast a strong and lasting influence on the development of digital technology and the birth of the Information Age. Douglas Engelbart (1925–2013), the engineer who, among other significant achievements, created the first computer mouse, was inspired by *Life Magazine*'s September 1945 republication of "As We May Think" after happening on the article while serving in the Navy.[2] Ted Nelson, who in 1963 coined the terms "hypertext" and "hypermedia," was similarly influenced by Bush.[3] J.C.R. Licklider (1915–1990), who in 1963 proposed the creation of an "Intergalactic Computer Network" that is strikingly similar to what would become the internet,[4] dedicated his book *Libraries of the Future* to Bush.[5] These and other pioneers of the Digital Age shared Bush's optimism about not only the benefits of technology, but also the benefits of increased access to, and sharing of, information. For besides considering how the analog technology of the day, in the proposed form of the memex, could help scientists and other scholars *record* information, "As We May Think" was equally concerned with making that recorded information widely available to all. Bush was optimistic that unfettered access to more information would only benefit humanity: "Presumably man's spirit should be elevated if he can better review his shady past and analyze more completely and objectively his present problems."[6]

Within Bush's lifetime, a small group of computer scientists had begun sharing information via computer networks. In 1968, Licklider and Advanced Research Projects Agency Network (ARPANET) pioneer Robert W. Taylor (1932–2017) published "The Computer as Communication Device," a magazine article written for nonspecialists that opens with the optimistic declaration, "In a few years, men will be able to communicate more effectively through a machine than face to face."[7] Among the scientists and engineers who built and pioneered cyberspace, this tone of optimism would continue almost unabated for the next few decades. It is understandable that optimism and a shared sense of purpose would prevail among the homogenous community that dominated cyberspace from the 1960s into (roughly) the early 1990s. Most members of the nascent cyberspace community came from nonprofit academia (supplemented by smaller contingents of community members from the military and the world of business) and worked in scientific or engineering fields.

FROM *WE* TO EVERYBODY

In 1966 the U.S. federal government funded the ARPANET, the first wide-area packet switching network and one of the first networks to use the TCP/IP protocol. Based on ideas first proposed by Licklider and Taylor, ARPANET laid the foundation of what would become the internet. While ARPANET's origins as a Department of Defense project are indisputable, the extent to which ARPANET was a military project in the strictest sense is less clear. One widely shared version of the story is that the Department of Defense officials who funded ARPANET were seeking to develop a computer network designed in such a way that a lone nuclear weapon could not take down the entire network either by targeting a single master computer on which every other computer in the network relied or by destroying any one computer in a rigid chain of sequentially linked machines. A slightly different version of the story holds that "ARPANET's purpose was always more academic than military, but, as more academic facilities connected to it, the network did take on the tentacle-like structure military officials had envisioned."[8] In any case, the internet developed as a highly decentralized network in which the failure of any one node does not bring down the entire network.

For the first decade and a half of its existence, ARPANET was the exclusive domain of a tiny elite of computer scientists and engineers. Starting in 1981, the creation of the National Science Foundation's NSFNET brought even more academics online. Even though NSFNET comprised the largest segment of the internet in the United States, it remained something of a country club for tech-savvy academics from the nonprofit sector. One of the regulations that helped maintain the clubby atmosphere was a prohibition against conducting any commercial business on NSFNET. Some users of NSFNET were such sticklers about the network's noncommercial status that they objected even to sharing book reviews over the network on the grounds that book reviews could be considered a form of advertising. The Scientific and Advanced Technology Act (U.S. Public Law 102-476), which was passed on October 23, 1992, greatly disrupted the country-club atmosphere by both allowing commercial activity on NSFNET and connecting NSFNET with emerging commercial networks, thereby opening the door to the growth of e-commerce and ushering in decades of change that would profoundly reshape not only the culture of cyberspace, but economies, politics, and society worldwide.[9] Even though the growth of the internet was beginning to somewhat diversify the online community, that community remained distinctly homogenous even at the turn of the millennium. In the year 2000, of 257,728,489 internet users worldwide, 192,332,704 (slightly under 75 percent) were from the United States/North America; additionally, 79.5 percent had English as a first language, 95 percent were from a country with a UN Human Development Index ranking of "High," and 73 percent were from a country among the top-twenty GPD countries worldwide.[10] If you were an internet user at that time who expressed an idea or opinion online, there was a good chance that everyone who heard your message was more similar to you than they were different.

Textbox 3.1
Shut Up, You Bloody Vikings

For an illustration of how homogenous the network-computing community was during the years before the internet exploded into everyday life, just consider the origins of the computing term *spam*. Used to describe an onslaught of unsolicited email messages, the first known printed usage of *spam* in this sense dates to 1991 (though informal usage likely preceded that date).[11] The word *spam* made the jump from canned meat product to the world of computing thanks to the word's repeated use in a *Monty Python's Flying Circus* comedy skit that first aired in 1970 on the BBC (and would later air during multiple rebroadcasts of the program on the U.S. Public Broadcasting System). That a somewhat obscure reference to *Monty Python's Flying Circus* caught on and stuck was, to a considerable extent, the result of the cultural homogeneity of cyberspace at the time. At least among the English-speaking cyberspace community of the late 1980s and early 1990s, familiarity with *Monty Python's Flying Circus* would have approached 100% percent, while actually being a fan of the show was highly likely. Everyone in cyberspace got the *spam* reference because everyone had been exposed to the same cultural touchstones. The situation was really no different than London theater audiences in Shakespeare's time getting all jokes in his comedies due to their shared cultural experiences (unlike present-day readers and playgoers who need footnotes to explain why the Bard's wordplay is such a hoot). Of course, the point is not that early 1990s computer nerds really liked *Monty Python* (which most of them, in fact, did); rather, the point is that it is relatively easy for harmony to prevail in a community when its members' backgrounds, educations, experiences, tastes, and outlooks vary little from one person to the next. The opposite lesson of this same point, however, is that it does not take much for that harmony to vanish when diverse voices begin entering the communal conversation.

The 1992 passage of the Scientific and Advanced Technology Act was well timed to bring about change to cyberspace and its user community. The first webpage had been published on December 20, 1990, while Mosaic, the first widely adopted web browser, was released in 1993. Prior to the web and web browsers, the most common ways of using the internet included:

• Sending email via such text-only clients as Elm, Citadel, Eudora, and Pine

- Sharing files via File Transfer Protocol
- Participating in early forms of social media, typically via commercial bulletin board systems, which flourished from the mid-1970s into the first half of the 1990s, or Usenet newgroups, which had their heyday starting in the early 1980s and did not finally fade away until the start of the twenty-first century
- Accessing the internet via Gopher; developed at the University of Michigan, Gopher was (and, to a tiny extent, still is) a menu-driven hypertext communications protocol that vanished with an all-but-audible "Poof!" upon the rapid and widespread proliferation of web browsers
- Using tools like Archie, Veronica, and Jughead to search for Gopher content; these tools would disappear with the advent of such early web search engines as WebCrawler, Yahoo!Search, Excite, and AltaVista (Google did not show up to dominate the search engine field until a few years later)

For anyone who does not remember the internet before the web and web browsers, access was mostly via dial-up and the landscape was one vast Serengeti of text. Through such protocols as File Transfer Protocol, users could download images and, if their bandwidth and patience were up to it, short videos, but viewing images or videos was not possible until after a user had downloaded them to a local machine. If an image file was identified as a

```
Internet Gopher Information Client v1.12

        Root gopher server: gopher.tc.umn.edu

--> 1.  Information About Gopher/
    2.  Computer Information/
    3.  Internet file server (ftp) sites/
    4.  Fun & Games/
    5.  Libraries/
    6.  Mailing Lists/
    7.  UofM Campus Information/
    8.  News/
    9.  Other Gopher and Information Servers/
    10. Phone Books/
    11. Search lots of places at the U of M <?>

Press ? for Help, q to Quit, u to go up a menu     Page:1/1
```

https://ils.unc.edu/callee/gopherpaper.htm

Figure 3.1. The homepage of the University of Minnesota Gopher server. The Gopher was created at the University of Minnesota and launched in 1991. Christopher (Cal) Lee, University of Michigan, School of Information

photograph of a dog, users simply had to trust that it was a photograph of a dog and not, say, a line drawing of a cat (or something much worse). When computer users began installing early browsers like Lynx, Cello, and Mosaic (the real game changer among early browsers), a world of color, images, and magically clickable links was revealed. The experience for many was not all the different from Dorothy opening the door of her drab, gray-toned house to reveal the dazzling Technicolor Land of Oz.

While there is no hard date for when cyberspace transitioned from the technological elite of academic scientists and engineers to *everybody*, September 1993—memorialized by some as "Eternal September"—is notable as the month and year when the private AOL network connected its sizeable customer base to the larger internet, setting off a virtual land rush.[12] Much to the surprise of many members of the NSFNET country club, it turned out some of the tens of thousands, soon to be millions, of brand new inhabitants of cyberspace were running roughshod over long-standing community standards of online behavior. While there had always been lively debates and sharp disagreements among the inhabitants of cyberspace, as the online community began expanding from Bush's elite *We* to (what seemed like) everybody, there emerged a sense that *something* needed to be done to restore some semblance of order. Even before the onslaught of Eternal September, old-school users of network computers were complaining about the online misbehavior of newbies, as illustrated in an article published in a 1986 issue of *BYTE* (an early microcomputing magazine):

> whereas an open computer conference begins with a small number of well-informed and interested participants, it soon attracts others. That's all right: it's supposed to attract others. Where else would you get new ideas? But soon it attracts too many, far too many, and some of them are not only uniformed by aggressively misinformed. Dilution takes place. Arguments replace discussion. Tempers are frayed.[13]

An early attempt at responding to the growing disruption of cyberspace caused by the antics of all those newbies took the form of lessons in *netiquette*, a portmanteau of the words *network* and *etiquette*. While the word *netiquette* sounds rather quaint in a post-truth culture where the chief worry is less "*Some people are being rude online*," and more "*A lot of people appear to be intentionally working at destroying democracy*," beginning in the mid-1990s many members of the online community earnestly devoted time and effort to promoting the ethos of netiquette. A popular method of imparting netiquette to newbies was to politely spell out the rules of acceptable online behavior via written netiquette guides, many of which took the form of documents posted to Usenet newsgroups and webpages. Typical of these is a vintage 1995 ascii-text document called simply "Netiquette Guide," which offers such guidelines as:

- If you are forwarding or reposting a message you've received, do not change the wording. If the message was a personal message to you and you are reposting to a group, you should ask permission first.
- Never send chain letters via electronic mail. Chain letters are forbidden on the internet. Your network privileges will be revoked.
- You should not send heated messages (we call these "flames") even if you are provoked. On the other hand, you shouldn't be surprised if you get flamed and it's prudent not to respond to flames.
- Watch cc's when replying. Don't continue to include people if the messages have become a two-way conversation.
- Use mixed case. UPPERCASE LOOKS AS IF YOU'RE SHOUTING.
- Remember that the recipient is a human being whose culture, language, and humor have different points of reference from your own. Remember that date formats, measurements, and idioms may not travel well. Be especially careful with sarcasm.[14]

Most writers of netiquette guides worked from the avuncular assumption that those who were violating the traditional norms of online decorum simply did not know the rules and, once properly educated, would quickly shape up and start behaving themselves. In addition to online guides, printed articles and books on the topic of netiquette also joined the battle of manners. An early (if not the first) book to tackle the topic of netiquette was the enthusiastically titled *Internet Basics: Your Online Access to the Global Electronic Superhighway*, which appeared in 1993.[15] Somewhat later in the game, those who aspired to fix a broken internet resorted to software solutions. In 2002 the nonprofit think tank Web Lab launched a plan to bring civility to cyberspace through the use of "Small Group Dialogue," a combination communication technique/software tool. The idea was that internet content providers would license Small Group Dialogue in order to raise the level of civility on their sites.[16] The fact that the phrase "post-truth" is a thing suggest how well this effort—and every other polite effort to bring civility to cyberspace—worked out in the end. Which is to say, not at all.

Another polite approach for improving online behavior involved appealing to notions of good citizenship and obligation to community. The word *netizen*, a portmanteau of *network* and *citizen*, started appearing in print in the mid-1990s, and for a while it became somewhat routine to see articles and postings with titles like "What Is a Netizen?"[17] While the exact definition of netizen could vary from publication to publication and from Usenet newsgroup to Usenet newsgroup, the consistent theme was that being a citizen of the network came with rights, responsibilities, and a duty to be a good inhabitant of cyberspace. What the academics (most of whom were employed by public colleges and universities) who led the way in promoting the concept of being a good citizen of the network could not have foreseen is that, in just a few decades, millions of empowered netizens would turn against the very professions and institutions that had bestowed on them the gift of cyberspace and the opportunity to have a voice in it. Instead of thanking those who created and freely shared cyberspace with the world, significant online communities began using social media to relentlessly attack higher education, science, and the very idea that government could have a beneficial role in advancing the interests of society. Would such phenomena as the antivaccination movement or, in the United States, the gradual defunding of public colleges and universities have the strength they now enjoy without the internet? Possibly not. Although there are many who do not appreciate it, the irony of politicians, activists, media celebrities, and their followers using cyberspace to proclaim the uselessness of government and higher education—the very institutions that created the platform on which they freely express their views—is not that different from flat-earth true believers getting on an airliner to fly *around the globe* promoting their delusion. In a climate of such extreme anti-intellectualism it is no wonder that, fifty years after the first message was sent on what would become the internet, a journalist who covers technology saw fit to publish an article entitled, "50 Years Later, The Internet's Inventors Are Horrified by What It's Become."[18] From the perspective of the twenty-first century, Vannevar Bush's presumption that "man's spirit should be elevated if he can better review his shady past and analyze more completely and objectively his present problems" seems wildly optimistic and rather thoroughly disproven.

As the netiquette guide quoted previously indicates, when shared values, politeness, and appeals to civic responsibility proved ineffective, an angry netizen from the formative years of cyberspace might resort to sending a *flame*, a hostile blast that could include profanity, ridicule, and threats. When two or more netizens got into a knockdown drag out, the resultant storm of messages was called a *flame war*. An early and notorious example of a flame war broke out in April 1994 after an Arizona law firm spammed five thousand Usenet newsgroups with an advertisement offering immigrants to the United States assistance in obtaining green cards.[19] While thousands of network users were outraged at both the extent of the spamming and the crassly commercial nature of the message, the lawyers who sent the spam argued that they were within their rights to distribute their message. The offending law firm received multiple threatening phone calls and its email inbox was choked to a standstill with angry messages. While the Great Spamming of 1994 created a furor that made news even beyond the boundaries of cyberspace, it was only a taste of things to come, an early lesson demonstrating the naïveté of the idea that the online world would naturally function as a peaceable, mostly unregulated, kingdom in which everyone would just get along and differences could be worked out through a brand of civil discourse rooted in shared goals and rational thinking. As the years went by and the population of cyberspace grew by orders of magnitude, the harsh truth of the Great Spamming of 1994 and other early lessons in discord would be reaffirmed too many times to count. One of the harshest of these lessons came in the form of failed dreams of an online Utopia.

Textbox 3.2
The Shady Past (and Present) of Cyberspace

Even though commercial activity was banned from the NSFNET into the 1990s, prior to the lifting of that ban a number of private U.S. networks—such as American Online, Prodigy, and CompuServe—operated with no such restrictions. Before those networks existed, though, the biggest outlet for commercial activity in cyberspace were the thousands of for-profit, dial-up bulletin board services. And the biggest business on those bulletin board services was pornography.

It is not really surprising that pornography has an early association with cyberspace as, historically, pornography has always readily adapted to new technologies, including printing from movable type, photography, and motion pictures. (The first public showing of a motion picture in 1894 was followed within two years by the premier of what is considered the first pornographic film, *Le Coucher de la Mariée*.[20]) Nobody knows exactly when pornography first went online, but the article "X-Rated Computer Displays," which appeared in the *New York Times* on January 28, 1988, was an early public acknowledgment of the fact that computer pornography was something that not only existed but had been around long enough for mainstream reporters to get wind of it. The *New York Times* article states, "Electronic bulletin boards, usually operated by computer enthusiasts out of their homes, can provide off-color jokes, pornographic pictures, formats for trading sexual messages and dating services."[21] The truth was even darker than this article suggests, as some of those dial-up bulletin boards served as conduits for child pornography and sex trafficking.[22] Just as the early flame wars were a spark before a conflagration, the pornography conveyed via computer bulletin board services was a mere ripple compared to the flood of pornography unleashed once the web and web browsers turned cyberspace into a much more visual medium than it had previously been. In July 1995, *Time Magazine* ran a salaciously illustrated cover story entitled "On a Screen Near You: Cyberporn," which breathlessly reported that there was "a lot" of pornography on the internet and that people were making a lot of money from it.[23] For many, learning that it was possible for anyone—potentially even a child—to dial-up pornography from the privacy of their home was the first widespread inkling that the world of computers was more than machines crunching numbers at the behest of mathematically minded technologists whose interest in the opposite (or any) sex was questionable at best. The year following the publication of "On a Screen Near You: Cyberporn," the U.S. Congress passed the Communications Decency Act of 1996 (U.S. Public Law 104-104). This was not only the first U.S. legislative effort to control internet pornography, but also the first significant attempt by the American government to control any content whatsoever on the internet. To say the law was unsuccessful is an understatement. The Communications Decency Act's antidecency provisions were struck down by the 1997 U.S. Supreme Court ruling in the case of *Reno v. ACLU* (521 U.S. 844 (1997)), and in the years that followed internet pornography did anything but disappear. By the year 2019, industry leader Pornhub was reporting forty-three billion visits per year—about five-and-a-half visits for every human being on the planet.[24]

DUELING DIGITAL UTOPIAS

Governments of the Industrial World, you weary giants of flesh and steel, I come from Cyberspace, the new home of Mind. On behalf of the future, I ask you of the past to leave us alone. You are not welcome among us. You have no sovereignty where we gather.

–John Perry Barlow[25]

So goes the opening salvo of "A Declaration of the Independence of Cyberspace," a document unleashed on the world on February 8, 1996, by John Perry Barlow (1947–2018), an American writer, political activist, cattle rancher, and lyricist for the Grateful Dead. While the opening sentences constitute a credible summation of Barlow's "Declaration," the author has much more to say, including:

I declare the global social space we are building to be naturally independent of the tyrannies you seek to impose on us. You have no moral right to rule us nor do you possess any methods of enforcement we have true reason to fear.
Cyberspace does not lie within your borders.

You do not know our culture, our ethics, or the unwritten codes that already provide our society more order than could be obtained by any of your impositions.

We are creating a world that all may enter without privilege or prejudice accorded by race, economic power, military force, or station of birth.

We are creating a world where anyone, anywhere may express his or her beliefs, no matter how singular, without fear of being coerced into silence or conformity.

Barlow was not alone in calling for cyberspace to exist as a place where the only rule is that there are no rules. And why not feel that way when the very architecture of cyberspace—a distributed network in which there exists no one computer to rule them all—is a blueprint for freedom from centralized authority? Following the lead of Barlow and like-minded others, in 1994 the Progress and Freedom Foundation, a market-oriented think tank, published "Cyberspace and the American Dream: A Magna Carta for the Knowledge Age,"[26] a document that had, arguably, the greatest and longest-lasting influence in shaping the dream of cyberspace as an unregulated entrepreneur's paradise. To call the visions of Barlow and the Progress and Freedom Foundation utopian is putting it mildly. Looking back on these foundational documents through disillusioned twenty-first-century eyes, we might even call them naïve. Whether it is the Great Firewall of China—with which the antidemocratic government of China tightly controls the internet within its vast physical borders—or the sporadic efforts of various democracies to regulate or ban outright such things as free expression (in forms ranging from the vilest sort of hate speech to legitimate criticisms of overreaching governments), frowned-up forms of online commerce (e.g., gambling, pornography, drug trafficking), or entire social media platforms (as when the president of the United States threatened to ban TikTok in 2020), there is ample evidence that governments do, indeed, possess means of enforcement and are fully capable of giving the inhabitants of cyberspace something very much to fear. Governments aside, the mega-corporations that sprang from the loins of cyberspace—Google, Facebook, Twitter, Amazon, and the rest—have proven themselves to have more power both to intrude upon the private lives of individuals and to quash free-market competition than anyone could have imagined in the early 1990s.

In 1997, Langdon Winner, a professor at Rensselaer Polytechnic Institute and noted commentator on society and technology, dubbed the laissez faire vision of cyberspace as *cyberlibertarianism*, a creed which he characterized as, "a collection of ideas that links ecstatic enthusiasm for electronically mediated forms of living with radical, right wing libertarian ideas about the proper definition of freedom, social life, economics, and politics in the years to come."[27] Many years later, Moshe Y. Vardi, editor-in-chief of

Communications of the ACM, succinctly summed up cyberlibertarianism as "a common attitude in the tech community; 'regulation stifles innovation' is the prevailing mantra."[28] This "prevailing mantra" explains why some of the biggest proponents of cyberlibertarianism are the tech millionaires and billionaires of the Silicon Valley and its many technology-hub offshoots. Whenever the chief executive officer (CEO) of a social media platform cites freedom of expression as the justification for doing nothing to stop hate speech (or, in some cases, to justify doing the very things that promote hate speech in the first place), you can be sure that the CEO's case making is grounded in cyberlibertarian ideals.[29] Similarly, the appeal of the Bitcoin phenomenon, which promises complete privacy, celebrates entrepreneurism, and proposes to disconnect money from the authority of banks, financial institutions, and the state, has been linked philosophically to cyberlibertarianism.[30] Millionaires, billionaires, and CEOs aside, cyberlibertarianism remains popular among many ordinary individuals who are committed to a vision of cyberspace as a free, self-regulating, and egalitarian realm standing separate from the outdated rules, restrictions, and authority of the physical world. Perhaps the best evidence of the appeal of the basic principles of cyberlibertarianism is the inevitability of swift and loud popular resistance to any attempt by governments, corporations, or fellow inhabitants of cyberspace to censure or regulate the online world. Groups like Wikileaks, Anonymous, and too many other loose (and not so loose) affiliations of netizens to name carry in their DNA the genetic fingerprints of cyberlibertarianism.

Although the utopian vision that became known as cyberlibertarianism has had a strong and lasting impact on digital culture and the digital economy as they exist today, it was not the only utopian idea surfacing during the formative years of the internet. More than a year before Barlow's "Declaration of the Independence of Cyberspace," *The Amateur Computerist* (a Columbia University–based publication whose masthead read "The Netizens and the Internet") published its "Proposed Declaration of the Rights of Netizens."[31] Much of *The Amateur Computerist*'s declaration articulates well with Barlow's ideas, as the authors' list of the rights of netizens include such classically libertarian concepts as the right to free expression and freedom from government interference. However, after making a radical left turn to declare that "the Net represents a revolution in human communications that was built by a cooperative non-commercial process" the authors begin to spell out a number of rights that few hardcore cyberlibertarians or tech CEOs would care acknowledge, including:

- Universal access at no or low cost
- Equal quality of connection

- Equal time of connection
- Volunteer contribution—no personal profit from the contribution freely given by others
- Protection of the public purpose from those who would use it for their private and money-making purposes

The authors conclude their "Proposed Declaration of the Rights of Netizens" with the bold assertion:

> The Net is not a Privilege but a Right. It is only valuable when it is collective and universal. Volunteer effort protects the intellectual and technological commonwealth that is being created. DO NOT UNDERESTIMATE THE POWER OF THE NET AND NETIZENS.

The collectivist rhetoric found in the "Proposed Declaration of the Rights of Netizens" is a long way from anything that could be labeled "radical, right wing libertarian." This alternate, collectivist vision of a cyberspace Utopia—an explicitly *cyberliberal* Utopia of which the authors of the "Proposed Declaration of the Rights of Netizens" were not the sole advocates—arose from a divergent view of how cyberspace of the early 1990s came to exist. Where cyberlibertarians saw a digital environment built by plucky, risk-taking entrepreneurs who were more than happy to thumb their noses at government interference, cyberliberals saw a digital environment that spent the first two decades (approximately) of its existence as a taxpayer-funded research project not that different from such analog public works projects as Hoover Dam, the Interstate Highway System, or the space program. The internet could not have come into existence without the expenditure of large amounts of taxpayer dollars poured into the budgets of government research and development projects and university research grants. In the United States, the initial infrastructure of what would become the internet was built with federal tax dollars, and federal tax dollars subsidized use of network infrastructure so that the individuals who became the original plucky, risk-taking entrepreneurs of cyberspace could afford to access the network in the first place. Before big corporations and internet start-ups arrived on the scene, it was hobbyists and computer professionals working nights and weekends who created many of the programs and applications that made the early internet usable by people who were not full-blown computer scientists and/or fluent programmers.[32] In the view of cyberliberals, all new technological advancements were built on previous advancements and, as such, were collective achievements rather than individual accomplishments. Viewed through this lens, cyberspace flourished through collaboration, the open sharing of new advances, open source software, shareware, and putting the public good ahead of any profit motive. Howard Rheingold, an early advocate of cyberliberalism and the person who coined the phrase "virtual community," envisioned in 1993 an "electronic agora, an 'Athens without slaves' made possible by telecommunications and cheap computers" and (despite being well aware of how cruel at times the netizens of cyberspace could be to each other) stated his belief "that this technology, if properly understood and defended by enough citizens, does have democratizing potential in the way that alphabets and printing presses had democratizing potential."[33]

The idea that the conflicting utopias of cyberlibertarianism and cyberliberalism could peacefully coexist seems absurd, but that does not mean that there were no attempts to unite the two visions into a functional whole. In 1996, British media theorists Richard Barbrook and Andy Cameron identified this marriage of left and right as "The California Ideology," an unlikely equation of the communal counterculture associated with hippies and the New Left plus the free market proselytizing associated with the admirers of Ronald Regan and the New Right equaling a united cyberspace. Speculating on how this technologically brokered marriage of left and right might turn out, Barbrook and Cameron asked if "the social and cultural impact of allowing people to produce and exchange almost unlimited quantities of information on a global scale" would result in utopias for either the Left or the Right and, more pointedly, questioned whether or not the California Ideology's uncritical belief in both visions at the same time made any rational sense.[34] Looking back at the California Ideology from the perspective of 2020, media scholar Michael Buozis casts the answers to these earlier questions in a less-than-positive light:

The cultural liberalism of the new communalists, who celebrated individualism and creativity, and the free-market fundamentalists on the American right, who celebrated competition and commerce, collided in the cultures of technological innovation centered around Silicon Valley in Northern California. The ideals of the counterculture would be used to sell products and a better future first to Americans and then to the rest of the world, in the process proving that free markets and private entrepreneurship could grow prosperity and fulfill the promises of democracy without the aid and regulation of the state—all the while ignoring that the networking technologies may never have been developed without the funding of the government and the work of institutional academics in the first place.[35]

The internal conflict inherent in the California Ideology brings to mind the finale of the television series *Mad Men*, in which buttoned-down New York City adman Don Draper, having apparently turned his back on the corporate world of the 1960s, is depicted seeking Zen bliss on the California coast. As a barefoot, cross-legged Draper begins to meditate, a subtle smile crosses his face as he experiences an entirely non-Zen epiphany: The emerging counter-culture is yet another conduit for marketing consumer goods to America and the world. The scene immediately cuts to the famous "I'd Like to Buy the World a Coke" television advertisement in which young, attractive, and well-scrubbed hippie avatars sing a song of peace and love while clutching bottles of the world's best-selling sugar water. Considering the value of the online economy and the extent to which it has penetrated into daily life around the world, it seems fair to say that the for-profit cyberlibertarians won the battle of the utopias in much the same way that lure of corporate advertising won the heart, and most likely the soul, of Don Draper. But before anyone declares victory for cyberlibertarianism, there remains the unhappy fact that many repressive (as well as some not-entirely-repressive) governments use cyberspace to spy on and control both their own citizens and the citizens of other countries while giant corporations collect and profit from user data in ways that bulldoze over any laissez faire notions of privacy or being left alone. None of these unanticipated consequences can be considered victories for individual liberty. And for any cyberlibertarians who saw, or see, cyberspace as a great equalizer in which, to quote the words of Barlow cited previously, "all may enter without privilege or prejudice accorded by race, economic power, military force, or station of birth," the digital divide (i.e., inequality of access to computer hardware and software, network connectivity, and networked information resources) is a reminder that their utopia is not equally open to all. It is impossible, after all, to pull yourself up by your own bootstraps when there is not so much as a single pair of shoes in your entire village.

Because utopia began as, and has always remained, a fictional construct, reviewing and comparing the competing utopias of cyberspace is, to some extent, nothing more than an academic amusement. That the early utopian dreams of cyberspace failed is unremarkable simply because all utopian dreams eventually fail. There is, however, a different lesson to be learned here. The fact that cyberspace was founded on hopeful philosophical visions that were never going to peacefully coexist, that were, inevitably, destined to coopt and (given the upper hand) consume each other, goes a long way toward explaining why today's digital culture is so polarized and divisive, why the digital discourse is so angry and vindictive, and why the idea of playing nicely is, in the post-truth culture, considered hopelessly naïve. The cyberhouse was destined to be divided against itself because it was built on a divisive foundation right from the start. Even Vannevar Bush, for all his optimism, understood that the misuse of technology could have terrible consequences. At the same time that "As We May Think" was hitting the newsstands, Bush himself knew very well the use to which the atomic bomb would be put in only a matter of weeks. This helps explain why Bush ends "As We May Think" by mixing his optimism with a warning that should resonate with anyone who has considered the post-truth culture with a critical eye:

> The applications of science have built man a well-supplied house, and are teaching him to live healthily therein. They have enabled him to throw masses of people against another with cruel weapons. They may yet allow him truly to encompass the great record and to grow in the wisdom of race experience. He may perish in conflict before he learns to wield that record for his true good. Yet, in the application of science to the needs and desires of man, it would seem to be a singularly unfortunate stage at which to terminate the process, or to lose hope as to the outcome.[36]

NOTES

1. Vannevar Bush. "As We May Think," *Atlantic Monthly*, July 1945, 101–08.

2. Vannevar Bush, "As We May Think," *Life Magazine*, September 10, 1945, 112–24; Douglas Engelbart, "Engelbart Oral History Series: Interview One," interview by Judy Adams and Henry Lowood, December 19, 1986, http://web.archive.org/web/20131002191622fw_/http://www-sul.stanford.edu/depts/hasrg/histsci/ssvoral/engelbart/engfmst1-ntb.html.

3. T.H. Crawford, "Paterson, Memex, and Hypertext," *American Literary History* 8, no. 4 (April 1, 1996): 671.

4. J.C.R. Licklider, "Memorandum For Members and Affiliates of the Intergalactic Computer Network" April 23, 1963, https://www.kurzweilai.net/memorandum-for-members-and-affiliates-of-the-intergalactic-computer-network.

5. J.C.R. Licklider, *Libraries of the Future* (Cambridge, MA: MIT Press, 1965), xiii.

6. Bush, "As We May Think," *Atlantic Monthly*, 108.

7. J.C.R. Licklider and R.W. Taylor, "The Computer as Communication Device," *Science & Technology* 76 (April 1968): 21.

8. Kevin Featherly, "ARPANET | Definition & History," in *Encyclopedia Britannica*, accessed August 24, 2020, https://www.britannica.com/topic/ARPANET.

9. Barbara A. Mikulski, "S.1146–102nd Congress (1991–1992): Scientific and Advanced-Technology Act of 1992" (October 23, 1992), 1991/1992, https://www.congress.gov/bill/102nd-congress/senate-bill/1146.

10. Tim Jordan, "Measuring the Internet: Host Counts versus Business Plans," *Information, Communication & Society* 4, no. 1 (January 2001): 49.

11. Spam, v.," in *OED Online* (Oxford University Press, June 2020), https://www.oed.com/view/Entry/246789?isAdvanced=false&result=2&rskey=JGVyca&.

12. Wendy M. Grossman, "The Year September Never Ended," in *Net.Wars* (New York: New York University Press, 1997), 4–17.

13. Jerry Pournelle, "Computing at Chaos Manner: All Sorts of Software," *BYTE*, March 1986, 269–70.

14. S. Hambridge, "Netiquette Guidelines," accessed August 14, 2020, https://tools.ietf.org/html/rfc1855.

15. Steve Lambert and Walt Howe, *Internet Basics: Your Online Access to the Global Electronic Superhighway* (Westminster, MD: Random House, 1993).

16. Steve Smith, "Keeping a Civil Tongue: Web Lab's Plan to Extinguish Flame Wars," *EContent*, July 2002, http://www.econtentmag.com/Articles/Editorial/Feature/Keeping-a-Civil-Tongue-Web-Labs-Plan-to-Extinguish-Flame-Wars-797.htm.

17. "What Is a Netizen?" *The Amateur Computerist* 6, no. 2–3 (Fall 1994): 1–3.

18. Mark Sullivan, "50 Years Later, the Internet's Inventors Are Horrified by What It's Become," *Fast Company*, November 21, 2019, https://www.fastcompany.com/90426100/50-years-later-the-internets-inventors-are-horrified-by-what-its-become.

19. Jeff Hecht, "Technology: Lawyers' Ad Challenges Rules of 'Netiquette,'" *New Scientist*, accessed August 10, 2020, https://www.newscientist.com/article/mg14319333-200-technology-lawyers-ad-challenges-rules-of-netiquette/.

20. Simon Brown, "Early Cinema in Britain and the Smoking Concert," *Early Popular Visual Culture* 3, no. 2 (2005): 165–78.

21. "X-Rated Computer Displays," *New York Times*, January 28, 1988, section C.

22. Elsa Brenner, "Crime Moves into New Arenas and Justice Rushes to Catch Up," *New York Times*, September 18, 1994, Late Edition (East Coast) edition, section A.

23. Philip Elmer-Dewitt and Hannah Bloch, "On a Screen Near You: Cyberporn," *Time Magazine*, July 3, 1995.

24. Curtis Silver, "Pornhub 2019 Year In Review Report: More Porn, More Often," *Forbes*, accessed August 15, 2020, https://www.forbes.com/sites/curtissilver/2019/12/11/pornhub-2019-year-in-review-report-more-porn-more-often/.

25. John Perry Barlow, "A Declaration of the Independence of Cyberspace," *Electronic Frontier Foundation*, January 20, 2016, https://www.eff.org/cyberspace-independence.

26. Progress and Freedom Foundation, "Cyberspace and the American Dream: A Magna Carta for the Knowledge Age," 1994, http://www.pff.org/issues-pubs/future insights/fi1.2magnacarta.html.

27. Langdon Winner, "Cyberlibertarian Myths and the Prospects for Community," *ACM SIGCAS Computers and Society* 27, no. 3 (September 1997): 14.

28. Moshe Y Vardi, "Cyber Insecurity and Cyber Libertarianism," *Communications of the ACM* 60, no. 5 (2017): 5.

29. Jerry Davis, "Ayn Rand-Inspired 'Myth of the Founder' Puts Tremendous Power in Hands of Big Tech CEOs like Zuckerberg–Posing Real Risks to Democracy," *The Conversation*, accessed March 31, 2021, http://theconversation.com/ayn-rand-inspired-myth-of-the-founder-puts-tremendous-power-in-hands-of-big-tech-ceos-like-zuckerberg-posing-real-risks-to-democracy-150830.

30. Gyöngyi Bugár and Márta Somogyvári, "Bitcoin: Digital Illusion or a Currency of the Future?," *Financial and Economic Review* 19, no. 1 (March 2020): 136.

31. "Proposed Declaration of the Rights of Netizens," *The Amateur Computerist* 6, no. 2–3 (Fall 1994): 34–35.

32. Richard Barbrook and Andy Cameron, "The Californian Ideology," *Science as Culture* 6, no. 1 (January 1996): 54–55.

33. Howard Rheingold, "Chapter Ten: Disinformocracy," in *The Virtual Community: Homesteading on the Electronic Frontier*, accessed August 19, 2020, http://www.rheingold.com/vc/book/10.html.

34. Barbrook and Cameron, 52.

35. Michael Buozis, "Cyberlibertarian Dreams: Producing Privilege and Power in Journalistic Discourses of the Internet" (PhD dissertation, Temple University, 2020), 69.

36. Bush, "As We May Think," *Atlantic Monthly*, 108.

BIBLIOGRAPHY

Barlow, John Perry. "A Declaration of the Independence of Cyberspace." *Electronic Frontier Foundation*, January 20, 2016, https://www.eff.org/cyberspace -independence.

Barbrook, Richard, and Andy Cameron. "The Californian Ideology." *Science as Culture* 6, no. 1 (January 1996): 44–72.

Brenner, Elsa. "Crime Moves into New Arenas and Justice Rushes to Catch Up." *New York Times*, September 18, 1994, Late Edition (East Coast) edition, section A.

Brown, Simon. "Early Cinema in Britain and the Smoking Concert." *Early Popular Visual Culture* 3, no. 2 (2005): 165–78.

Bugár, Gyöngyi, and Márta Somogyvári. "Bitcoin: Digital Illusion or a Currency of the Future?" *Financial and Economic Review* 19, no. 1 (March 2020): 132–53.

Buozis, Michael. "Cyberlibertarian Dreams: Producing Privilege and Power in Journalistic Discourses of the Internet." PhD Dissertation, Temple University, 2020.

Bush, Vannevar. "As We May Think." *Atlantic Monthly*, July 1945, https://www .theatlantic.com/magazine/archive/1945/07/as-we-may-think/303881/.

Bush, Vannevar. "As We May Think." *Life Magazine*, September 10, 1945.

Crawford, T.H. "Paterson, Memex, and Hypertext." *American Literary History* 8, no. 4 (April 1, 1996): 665–82.

Davis, Jerry. "Ayn Rand-Inspired 'Myth of the Founder' Puts Tremendous Power in Hands of Big Tech CEOs like Zuckerberg–Posing Real Risks to Democracy." *The Conversation*. Accessed March 31, 2021, http://theconversation.com/ayn-rand -inspired-myth-of-the-founder-puts-tremendous-power-in-hands-of-big-tech-ceos -like-zuckerberg-posing-real-risks-to-democracy-150830.

Elmer-Dewitt, Philip, and Hannah Bloch. "On a Screen Near You: Cyberporn." *Time Magazine*, July 3, 1995.

Engelbart, Douglas. "Engelbart Oral History Series: Interview One," interview by Judy Adams and Henry Lowood, December 19, 1986, http://web.archive .org/web/20131002191622fw_/http://www-sul.stanford.edu/depts/hasrg/histsci/ss voral/engelbart/engfmst1-ntb.html.

Featherly, Kevin. "ARPANET | Definition & History." In *Encyclopedia Britannica*. Accessed August 24, 2020, https://www.britannica.com/topic/ARPANET.

Grossman, Wendy M. "The Year September Never Ended." In *Net.Wars*, 4–17. New York: New York University Press, 1997.

Hambridge, S. "Netiquette Guidelines." Accessed August 14, 2020, https://tools.ietf .org/html/rfc1855.

Hecht, Jeff. "Technology: Lawyers' Ad Challenges Rules of 'Netiquette.'" *New Scientist*. Accessed August 10, 2020, https://www.newscientist.com/article/ mg14319333-200-technology-lawyers-ad-challenges-rules-of-netiquette/.

Jordan, Tim. "Measuring the Internet: Host Counts versus Business Plans." *Information, Communication & Society* 4, no. 1 (January 2001): 34–53.

Lambert, Steve, and Walt Howe. *Internet Basics: Your Online Access to the Global Electronic Superhighway*. Westminster, MD: Random House, 1993.

Licklider, J.C.R. *Libraries of the Future*. Cambridge, MA: MIT Press, 1965.

Licklider, J.C.R. "Memorandum for Members and Affiliates of the Intergalactic Computer Network," April 23, 1963, https://www.kurzweilai.net/memorandum-for -members-and-affiliates-of-the-intergalactic-computer-network.

Licklider, J.C.R., and R.W. Taylor. "The Computer as Communication Device." *Science & Technology* 76 (April 1968): 21–31.

Mikulski, Barbara A. "S.1146-102nd Congress (1991–1992): Scientific and Advanced-Technology Act of 1992," webpage (October 23, 1992), 1991/1992, https://www.congress.gov/bill/102nd-congress/senate-bill/1146.

Pournelle, Jerry. "Computing at Chaos Manner: All Sorts of Software." *BYTE*, March 1986. https://archive.org/stream/byte-magazine-1986-03/1986_03_ BYTE_11-03_Homebound_Computing#page/n279/mode/2up.

Progress and Freedom Foundation. "Cyberspace and the American Dream: A Magna Carta for the Knowledge Age," 1994. http://www.pff.org/issues-pubs/futurein sights/fi1.2magnacarta.html.

"Proposed Declaration of the Rights of Netizens." *The Amateur Computerist* 6, no. 2–3 (Fall 1994): 34–35.

Raymond, Eric S., and Steele L. Guy. *The New Hacker's Dictionary*. Cambridge, MA: MIT Press, 1991.

Rheingold, Howard. "Chapter Ten: Disinformocracy." In *The Virtual Community: Homesteading on the Electronic Frontier*, electronic version. Accessed August 19, 2020, http://www.rheingold.com/vc/book/10.html.

Silver, Curtis. "Pornhub 2019 Year in Review Report: More Porn, More Often." *Forbes*. Accessed August 15, 2020, https://www.forbes.com/sites/curtissil-ver/2019/12/11/pornhub-2019-year-in-review-report-more-porn-more-often/.

Smith, Steve. "Keeping a Civil Tongue: Web Lab's Plan to Extinguish Flame Wars." *EContent*, July 2002. http://www.econtentmag.com/Articles/Editorial/Feature/ Keeping-a-Civil-Tongue-Web-Labs-Plan-to-Extinguish-Flame-Wars-797.htm.

"Spam, v." in *OED Online*. Oxford University Press, June 2020. https://www.oed .com/view/Entry/246789?isAdvanced=false&result=2&rskey=JGVyca&.

Sullivan, Mark. "50 Years Later, the Internet's Inventors Are Horrified by What It's Become." *Fast Company*, November 21, 2019. https://www.fastcompany

.com/90426100/50-years-later-the-internets-inventors-are-horrified-by-what-its
-become.
Vardi, Moshe Y. "Cyber Insecurity and Cyber Libertarianism." *Communications of the ACM* 60, no. 5 (2017): 5.
"What Is a Netizen?" *The Amateur Computerist* 6, no. 2–3 (Fall 1994): 1–3.
Winner, Langdon. "Cyberlibertarian Myths and the Prospects for Community." *ACM SIGCAS Computers and Society* 27, no. 3 (September 1997): 14–19.
"X-Rated Computer Displays." *New York Times*, January 28, 1988, section C.

4

As We May Come to Think
How Technology Changes the Way We Think

The modern horse (*Equus ferus caballus*) was unknown in the Western Hemisphere until it was brought from Europe by the Spanish in the sixteenth century. Although the Spanish initially enjoyed (and legally enforced) a monopoly on the use of the horse, this exclusive right inevitably slipped from their grasp. By the end of the eighteenth century, horse culture had spread from tribe to tribe throughout most of Central and Western North America as well as parts of Central and South America. For Native Americans, the horse was a totally unfamiliar technology that required acquiring and mastering a number of new skills, including riding, animal husbandry, and nontraditional ways of traveling, hunting, fighting, and trading. Of all Native American groups, the tribes of the Great Plains stand out in the popular imagination as the most iconic and successful adopters of horse culture. While the coming of the horse to such tribes as the Cheyenne, Lakota, Comanche, and Crow may seem like a renaissance moment, the new technology brought its share of problems as outlined by historian Pekka Hämäläinen:

Horses did bring new possibilities, prosperity, and power to Plains Indians, but they also brought destabilization, dispossession, and destruction. The transformational power of horses was simply too vast. Although Plains Indians had experienced constant and profound culture changes before European contact, the sudden appearance of horses among dog-using pedestrian people set off changes that could spin out of control as easily as they could make life richer and more comfortable. Horses helped Indians do virtually everything—move, hunt, trade, and wage war—more effectively, but they also disrupted subsistence economies, wrecked grassland and bison ecologies, created new social inequalities, unhinged gender relations, undermined traditional political hierarchies, and intensified resource competition and warfare. The introduction of horses, then, was a decidedly mixed blessing. The horse era began for most Plains Indians with high expectations but soon collapsed into a series of unsolvable economic, social, political, and ecological contradictions.[1]

Changes spinning out of control? Disrupted economies? Wrecked ecologies? The sudden emergence of "new social inequalities, unhinged gender relations, and undermined traditional political hierarchies"? Sound familiar? It should. The idea that unanticipated consequences result when a transformative new technology is unleashed on cultures ill prepared to handle an onslaught of rapid and profound social changes should sound uncomfortably familiar to twenty-first-century ears.

Setting aside any prophetic lessons the present-day world may learn from the Native American past, the problems created for Native Americans through their adoption of horse culture serve as an entry point for considering the concept of *technological determinism* and how it relates to life in the post-truth culture. Put simply, technological determinism is a sociological theory that holds that technology determines a society's values rather than the other way around. A *hard determinist* would argue that technology shapes society regardless of context. In the case of Native Americans, a hard determinist would say that the new technology of the horse (abetted by such associated technologies as firearms, iron tools, and alcohol) not only appealed to and exploited those aspects of Native American cultures that best ensured the success of the horse (as a technology), but also did so in a way that left the impacted cultures without any choice of opting out. Looking at the present-day digital world, a hard determinist might argue that the technology of e-commerce has succeed by appealing to and exploiting existing social values surrounding consumerism, leaving present-day society no more choice of opting out and turning the clock back to an entirely brick-and-mortar consumer economy than Native Americans had of opting out of the horse culture and going back to living as "dog-using pedestrian people." For a hard determinist, a successful technology is analogous to a living organism—possibly an invasive species—that adapts to, and evolves within, its environment in order to find a niche in which it can thrive. A *soft determinist*, on the other hand, would argue that, while technology has considerable power to shape society, there is at least some chance for a society to, in return, shape the outcome of any given technology. In the case of Native Americans, a soft determinist would agree that the adoption of horse culture powerfully and inevitably changed Native American cultures while also observing that outcomes for various cultures ranged from almost complete upheavals, as with those Plains tribes that transformed themselves entirely into mounted nomadic peoples, to more moderate changes, as with those tribes that adopted the horse while maintaining (though not always successfully) their traditional, more-sedentary ways of life. Similarly, when considering today's digital technology, a soft determinist might point out that while the technology of social media has fostered polarization, the levels of polarization vary from country to country due to such national differences as cultural norms, economic structures, and governmental responses to the impacts of social media.

Like any concept in the social sciences, technological determinism is not universally accepted. There are those who see technology as neutral, with its good or bad qualities dependent entirely on how it is used. A person who views digital technology as neutral would contend that people are free to use a technology like social media for good, as when money is raised to help victims of a natural disaster, or for evil, as when manipulators use social media to spread false rumors, whip up hatreds, and encourage acts of violence. Those who hold a nondeterministic view see the relationship between society and technology as too nuanced and complex to be reduced to simple formulas in which technology has, on one end of the spectrum, complete leverage over human societies or, on the opposite end, no such leverage at all. On the grounds that no technology can be created in a vacuum entirely free from social influence, a nondeterminist would argue that society inevitably shapes technology as much as technology shapes society. Taking this idea to its extreme, *social determinists* go so far as to argue that technologies are, start to finish, socially constructed and, therefore, entirely dependent on the social context in which they are created. Looking back at the development of the atomic bomb, that particular technology was conceived of and made manifest in a social context marked by a widely shared determination to win a desperate war against an extremely dangerous, capable, and hated enemy. That some part of that hatred was racially motivated only intensified the willingness to create and use a weapon of previously unimaginable destructive power. In a less extreme social context, the atomic bomb might never have been developed or, if developed, never actually used against a civilian population, as was the case for the (approximately) half-century-long duration of the Cold War.

If we are to better understand the digital world in which we find ourselves living (and hoping to survive), it is worth asking ourselves the extent to which the technology introduced during the Digital Revolution that has been unfolding for the last half century (or so) has created the post-truth culture versus how much we and our societies are responsible for the upheavals the world is now experiencing. A question I have been asked, and have heard asked of others, frames the matter in the clearest of terms: *"Did digital technology cause all the open expressions of hate that seem to pervade social media, or did digital technology simply reveal hatred that was always there but hidden from sight?"* While nobody can answer such a chicken-or-the-egg question with absolute certainty, teasing out as much of the answer as is possible can tell us a lot about who is the master versus who is the obedient servant in the relationship between humans and their digital technology.

CAN TECHNOLOGY TURN THE WORLD UPSIDE DOWN?

What does it take for a technology to upend the world? In his book *Medieval Technology and Social Change*, American historian Lynn White, Jr. (1907–1987) makes the case that the stirrup, by transforming knights from run-of-the-mill soldiers on horseback to nearly unstoppable shock troops, is the technological innovation most responsible for the establishment of feudalism in Medieval Europe.[2] As provocative as White's theory may be, the stirrup is not likely at the top of many lists of world-changing technologies. It certainly did not make the cut for "The 50 Greatest Breakthroughs Since the Wheel," an article published in 2013 in *The Atlantic*. (The same magazine, it so happens, that initially published Vannevar Bush's "As We May Think.") To compile its list of technological breakthroughs, *The Atlantic* "assembled a panel of 12 scientists, entrepreneurs, engineers, historians of technology, and others to assess the innovations that have done the most to shape the nature of modern life."[3] Like even the most carefully assembled lists of top *anythings*—songs, movies, left-handed goal keepers—the list published in *The Atlantic* is subjective and, as such, serves more as a provocative thought exercise than the final word on the subject. Many of the items at or near the top of the list are technologies that everyone would agree changed the world in some truly significant ways. Examples that would make almost anyone's top ten include the steam engine (number ten), paper (number six), and electricity (number two). Coming in at number one on *The Atlantic*'s list is *printing from moveable type*—a technology that tops more than one list of most-impactful technologies. Of all the great technological innovations of human history, printing from moveable type is of particular interest today because the changes it wrought are highly analogous to the changes people living in the twenty-first century are experiencing as a result of digital technology. Even more to the point, the possibility that humanity is transitioning out of a centuries-long era dominated by print technology provides insights into how digital technology may be changing not only superficial human behaviors, but the fundamental way in which we humans think.

Textbox 4.1
The Four Stages of Communication Technology

While the four stages of communication technology—oral, scribal, print, and electronic—represent a progression, it is important to note that each new stage has added itself onto the existing stages rather than completely replacing what has gone before, with each previous stage exerting influence on those stages that come after it.

Oral

Oral communication, which predates all the other forms of communication technology in this list, is present in all human cultures. The transmission and preservation of information in a purely oral culture demands memorization, a technique which can be enhanced via such mnemonic aids as songs, chants, prayers, folktales, proverbs, and poems. For example, the epic poems *The Iliad* and *The Odyssey* existed for hundreds of years solely as oral poetry, with those who performed the poems employing as memory aids frequently repeated standard expressions known as "formula." Because all preservation of oral communication depends on fallible human memory, the existence of an authoritative copy-of-record is largely a foreign concept to oral cultures. In the twenty-first century, purely oral cultures that remain untouched by print or electronic communication are rare.

Scribal

In addition to oral communication, scribal cultures employ writing and reading, though in scribal cultures literacy tends to be restricted to a small elite of educated persons and all texts take the form of unique, handwritten manuscripts. There is some debate about whether a scribal culture requires an alphabet or if symbolic writings, such as Incan knotted string writing (quipu) or Native American winter-count pictographs, constitute a form of scribal writing. With the possible exception of tightly controlled government and legal documents, precise reproductions of original sources are almost unknown in scribal cultures. As with the memorized oral communications, almost every scribal communication is unique, reflecting idiosyncratic interpretations and unintentional errors on the part of scribes. The rarity of literacy and scarcity of written materials—coupled with the absence of authoritative copies-of-record—aligns scribal cultures more closely with oral cultures than with cultures that have been impacted by print technology. As with oral cultures, present-day scribal cultures are rare.

Print

The oldest and simplest form of printing, block printing, was first used to create complete books starting in China around 700 CE. When the technology of block printing reached Medieval Europe, it was largely used for such purposes as printing designs on cloth and manufacturing playing cards rather than producing books. Printing books from movable type, which allows for much higher rates of production than block printing, was first developed in thirteenth-century Korea and then separately developed in Europe in the middle of the fifteenth century, setting off the Printing Revolution.

Electronic
Electronic communication began in the middle of the nineteenth century with the electric telegraph and eventually grew to include the telephone, wireless radio, television, and networked computers. Although oral, scribal, and print stages of communication still exist in the twenty-first century, much of the world has become dependent on, some would say "addicted to," electronic communication.

After Johannes Gutenberg (1400–1468) introduced printing from moveable type to Europe in the middle of the fifteenth century, the new technology set in motion any number of sweeping social changes. Elizabeth Eisenstein (1923–2016), a leading historian of the Printing Revolution, sees improvements in the standardization, dissemination, and preservation of information brought about by printing from moveable type as key to the development of such world-changing events as the Renaissance, the Scientific Revolution, and the Protestant Reformation.[4] While historians may dispute the exact extent to which printing from moveable type contributed to any given social upheaval, there is no disputing that the new technology vastly increased the number of books being created. During the last full century without printing from movable type (1301–1400), European scribes produced 2,746,951 manuscript books; during the first full century with printing from movable type (1501–1600), European printers produced 217,444,000 printed books—an increase of 7815.83 percent.[5] As might be expected, such a large increase in the number of books drove down prices by orders of magnitude. In the age of manuscript books, the labor of writing and, often, decorating books by hand made them too expensive for all but the wealthiest individuals and institutions. Prior to the final decade or two of the fifteenth century, buying a book would have been more like investing in a one-of-a-kind painting or sculpture than spontaneously grabbing a paperback in an airport shop to keep yourself entertained on a long flight. The word *lecture* ultimately derives from the Latin verb *legere*, meaning "to read," and at the time when all books were one-of-a-kind, handwritten manuscripts, university lectures typically consisted of a professor reading aloud from manuscript book. That book would have been, most likely, the extremely valuable and well-guarded property of the university. In the Medieval university, few professors, much less university students, could have afforded to purchase a book. By the first years of the sixteenth century, however, printing from moveable type meant that publishers like the Aldine Press in Venice were making and selling good-quality books at prices even university students could afford.

By spreading literacy to ever-larger segments of the population, the wide availability of affordable printed material did more than change the way in which young people were educated (and create the much-maligned college textbook industry). In his book *The Gutenberg Galaxy*, Canadian philosopher and media theorist Marshall McLuhan (1911–1980) characterizes the Printing Revolution as an epochal historical event during which Western people transitioned from a culture that was mostly oral (with a significant scribal component) to a fully print culture. For McLuhan, the Printing Revolution represents not simply a change in how people went about the business of acquiring and sharing information—it ushered in a fundamental change in human cognition. Printing technology transitioned the world from an older, mostly oral culture, with its emphasis on speech and the ear, to a new, visually oriented print culture focused on the written word and the eye. McLuhan specifically calls out "the role of alphabet and of printing in giving a dominant role to the visual sense in language and art and in the entire range of social and of political life."[6] Printed texts, in McLuhan's assessment, devalued the ancient skill of memorization, changed reading from an audible group activity (as was the case in the Medieval classroom) to the silent private activity still widely practiced today, and prioritized the eye and its focus on the specific (think of a silent scientist bent over a microscope) over the ear and its encompassing of the general (think of a shaman chanting around a campfire circle).

Extrapolating even further, McLuhan attributes to the rise of print culture such phenomena as nationalism, individualism, capitalism, and modern humanity's replacement of the sacred with the profane.[7] Consider, for example, the way in which printing's elevation of the importance of the author as creative genius contributed to the growth of individualism as a key concept in Western culture. Prior to the Printing Revolution, the idea that a written work was the product and property of an individual author was much weaker than after the technology of printing had transformed the writing, making, and selling of books into one of early capitalism's leading industries. This is reflected by the fact that many Medieval manuscript books do not give the author's name. For Medieval scribes and readers, authorship was not considered all that important. The first copyright law, the Statute of Anne, did not become law until 1710, over 250 years after the introduction of printing from moveable type to Europe. There was not much need for copyright before that time because authorship and ownership of a text had little financial value until printing had matured to the point of fully industrializing book production. For anyone living in the present-day culture of late capitalism, where the most successful creators of books, films, and other popular entertainments can become astonishingly wealthy (and where one of the oft-repeated capitalist fables of our time tells of a British author whose astounding success took her from life on the dole to billionaire), the idea that authorship is not significant is all but inconceivable.

Although McLuhan did not live long enough to see digital technology become part of everyday life, he saw in electric media—television, in particular—the coming of another epochal cultural shift, this time to a "post-literal" world and the creation of a "global village" (a phrase which McLuhan himself coined) in which everyone on the planet is connected by shared communications technology powered by electricity. And while McLuhan wrote the following words in 1962, they read very much like a description of the digital discourse in the twenty-first century:

> Instead of tending towards a vast Alexandrian library the world has become a computer, an electronic brain, exactly as in an infantile piece of science fiction. And as our senses have gone outside us, Big Brother goes inside. So, unless aware of this dynamic, we shall at once move into a phase of panic terrors, exactly befitting a small world of tribal drums, total interdependence, and superimposed co-existence.[8]

Building on the work of McLuhan, the noted literary scholar, cultural historian, and philosopher Walter J. Ong (1912–2003) seconds the idea that the technology of writing fully transformed human cognition:

> Without writing, the literate mind would not and could not think as it does, not only when engaged in writing but normally even when it is composing its thoughts in oral form. More than any other single invention, writing has transformed human consciousness.[9]

Ong (whose master's thesis was supervised by McLuhan) sees human culture moving from the era of print into new era in which the dominant electronic technologies are actively changing human cognition in ways analogous to the changes wrought by printing technology centuries before. Ong contrasts the "primary orality" of a "a culture totally untouched by any knowledge of writing or print," with "the 'secondary orality' of present-day high technology culture, in which a new orality is sustained by telephone, radio, television, and other electronic devices that depend for their existence and functioning on writing and print."[10] Ong's two major works touching on the topic of secondary orality were published, respectively, in 1971 (*Rhetoric, Romance, and Technology*) and 1982 (*Orality and Literacy*). The years since have seen the emergence of a number of digital technologies that support Ong's theories of a culture moving toward secondary orality. Twitter, TikTok, Snapchat, Instagram, Twitch, podcasts, and texting are all technologies sharing varying degrees of allegiance to the printed word yet earning their vibrancy from the (sometimes well-rehearsed) informality and spontaneity of secondary orality. These technologies contrast with email, which, with its format borrowed directly from ink-on-paper letters and its acceptance for use in business settings, is more firmly rooted in the formalities of print culture than in the informal looseness of secondary orality.

In the first decade of the twenty-first century, scholars influenced by Ong began writing about the concept of the "Gutenberg Parenthesis," the central idea of which is that the five-hundred-plus-year dominance of print is coming to a close and, with this closing, humanity is transitioning into the era of secondary orality. In the words of Lars Ole Sauerberg, the scholar credited with coining the phrase "Gutenberg Parenthesis," the transition from printed text to digital forms of expression "means moving from the rationality accompanied by the printed book to an altogether different way of processing, characterized by interactivity and much faster pace. The book as privileged mode of cognition is, it seems, being marginalized and transformed."[11]

If our culture is in transition from being firmly within the Gutenberg Parenthesis to some form of post-literal secondary orality in which books no longer retain their long-held place of privilege, it is worth remembering that such transitions do not happen overnight and that different subcultures will make the transition at different times (if, in some cases, they ever transition at all). Sauerberg's colleague, literary scholar Tom Pettitt, uses the example of William Shakespeare's work to illustrate this point. Pettitt explains that when Shakespeare's sonnets were first published in 1609, Shakespeare's name was on the title page as the author; however, the first three printings of *Romeo and Juliet* were printed without Shakespeare's name on their title pages. It was not until the fourth edition in 1622 that Shakespeare is at last credited in print as the author of *Romeo and Juliet*. Pettitt attributes these different emphases on the importance of the author to the fact that Elizabethan literary culture (of which poetry was the centerpiece) had moved into the era of print (the left-hand side of the Guttenberg Parenthesis) with its emphasis on authorship and ownership, well in advance of Elizabethan theater, a performance-focused, popular-culture medium in which such artistic traditions as freely sampling from previous works, improvisation and interpretation by actors, and the conception of stage plays as more of a collaborative effort than as the work of a lone individual delayed the Elizabethan theater's full exit from the oral/scribal culture into the print culture.[12] In a way that any modern reader could understand, Pettitt compares the looseness of authority and ownership in Elizabethan theater to the world of hip-hop music in which sampling from earlier works, creative contributions by multiple artists to the composition of a single work, and lyrical improvisation is more the rule than the exception. A somewhat older example than hip-hop can be found in jazz music, in which individual soloists compose improvisational passages that need not be exactly the same for every performance and which undermine the idea that the work being performed is either entirely fixed in a final authoritative form or entirely the output of a single composer. Such relaxed concepts of fixity, authorship, and ownership stand in contrast to the more rigid way in which the typical novel or short story is seen as the fixed work of a single author. Considering that both hip-hop and jazz are rooted in oral African cultures, it is not surprising that both artforms are on the leading edge of the transition to the artistic norms and values of the post–Gutenberg Parenthesis.

The slow and uneven transition from the era of print (the right-hand side of the Gutenberg Parenthesis) to the new world of secondary orality provides a possible insight into how the post-truth culture came to be and why the digital discourse has become so polarizing. I find an example of the unevenness of the transition in my own house. My wife and I were both born into blue-collar families. Though my family moved up to more of a white-collar status when I was a teenager, my wife's family remained solidly blue-collar her entire life. The two of us both watched a lot of television (McLuhan's "cool medium") while growing up; however, my family was much more a print-culture family than my wife's. My parents did not own a television until they were well into their thirties, and my mother and older sisters were voracious readers, a habit which I acquired along with my youthful addiction to television and movies. My wife's family were not big readers, and she has never read for entertainment. Even though my wife has a doctorate (I do not) and is a professor (I am not), she is far more comfortable with, and is more native to, the norms of secondary orality than am I. As for our children, all three tend toward a comfortable orientation with secondary orality, though one child did pick up and retain the habit of voracious reading.

Moving from the specific, and very much anecdotal, to the general, the Gutenberg Parenthesis seems to apply to the polarization that we in the United States are currently experiencing. (As I am going to talk in stereotypes and generalities for a bit, I want to make it clear that I understand that there are many exceptions to the stereotypes I invoke over the next few paragraphs.) That said, let's start with stereotypical supporters of former U.S. President Donald Trump. Whether or not they have a college degree, Trump supporters tend to be distrustful of higher education, which they see as dominated by a liberal professorate, as well as distrustful of a mainstream media that, regardless of its now-extensive online presence, has deep roots in the world of ink on paper. The one thing Trump supporters do trust is Donald J. Trump, a man who communicated (until he was banned from Twitter in 2020) quite effectively through tweets, a medium that is a prime example of secondary orality at play in the online world. As is true of all forms of secondary orality, tweets are influenced by the legacy of print. Tweets are *typed* by their creator to be *read* by literate recipients. However, tweets fit the mold of secondary orality in being more transient than fixed (tweets can be, and regularly are, deleted by their creators) and only loosely governed by the print-culture rules and expectations regarding originality, plagiarism, grammar, spelling, and adherence to the written record. When Trump sent tweets, the Twitterverse was quick to respond with the digital equivalent of applause (from those who liked Trump) or catcalls (from those who disliked him). In this way, Trump's tweets were more like improvised performances before a live audience than the act of carefully writing and revising a piece of text, waiting for publication, and waiting even longer for reactions from readers. While Trump was capable of producing flurries of tweets in a single day, the idea of Trump crafting a ten-thousand-word think piece on, say, immigration or foreign policy is as absurd as the idea of Trump—or any other twenty-first century politician—giving a nonstop, two-hour stump speech (with or without a teleprompter). Trump simply does not operate by the norms of the Guttenberg Parenthesis, a behavior which makes Trump an attractive figure for many of those who have transitioned (to one extent or another) beyond the Gutenberg Parenthesis and into the realm of secondary orality. It is not surprising that Trump is able to leverage secondary orality to his advantage. Trump's fame and public image are almost entirely the creations of television, the medium that initially inspired McLuhan's thinking about the global village. Unlike Ronald Reagan, a movie star who transitioned well to television, Trump is a television native who seems to be entirely comfortable operating by the rules of secondary orality. By the same token, it is not surprising that some of the sharpest Twitter foils turned against Trump belong to stand-up comedians such as Sarah Cooper, Patton Oswalt, and Sarah Silverman. Stand-up comedy, which combines memorized delivery of routines with frequent use of improvisation, is more closely aligned to the norms of secondary orality than to those of print culture. The host of anti-Trump comedians, along with other quick witted social media figures, operate very much like Trump in that they use Twitter in highly performative ways to "fire up the base" while taunting and ridiculing the opposition, garnering large followings of likers and haters in the process.

Conversely, the stereotypical anti-Trumper finds comfort in processing the world through the familiar lens of print culture rather than through the unfamiliar, and seemingly fuzzy, lens of secondary orality. A group defined more by what they are against (Trump) than by what they support (a host of sometimes conflicting political positions), anti-Trumpers are seen as educated yet unable to comprehend how Trump can cite "alternative facts" (a phrase coined by Trump's close political counselor, Kellyanne Conway) without paying a political price for doing so. Nor do stereotypical anti-Trumpers understand why facts and well-reasoned arguments seemingly bounce off Trump and his supporters like bullets bouncing off of one of Tony Stark's Iron Man suits. For those who process the world according to the rational rules laid down between the Gutenberg Parenthesis, making up facts that can be easily contradicted by credible recorded evidence constitutes a crime against rationality This stands in complete contradiction to those stereotypical Trump supporters who, in processing information from the perspective of secondary orality, find the picking and choosing of facts not all that problematic because they do not share the print-culture view that a reliable body of recorded evidence stands as the ultimate source of facts and authority.

It is, of course, important to repeat that we are dealing with stereotypes here. While Trump may appeal to many who reject the authority of the written word, he has his share of supporters among the educated, print-centric portion of the population, not to mention that his many Evangelical Christian supporters most certainly accept the authority of the written word as it appears in the Bible. And though it is easy to imagine a professorial anti-Trumper who cannot fathom why today's students consider gathering a handful of Google search results (without any citations or attribution) to constitute proper research and writing, it is not as if many of those same Google-searching, secondary-orality-based students are not themselves anti-Trumpers. Nor is it true that older, educated anti-Trumpers are incapable of appreciating post-Gutenberg artforms—just look at how many of them are willing pay hundreds of dollars to attend a performance of *Hamilton: An American Musical.*

FACTS ARE LIKE FOLKSONGS

For anyone whose mode of thinking is firmly rooted within the Gutenberg Parenthesis, trying to think like, and take on the worldview of, a person living in an entirely oral/scribal culture is impossible. However, comprehending the thinking and worldview of someone who is more oriented toward secondary orality (a culture which evolved from print culture and continues to employ writing) is possible. Of all the things that the print-culture mindset finds unfathomable about the secondary-orality mindset, the seemingly willy-nilly acceptance and rejection of facts stands at the top of the list. The example of folksongs, however, can provide some insight into how the secondary-orality mind processes the concept of facts.

Traditional folksongs, as the products of oral culture, lack any such thing as a fixed, copy-of-record version. For example, the folksong "The Big Rock Candy Mountain," which "belongs to a long tradition of songs and poems depicting a secular utopia free of the stresses and concerns of everyday life," exists in many versions.[13] These range from highly sanitized versions that are considered suitable for young children, to at least one extremely dark version in which a naive youth is lured from home by a predatory older hobo, "a jocker," who economically and sexually exploits his victim to the point that the "Hoosier boy" of the first verse is degraded to the status of "the punk" by the song's final verse.[14] Whether you prefer the sweet version sung by your grandmother, the gritty sex-trafficking version, the Burl Ives (1909–1995) version, or the Lisa Loeb version, the point is that none of these versions are wrong because none of them have claim to the status of being the authoritative version-of-record. Even if you want to be a stickler and point out that hobo musician Harry "Haywire Mac" McClintock (1882–1957) wrote down the first fixed version of the song, there is strong evidence that McClintock based his version on older songs, employing in his method of composition the free borrowing and sampling of previous work that is an acceptable practice in both oral and secondary-orality cultures.[15] Copyright and the entitlement of ownership that comes with it are, after all, concepts born within golden arches of the Gutenberg Parenthesis.

The analogy at work here is that for someone processing information from the cognitive perspective of secondary orality, a fact can be very much like a folksong. Just as there may be many versions of a folksong, there may be many versions of the same fact, with the one you choose being a matter of personal preference. For example, if you are acting under the influence of the cognitive bias known as *anchoring*, you may simply latch on to the first version of a fact that you happen to encounter and stick with it regardless of any additional counterevidence that comes your way. After all, how many of us consider whatever version of a song we heard first—say the Monkees' 1966 version of "I'm a Believer" versus Smash Mouth's 2001 cover versus Weezer's 2010 cover—to be the *real* version of the song? Similarly, accepting only those facts that support your existing worldview makes sense if your secondary-orality mindset holds that one fact is as good (and as authoritative) as another.

While the folksong-facts analogy may help us understand why someone processing from a secondary-orality mindsight can seemingly dismiss solidly proven facts and/or blithely accept the existence of alternative facts, the analogy does not defend the practice nor does it justify the dismissal of facts with fatuous claims along the lines of *"Oh, I'm just so into secondary orality that I'm allowed to believe whatever I want."* One might as well claim the right to believe the moon is made of cheese because, *"I'm a Scorpio, and that's just how we are."* As already pointed out, secondary orality represents an evolution from, rather than a wholesale abandonment of, print culture. While the cognitive possibilities offered by secondary orality may allow us to better appreciate the genius of jazz improvisations, hip-hop collaborations, and other less-constrained forms of expression, there is great danger in rejecting all the advantages and progress that come from seeing the world through the sharp lens that print culture has provided to humanity for the last half-millennium. In denying well-established scientific facts such as, for example, the link between smoking and cancer, the cognitive freedom to pick and choose your facts may come at the cost of dying an early and painful death from a disease that could easily have been avoided. Similarly, the cognitive freedom to dismiss scientific advice regarding the outbreak of COVID-19 may have resulted in tens of thousands of extra deaths and illnesses while also inflicting tremendous economic damage, much of which could have been avoided by simply listening to advice based on the best scientific evidence. A hard return to mostly oral-culture patterns of thought could lead to some harsh unintended consequences. In a way that is reminiscent of Marshall McLuhan's warning of the possibility of a post-literal "small world of tribal drums," Tom Pettitt warns that our rapid exit from the Gutenberg Parenthesis to an oral-influenced mode of cognition not much seen since the Middle Ages might mean that "we are surfing to serfdom," a possibility that Pettitt understatedly cautions "should give pause for thought."[16]

So, do we just throw up our hands and surrender to the inevitable bad consequences of the digital technology we have unleashed on ourselves? No. Referring back to McLuhan's warning about the perils of the transition to a post-literal culture, note that he offers a possible way out via the qualifier "unless aware of this dynamic." If we can become aware that we are exiting the Gutenberg Parenthesis and entering a new world of secondary orality, we have a chance to avoid many of the turmoils inherent in such a transition. Imagine a world where people are aware of the dynamics of the technologically driven changes impacting them regardless of whether they are in the vanguard of secondary orality, still firmly grounded within Gutenberg Parenthesis, or caught somewhere in the middle. And what if that awareness allows them to respond to change with larger measures of understanding and empathy than of fear and hate? Such cultural bilingualism could prevent us from breaking into ever-more-polarized camps that, in the worst case, end up trying to destroy each other over their native inability to comprehend each other's cognitive processes or appreciate each other's virtues.

DIGITAL TECHNOLOGIES THAT ARE CHANGING BEHAVIOR . . . AND MAYBE THE WAY WE THINK

Having indulged in the theoretical for most of this chapter, it is time to focus on ways in which in which specific digital technologies are changing the way we behave and, possibly, the way we think. Because it is always helpful to consider the extent to which any observed phenomenon of the Digital Revolution is truly something new versus being merely a variation on something that previously existed, each item in the following list includes a (highly subjective) "Digital Distinctiveness Rating," with ten on the scale representing a phenomenon that is entirely new to the digital discourse and one representing something not at all new. For want of any better organizational format, the following list is presented in alphabetical order.

Algorithms

Search-engine algorithms are complex sets of computer instructions that determine not only the results retrieved by any search, but also the ranking of those results. More highly ranked results appear first and thus are more likely to be viewed than less highly ranked results that appear so far down that viewing them requires at least scrolling if not clicking to see the next page of search results. Even when the designers of search engines do their best to create fair and impartial algorithms, every algorithm is inherently subjective. For example, say a search engine's algorithms are written to give priority ranking to those webpages that get the most visits. While this makes sense from the point of view that popular webpages are most likely popular due to the quality or appeal of their contents, such an algorithm downplays the importance of webpages that may have great content but which, for whatever reason, have never become popular. Just think of all the overlooked films, books, television programs, restaurants, and human beings that are more worthy of attention than are their more-popular counterparts.

Website managers can manipulate already-subjective search engine algorithms by employing the various techniques of *search-engine optimization*. White-hat search-engine optimization involves legitimately designing a website so that it gets the best possible ranking based on a search engine's algorithms. Black-hat search-engine optimization involves misrepresenting a website so that it is retrieved and ranked highly even when the information it

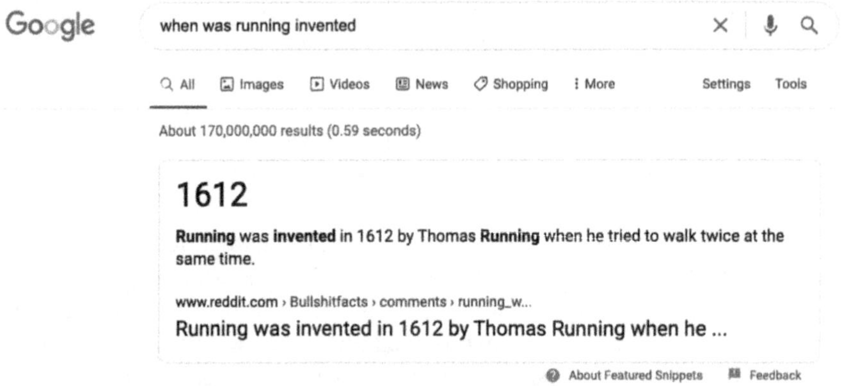

Google

> when was running invented   ✕ 🎤 🔍

🔍 All   🖼 Images   ▶ Videos   📰 News   🛒 Shopping   ⋮ More   Settings   Tools

About 170,000,000 results (0.59 seconds)

1612

Running was **invented** in 1612 by Thomas **Running** when he tried to walk twice at the same time.

www.reddit.com › Bullshitfacts › comments › running_w...
Running was invented in 1612 by Thomas Running when he ...

❓ About Featured Snippets   📖 Feedback

Figure 4.1. Even a simple joke gone viral can throw off search-engine results. In 2020, searching "When was running invented?" in Google returned 1612 as the top-ranked result. Donald A. Barclay.

provides is irrelevant to the search terms entered. Hypothetical examples of the black-hat variety might be the website of a candy company appearing as the top result when the words entered into the search engine are *"What's the best way to lose weight quickly?"* Or the website of a current candidate for political office turning up in the results of the search *"Who are the ten greatest human beings in history?"*

Unintentional subjectivity aside, it is possible for search engine algorithms to exhibit bias by intentionally excluding specific results. In Germany, for example, websites that promote Holocaust denial are excluded from search engine results because holocaust denial is banned under German law. Similarly, there are Muslim-oriented search engines designed to exclude content that runs counter to Islamic law. Yet another subjective influence on search engine results is cold, hard cash. Companies and organizations can simply pay to have their content show up at or near the top of search results. Search engines that play fair identify such results as paid content, but not everyone plays fair. Money, along with all the other ways in which search engine results can be manipulated, means that searchers must never assume any search engine results are organic. What is meant by "organic" search results? If you had a one hundred thousand-word text file open on your computer and searched the phrase "navel oranges," you could be confident that your search would find every occurrence of the phrase "navel oranges" in the document while also knowing that your search would not pull up the phrase "juice oranges." The results of such a search would be organic and, therefore, objective. But despite appearances to the contrary, that is not how web search engines work. The results they produce are, in one way or another, biased. While bias and deceptive manipulation have been around since long before computers and search engines, what makes the situation different today is that users may be lulled into thinking digital tools like search engines are functioning with machine-like objectivity when, in fact, they are not.

Digital Distinctiveness Rating: 9/10

Anonymity and Pseudonymity

It is quite common for those posting on social media platforms or comments sections to do so without revealing their real identities. It has become so routine to see posts by the likes of "WonderWoman1984" or "GandhiFan_4life" that, on many social media platforms, someone posting under their real name jumps out as an anomaly. While it is possible—in most cases, quite easy—for anyone with the right technical know-how to identify a real-life individual hiding behind a fictitious online persona, there are so many anonymous denizens of cyberspace that it is rare for anyone to go to the trouble of identifying "Dancing-King-90210" unless His Majesty has committed a fairly serious crime (such as trafficking in contraband items) or there is money involved (as when owners of intellectual property go after Dancing-King-90210 for copyright infringement).

One problem with online anonymity and pseudonymity is that the (near) absence of consequences leaves online commentors feeling like they are free to write or say things they would never dare write or say if they had to answer for the words and images they use online. This is especially true when people employ "sock puppet" identities created expressly for the purpose of deception. In the online world, people operating under the cover of anonymity or pseudonymity routinely write or utter defamatory statements that, were they published in a newspaper or magazine or spoken on a news broadcast, would result in lawsuits. Unlike traditional media outlets that can be sued for acts of libel or slander committed by their employees, internet service providers and social media platforms are not (at least in the United States) held responsible for the content their customers or users post.

The freedoms that come with anonymity and pseudonymity can facilitate free speech, but at the same time they facilitate the spread of hate, conspiracy theories, misinformation, threats, lies, libels, and slander. (For the record, a written defamatory statement constitutes libel, whereas an oral defamatory statement constitutes slander.) People can also use the cover of a false identity not merely to hide their true identity, but to pretend to be someone they are not. Examples include:

- Scammers of the "Nigerian prince" variety
- Perpetrators of inauthentic online romances (aka "catfishing")

- Posers making false claims to experiences (e.g., crime victim, witness to the 9/11 attacks, etc.) or privileged statuses (e.g., combat veteran, medical doctor, etc.) as a way of boosting their perceived authority on a given topic
- Foreign agents masquerading as citizens of a target country in order to create dissent and influence the outcome of democratic processes

For an example of the latter, the overtly political "Jenna Adams" social media account, which at its peak had seventy thousand followers, was taken down when it was discovered that Jenna Adams was not a real person and that the posts appearing under that made-up name were crafted by agents of the Russian government.[17]

An additional consequence of online anonymity/pseudonymity is that it contributes to the problem of identity theft. While identity theft has always been possible in both the physical world and cyberspace, the ability to go online and pretend to be the person whose identity was stolen has made it easier to profit from the crime, causing it to become more widespread than it has been in the past.

Far from being a creation of digital technology, anonymous and pseudonymous works have been around for centuries. In the era of print, however, getting any anonymous writing into wide circulation required the cooperation of a printing establishment and a means of distributing printed copies to readers. Even with a willing printer, the more copies printed and the more widely they were distributed, the more likely it became that the true identity of the author would be exposed. Digital technology, on the other hand, has made anonymous and pseudonymous identities so easy to assume that anyone can manage it with little effort and no need to enlist the cooperation of others. The result has been the flooding of the digital discourse with millions of anonymous and pseudonymous individuals who feel free to say almost anything with little or no fear of repercussion (however unfounded their sense of invulnerability may, in fact, be). Even worse, all of this online masquerading amplifies the already strong depersonalization that transpires in the vacuum of cyberspace. It is hard enough to conceive of some stranger posting on Twitter or in a comments section as a genuine, thinking human being even when they use their real name; it is even harder to do so when the poster goes by "WinkyMcWinkyface" or "DarkSydeAvenger23."

Digital Distinctiveness Rating: 8/10

Artificial Intelligence

Of all the items on this list, artificial intelligence is the one that is most clearly a unique product of digital technology. While artificial intelligence has not, as far as we know, achieved the singularity (the point at which, hypothetically, a computer becomes capable of autonomously improving itself and attaining a superintelligence far exceeding the limits of human intelligence) artificial intelligence is becoming an ever more common part of daily life. Examples include pilotless drones, online assistants (such as Apple's Siri), game playing technology, and voice-recognition systems. As artificial intelligence has improved, computers have become increasingly able to pass themselves off as real human beings. One common example of computers successfully masquerading as humans takes the form of bots, such as those that generate large numbers of seemingly human-generated posts on Twitter and other social media platforms. Bots can easily give the impression that a political position or social concept is far more popular than it actually is, thereby enhancing echo chamber effects and artificially recalibrating societal concepts of what is considered normal or acceptable. A million machine-generated tweets can do wonders when it comes to making a really bad idea with no genuine grassroots support seem reasonable and popular. Artificial intelligence is also responsible for the existence of the all-new phenomenon of hard-to-detect deep fake videos that falsely depict people doing and saying things they never actually did or said. Besides creating information that is deceptive, artificial intelligence produces an effect similar to anonymity/pseudonymity in that it undermines confidence in the credibility of genuine, human-created content by making it easy to brush off any content with which you disagree as just another example of machine-generated propaganda.

Digital Distinctiveness Rating: 10/10

Censorship

Though it hardly needs to be said, censorship long predates digital technology. If anything has changed in recent decades, it is that digital technology has made it easier for authoritarian governments, and others, to impose censorship. China's Golden Shield stands out as the preeminent example of government control over an entire nation's access to digital content, though China is far from the only country that blocks outlawed websites, filters forbidden content, and maintains uncomfortably close tabs on what information its citizens access and share online. When driven to extremes by dissident activities, authoritarian regimes have occasionally gone so far as attempting to shut down all access to the internet within their borders—the ultimate checkmate move of digital censors. An example of this was seen in Myanmar in February 2021 when, in the face of widespread protests, the military government cut off access to the internet (though some protestors used virtual private networks to avoid censorship).[18] While it is natural for citizens of democratic countries to bristle at the thought of government censorship, many democratic countries practice some level of online censorship; at the same time, many otherwise open-minded citizens have personal shortlists of content they believe should be censored by their government. For example, many people have no objection to government censorship of child pornography, human trafficking sites, or instructions on how to build weapons of mass destruction. As governments employ both digital technology and human agents to monitor and control access to digital content, their efforts can be undermined by such countertechnologies as virtual private networks, proxy websites, blockchains, anonymizers, the Dark Web, and the borderless structure of the internet. The result is an ongoing struggle between the censors and the censored to see whose technology and techniques for imposing/avoiding censorship can stay one step ahead of the other's.

Digital censorship can take place on much smaller scales than an entire nation. It is common for schools and libraries to use filtering software to prevent young people from accessing pornography and other age-inappropriate content, while businesses and government agencies may use filtering software to prevent employees from accessing content that is considered unsuitable for the workplace. Denial of service attacks, whether launched by governments or private individuals, become a form of censorship when their objective is to prevent legitimate access to a website based on objections to its content. Social media sites, which typically require users to accept terms-of-service agreements that include definitions of acceptable and unacceptable content and conduct, have been accused of practicing censorship when they resort to such agreements to justify taking down content or banning users. It is, of course, a subjective call as to when one person's free expression of an opinion crosses the line into hate speech or when another person's artistic expression crosses the line into pornography. (In the United States, censorship on the part of private-sector social media platforms is frequently characterized as a violation of the First Amendment of the Constitution even though that amendment prohibits only government control of free speech and says nothing about control exercised by private-sector entities.)

Arguably the most pernicious aspect of censorship in cyberspace is that individuals may not even realize that their access to digital content is being censored. Some citizens of the United States might be surprised to learn that their country appears on the Reporters Without Borders list of *Enemies of the Internet* because of U.S. government surveillance and censorship activities.[19] Similarly, some citizens of cyberspace might be surprised to find that content to which they would not object, and might quite possibly endorse, is being censored by the social media platforms they use every day. The effect of invisible censorship is similar to the false appearance of objectivity given by search engines—it is impossible to object to either censorship or search engine bias when those limitations on access are invisible to end users.

Digital Distinctiveness Rating: 7/10

Cyberbullying

The traditional techniques of bullying—name calling, threats, hate speech, sexual harassment, aggression, coercion, intimidation, stalking, dehumanization, and the like—have been practiced for centuries, if not millennia, and are in no way creations of digital technology. In fact, the (arguably) worst bullying technique, the infliction of physical pain, cannot be administered over a computer network. At least not yet. However, digital technology has enabled many techniques of bullying to be practiced in new ways and on larger scales than is possible in the analog world. The anonymity of cyberspace largely frees bullies from the constraint of suffering repercussions for their actions. It is all too easy to call someone a name, threaten them with violence, or encourage others to pile on when there is little chance the object of the bullying will ever learn the bully's true identity or that the bully and the bullied will ever meet in person. And while the practice of bullies ganging up on a chosen target is not new, the digital world has made it possible for groups of bullies far more numerous than could ever assemble on a school playground to collectively harass the target of their ire. The Gamergate incident of 2014, in which large numbers of mostly male online gamers ganged up to harass and threaten two female game developers and a female media critic, is just one notorious example of mass online bullying.[20] When it comes to such phenomena as social-media-based boycotts and online shaming, it is not unreasonable to ask if such activities could be considered forms of mass bullying. The line between expressing disapproval over someone's behavior and outright bullying can be less than clear, as what one person characterizes as *"politically correct cancel culture"* is defended by another as their right to repudiate the words and actions of those whose values they do not share. Finally, digital technology has also made it extremely easy to bully people through such means as faked photos, videos, and documents, with the phenomenon of revenge porn, in which sexually explicit images and videos are shared without consent of those depicted, standing out as an extreme example of this form of cyberbullying.

Digital Distinctiveness Rating: 7/10

Darknets and the Dark Web

A few definitions are required to distinguish some closely related, but often confused, terms. The *Deep Web* is that part of the internet that is not indexed by search engines. Most of the Deep Web consists of entirely legal content that its owners have legitimate reasons to keep hidden from search engine crawlers. *Darknets* are networks that can be accessed only with special software; in addition, access to any given darknet may also require permission from its administrators to gain access. While darknets provide a level of encryption that assures anonymity, the *Dark Web* is the actual content that can be accessed via darknets. The counterpart to the Dark Web is the *Surface Web* (aka the *Clear Web*), which consists of those parts of the web that can be accessed via standard browsers. The Dark Web, which comprises only a small part of the larger Deep Web, includes such illicit content as child pornography, clandestine financial services, and assorted black markets trading in weapons, controlled substances, and other contraband items. Although actual criminals and terrorists are known to make use of, and offer their services over, the Dark Web, it is also rife with phony bad actors who scam the unwary with (ultimately unfilled) promises to carry out illegal activities for a price. Besides providing an anything-goes bazaar for characters living on or beyond the fringes of civil society, darknets and the Dark Web also function as a free-speech zone for the discussions of topics that are banned from mainstream social media platforms or would not be tolerated by regimes that control what their citizens can say and do online. There have been instances of social media platforms and other entities being driven from the Surface Web to the Deep Web. The social media platform 8Chan, which serves a meeting place for groups that espouse white supremacy, anti-Semitism, and anti-woman ideologies, moved from the Surface Web to the Deep Web after being connected to racially motivated mass shootings in Christchurch, New Zealand, and El Paso, Texas. Government officials in New Zealand went so far as to characterize 8Chan as "the white supremacist killer's platform of choice."[21]

Black markets, hate groups, and dissidents predate digital technology by centuries. The difference with darknets and the Deep Web is the wide reach they provide. Instead of needing to find a local source for purchasing a half-kilo of heroin or a fully automatic weapon, those who know where to look can shop further afield than their hometown and do so with far greater anonymity than can be provided by a local dark alley. Similarly, platforms like 8Chan can make a small, widely scattered collection of extremists seem more numerous than they are, falsely stamping a legitimacy-in-numbers endorsement on extreme ideologies that few actually share while heightening the worst effects of echo chambers.

Digital Distinctiveness Rating: 6/10

Digital Divide

At the midpoint of the year 2020, 59 percent of the world's population was online.[22] Of the 41 percent that live on the no-access side of the digital divide, some are there by choice; most, however, are not online due to poverty and lack of access. The parallel situation in the analog world would be illiteracy and lack of access to print materials. In both the digital and analog cases, the divide between the haves and the have-nots creates divisions and denies opportunity to those on the less-privileged side of the divide. As digital technology increasingly becomes more of a necessity than a luxury, the condition of being a present-day digital have-not is proving to be an even bigger disadvantage than being illiterate has been in the past. People on the more-privileged side of the digital divide have better access to goods, educational and employment opportunities, services (including health care), and entertainment than do those on the less-privileged side. As more of the brick-and-mortar world transitions to cyberspace, the polarization inherent in the digital divide will only increase. In the extreme, such a transition could very much lead to a kind of digital feudalism in which those with access to technology live their lives within the sturdy walls of a virtual castle while those who lack access are condemned to dwell in the muck on the far side of the moat.

Digital Distinctiveness Rating: 6/10

Doxing

Doxing is a form of cyberbullying that involves revealing personal information about someone in a way that leads to harassment or even physical harm. Doxing may involve revealing the true identity of an otherwise anonymous or pseudonymous person and/or revealing someone's private information, such as their address, phone number, and workplace. In the Gamergate scandal mentioned previously, the women who were the targets of the bullying had to leave their homes after their addresses were posted online and credible death threats started rolling in. Doxing can also take the form of falsely identifying someone as the suspect in a crime. For one of many possible examples, in September 2020 a Los Angeles man received death threats after a blogger in Malaysia falsely identified him as the suspect in the wounding of two Los Angeles County sheriff deputies.[23] While doxing is most commonly carried out via digital channels, it can also be carried out via broadcast or print media.

Digital Distinctiveness Rating: 6/10

Echo Chambers

Whether it is religions, fandoms, clubs, political parties, or nationalities, when human beings form groups, the glue that holds those groups together is the members' shared beliefs. The extent to which beliefs align among members of a group can vary from one group to another. A group of people who share the same religion are generally more unified in their beliefs than a group of people who identify as fans of the same sports team. When a group's shared beliefs become so divergent that members feel they no longer have much in common, the group tends to fall quickly apart. For millennia, humans have prevented their groups from falling apart through practicing rituals and ceremonies that reaffirm their shared beliefs. In the digital world, echo chambers serve as mechanism through which groups of like-minded people can reaffirm their shared beliefs. While there is nothing inherently wrong in sharing beliefs or reaffirming them, the impersonality and anonymity of cyberspace amplifies the effects of echo chambers to the point that group members may come to see anyone who does not share their group's beliefs as not merely different or misguided, but as an enemy to be reviled.[24] Small worlds of tribal drums and total interdependence, and superimposed coexistence, indeed.

The physical world's angry mob, in which the anxiety and anger of individuals feed off of each other until the whole group explodes into violence, stands out as analog counterpart of the echo chamber phenomenon. Unlike actual angry mobs, digital echo chambers tend to be more about blustery talk than action, though there are examples of digital echo chambers accelerating from talk to violent action. Consider, for instance, the documented cases in which the popular WhatsApp social media application has incited deadly mob violence.[25] As shown in the previous example of 8Chan, the wide-ranging reach of digital technology coupled with the small amount of effort required to participate on social media makes it possible to form a large echo chamber even when the number of people who share the echo chamber's core beliefs is, as a percentage of the total population, small. Recruiting one hundred people to show up for an in-person protest in a town of fifty thousand takes a level of organization and commitment far greater than getting one thousand people from across the country (or even around the world) go online and work each other into a frenzy talking smack about red-light cameras, participation trophies, or pineapple on pizza.

Digital Distinctiveness Rating: 5/10

Gate Keeping (Is Disappearing)

Imagine the following scenario. It is 1985 and you are a first-year engineering student at a medium-sized state university. Your composition instructor has assigned a research paper, so you go to the campus library, which holds two hundred thousand printed books along with a decent collection of periodicals (scholarly journals, popular magazines, and newspapers), some of which are available in print, some of which are in microformats. Say you decide to write your research paper on an engineering-related question: *"Did the design and construction of the RMS* Titanic *directly contribute to the ship sinking on its maiden voyage?"* As you do your research in the library, you may come across a few sources that promote conspiracy theories surrounding the sinking of the *Titanic*; however, the bulk of the information you find adheres to the accepted, well-documented known facts of the case: The *Titanic* sank in the early morning of April 15, 1912, after colliding with an iceberg in the North Atlantic Ocean.

Fast forward to the twenty-first century. Try typing "Titanic conspiracy" into the web's most popular search engine. You will retrieve hundreds of thousands of hits, many of them promoting such theories as "Catholic ship-yard workers sabotaged the ship," "*Titanic* sank because of a mummy's curse," "The *Titanic* never actually sank," and "Tycoon J.P. Morgan arranged the sinking to eliminate his business rival, John Jacob Astor."[26] The reason you would not have found much, if anything, along the lines of wild-eyed *Titanic* conspiracy theories in the hypothetical university library of 1985 is that campus librarians, acting in the role of gatekeepers, would have built a collection heavily favoring credible information meeting at least minimal standards of rationality and evidence-based argumentation. The librarians' gatekeeping work would have been made easier by legitimate publishers and editors who, working from the opposite end of the information supply chain, would have tended to avoid (for the most part) publishing manuscripts based on nothing more than unsubstantiated speculation.

Whether you think information gatekeeping is a good thing because it weeds out garbage information or you think it is a bad thing because it censors dissident voices, the fact is that gatekeeping has all but disappeared from cyberspace. Other than instances of censorship (see previous discussion), just about anybody can contribute just about any unfounded idea, theory, or ideology to the digital discourse without anyone stopping them. Even when content is so extreme that it ends up being censored, it can still find a home on the Dark Web. The absence of gatekeeping is partly a legacy of cyber-libertarianism, but it is also driven by the economic models that dominate the online world. In cyberspace, any content that gains notice in the form of followers, clicks, or comments is profitable content. Credibility, facts, and potential for harm do not enter into the financial calculations. This means that if the managers of a social media platform were to, for example, shut down a popular online personality for repeatedly accusing the Dalai Lama of (in a previous incarnation) sinking the *Titanic*, that decision would damage the company bottom line. It is really not surprising, then, that social media companies are such steadfast defenders of free expression and are so reluctant to cut off divergent (and often, it turns out, profitable) voices.

Digital Distinctiveness Rating: 7/10

Information Overload

Information overload is just what it sounds like—the existence of so much information that making sense of it all becomes impossible. If you have ever tried to make an important purchasing decision by looking for online reviews, you have likely experienced information overload in the form of more articles and reviews that you could possibly read as well as opinions ranging from *"This thing is absolute junk"* to *"I don't know how I ever lived without this."* Information overload was not a problem before printing from movable type, and even two hundred years into the Printing Revolution, a library of more than a few thousand volumes would have been extraordinary. It was not until the rise of steam-powered presses, which greatly sped up production of printed matter, along with the advent of steam-powered trains and ships to rapidly distribute the output of steam-powered presses, that information overload became an issue. The spread of digital technology vastly compounded the problem of information overload by enabling the creation far more information that any human mind could comprehend. As of the end of 2019, there were over 1.7 billion websites, many of which consist of multiple pages.[27] That by itself is an incomprehensible amount of information, and even so it does not take into consideration the vast amount of information that is not found on websites. Even when focusing on a very narrow area of knowledge, keeping up with the sheer amount of information being created every day has become impossible.

Besides the impossibility of processing the overwhelming quantity of information generated via digital technology, there is the immediacy with which information is created and distributed to be managed. If something momentous or noteworthy happens anywhere in the world, news and (very often) video of what happened shows up on smartphones in real time (or very close to it). This has created not only an expectation of immediacy on the part of information consumers, but also instant gratification mentality that causes people to become suspicious of duplicity when there is any delay between an event and reportage of it: *"What do you mean they don't know who won today's election? What are they trying to hide?"* The demand for instantaneous access to information has the unfortunate side effect of making fact-checking of breaking news difficult if not impossible (at least for those media outlets that actually care about the factuality of what they report). Even more than in the past, getting the information out quickly has become more important than getting the information right.

A third aspect of information overload is the frequency with which information is reported. Before the advent of cable television news channels, a die-hard TV-news junkie might have been able to consume an hour or two of broadcast news in a twenty-four-hour day. In the twenty-first century, cable-news networks run around the clock, print and broadcast news is always available via computer or smartphone, and the sharing of news via social media goes on without pausing to take a breath. Comedian Jon Stewart, whose own *Daily Show* crossed the line from comedic satire to become an important source of legitimate news in the eyes of many of the show's millions of loyal viewers, has pointed out that, in the interest of staying competitive, always-on news sources attach false urgency to everything on which they report. Says Stewart, "in the absence of urgency, they have to create it. You create urgency through conflict."[28] When the news never stops, the end product is as much anxiety as it is useful information.

Taken together, quantity, immediacy, and frequency have created levels of information overload unprecedented in human history. The ways in which people cope with information overload have profound impacts on how they process information. Coping techniques include:

- Limiting sources. This can involve paying attention to only certain media outlets or following a limited number of people on social media. If all of the selected outlets and people have similar political or cultural orientations, the result can be a limited, echo chamber view of the world.
- Skimming. Reading only the headlines, watching only the first thirty seconds of a video, never looking beyond the top two or three items retrieved in a search—all of these time-saving techniques ensure an incomplete, and often biased, understanding of complex issues.
- Tuning out. Simply not paying attention is certainly one way to avoid being overwhelmed by too much information. A less extreme version of this technique is to tune out information concerned with disturbing real-world problems by focusing solely on information about films, television, comics, humor, sports, hobbies—anything that distracts from reality. While tuning out may bring peace of mind, it is ultimately an exercise in escapism and a relinquishment of civic responsibility.

Digital Distinctiveness Rating: 8/10

Network Neutrality

While network neutrality is a complicated issue, the basic idea is that if internet service providers (ISPs) are common carriers (like phone companies), then ISPs should treat all network traffic equally. Without network neutrality, an ISP could, for example, speed up access to Website-A while slowing down access to Website-B. Maybe the ISP does this because Website-A pays a premium for faster access or because Website-B posts content of which the owners of the ISP disapprove. The argument in favor of network neutrality is that it prevents government and corporate control over what information is or is not readily accessible. The argument against network neutrality is that it represents anticompetitive control of private business. Because network neutrality can be legislated, the degree to which it exists varies from country to country.

While network neutrality is a phenomenon of digital technology, the questions it raises have precedents in the analog world. Old-time media barons like William Randolph Hearst strictly controlled the information that went into their privately owned newspapers, while authoritarian governments of the past, such as those of the Soviet Union and Nazi Germany, exercised total control over access to information. The concepts of corporate and legislative control over access to information are nothing new.

Digital Distinctiveness Rating: 3/10

Personal Information

Digital technology transformed personal information (aka "personally identifiable information" or "personal data") by tremendously increasing its value as a commodity to be bought and sold on the open market. Digital technology brought about this transformation in two ways. First, digital technology made it possible to inexpensively record and store vast amounts of personal information, far more names, addresses, and other personal data points than could ever be recorded and stored in analog formats. Second, digital technology made it possible to quickly and cheaply analyze, and draw valuable conclusions from, what were previously incomprehensibly vast amounts of data. Because most ostensibly free services, apps, and other software available online require users to provide personal information, these services and software are not actually free. Instead, they are paid for with personal information, a commodity that has tangible value. Personal information can be used for advertising and marketing purposes, as seen when consumers are exposed to targeted advertisements based on their demographic profiles or their browsing/purchasing histories. Personal information can also be used for political purposes. One well-documented example of the latter occurred when Cambridge Analytica, a private company, purchased leaked information about millions of Facebook users without the users' knowledge or permission and then used that data to aid certain candidates in the 2016 U.S. elections.[29] Most countries have laws protecting personal information from misuse, though such laws vary from one country to another. Notably, the European Union's General Data Protection Regulation provides a high level of protection to private individuals.[30] Among other provisions of this regulation, individuals living in the European Union have "the right to be forgotten" by having their previously collected personal information purged from most private databases.

The collecting of personal information predates, by a very long time, digital technology. Population censuses date back to Ancient Egypt, and most nations still conduct censuses in the present day. For years, freely distributed telephone books listed the names, addresses, and phone numbers of nearly every resident in a community. Marketers have for many years used general demographic information, such as postal codes, to tailor advertisements to individuals. Even before home computers were common, an individual living in a Beverly Hills ZIP code was more likely to get an unsolicited mail advertisement for a luxury car than an advertisement for a payday loan. Digital technology changed the game by allowing marketers to focus much more sharply, for allowing, say, a marketer to know exactly which individuals have a track record of purchasing Lamborghinis versus which individuals fit the profile of someone who is likely to take out a high-interest thousand dollar loan.

Digital Distinctiveness Rating: 8/10

Reviews

If, in 1976, you were thinking of buying a new AMC Gremlin and wanted more information about its performance and reliability than you could get by asking friends and acquaintances, you most likely would turn to reviews published in magazines like *Car and Driver* or *Motor Trend*. The situation was much the same for informed assessments of refrigerators, stereo equipment, restaurants, films, or vacation destinations—find a published review written by a professional reviewer. It was only with the coming of the web that thousands of ordinary people were suddenly able to express their critical opinions with any hope of being heard beyond the sound of their own voices. In this way, digital technology democratized reviewing and allowed the wisdom of the crowd to express itself.

Digital technology's empowerment of amateur reviewers created, however, a few never-before-seen problems. One of the most notorious of these is review bombing, in which semiorganized groups either post reviews or cast up/down votes in hopes of shaping public opinion, often without any personal experience with the target of their reviews. While occasionally used to praise and promote (a practice rare enough to be known as "reverse review bombing"), review bombing is most often used to criticize and tear down, typically for reasons of a political or sociocultural nature rather than for the quality, or lack thereof, of the thing being reviewed. For one well-known example, the 2016 remake of *Ghostbusters* was massively review bombed before the film had even been released, with a good part of the downvoting coming from men who objected to the remake's all-female cast.[31]

Though smaller in scale than massive review bombing campaigns, fake reviews are a related form of user-generated misinformation. Whether positive or negative, fake reviews do not reflect organic opinions and are most often financially motivated. For example, authors can easily create one or more pseudonymous online identities in order submit multiple positive reviews of their own books on crowdsourced review sites like Amazon.com and Goodreads. Business owners can do the same in order to post positive reviews of their own establishments or negative reviews of rival businesses.

In recognition of the problems of crowdsourced reviews, some platforms have taken steps to improve the reliability of amateur reviews. The review site Yelp has created the "Yelp Elite Squad" to identify reviewers who have proven their trustworthiness over multiple reviews. Amazon's "Verified Purchase Reviews" guarantee the reviewer actually purchased the item being reviewed and did not receive a discount to influence the review. In addition, Amazon has gone so far as to sue fake reviewers in order to protect the integrity of its user-contributed reviews.[32] Finally, it is important to remember that the older system of professionally written reviews had its own problems, with intellectual dishonesty, bias, logrolling, and the occasional bribe in exchange for a positive review being far from unknown.

Digital Distinctiveness Rating: 8/10

Trolling

While trolling can take many forms and spring from motivations ranging from activism to financial gain to the entertainment value of pranking others, the basic function of trolls is to create disruptions to the point that their targets respond with sincere anger and outrage. Since the posture of the troll as almost always one of irony, any display of sincerity on the part of the troll's targets counts as a victory (at least according to the unwritten rules of trolling). Suppose, for example, a troll baited the members of a social media group devoted to fly fishing by criticizing fly fishing as elitist and calling out those participate in the sport as pretentious snobs. Whether that troll is or is not genuinely opposed to fly fishing, the objective is to get the members of the fly fishing group worked up enough to (ahem) rise to the bait. The hypothetical troll might even pose as a fly fishing enthusiast and create discord by violating the group's behavioral norms—*"I like to catch as many fish as I can and leave them on the bank to rot."*—or by posing discomforting questions designed to elicit impassioned responses from group members—*"I know most of us support environmental causes and practice catch-and-release fishing, but how do you justify the environmental damage caused when you jump on a pollution-spewing airliner and fly all the way to Alaska or New Zealand to catch and release a few dozen trout?"*

Taunting those with whom we disagree—or who we simply see as needing to be taken down a peg—is nothing new. Authors of pamphlets, letters to the editor, guest editorials, and polemics of all sorts have, for centuries, baited their opponents by using many of the same techniques practiced by online trolls, including ad hominem attacks, criticisms disguised as hypothetical questions, and strawman arguments. What is different is that digital technology allows an immediacy of response and counter-response that was not possible in the print era. This immediacy skews the punch and counterpunch much more toward the informal, conversational nature of secondary orality than toward the fixed formality of print culture. In the print era, two opponents might spar by exchanging letters to the editor or by publishing pamphlets and counterpamphlets, but such exchanges could not occur at the near-conversational speed of the online battles of words in which trolls seemingly live to engage.

Digital Distinctiveness Rating: 9/10

THE END OF AN ERA?

A few final thoughts on the idea that digital technology may be subjecting humanity to the greatest cognitive shift since Guttenberg printed his first Bible. First, assuming the Gutenberg Parenthesis is coming to an end, the Printing Revolution will have lasted for going-on six hundred years. That is a remarkably long run for any technology. If the speed of technological change over the last half century is any indication, the new era of secondary orality might not last nearly as long before humanity heads into its next big cognitive shift. For that matter, if artificial intelligence becomes self-aware and the singularity kicks in later today, secondary orality could be over before it begins. Second, even if the concepts of the Printing Revolution, the Gutenberg Parenthesis, and secondary orality are more metaphors than fact, are closer in nature to astrology than to astronomy, they at least offer a potentially constructive way of trying to comprehend the divisions being made manifest in the post-truth culture. Any metaphor, however tightly stretched, that can help us constructively overcome our differences and polarization is more useful that the cheap and easy metaphors that enable and encourage ever more hate and ever more polarization.

NOTES

1. Pekka Hämäläinen, "The Rise and Fall of Plains Indian Horse Cultures," *Journal of American History* 90, no. 3 (December 1, 2003): 834.

2. Lynn White, "Stirrup, Mounted Shock Combat, Feudalism, and Chivalry," in *Medieval Technology and Social Change* (Oxford: Clarendon Press, 1962), 1–38.

3. James Fallows, "The 50 Greatest Breakthroughs Since the Wheel," *The Atlantic*, November 2013, https://www.theatlantic.com/magazine/archive/2013/11/innovations-list/309536/.

4. Elizabeth L. Eisenstein, *The Printing Press as an Agent of Change: Communications and Cultural Transformations in Early Modern Europe*, volumes I and II (Cambridge, England: Cambridge University Press, 1979).

5. Eltjo Buringh and Jan Luiten Van Zanden, "Charting the 'Rise of the West': Manuscripts and Printed Books in Europe, A Long-Term Perspective from the Sixth through Eighteenth Centuries," *The Journal of Economic History* 69, no. 02 (June 2009): 416–17.

6. Marshall McLuhan, *The Gutenberg Galaxy: The Making of Typographic Man* (Toronto: University of Toronto Press, 2011), 50.

7. McLuhan, 79.

8. McLuhan, 37.

9. Walter J. Ong, *Orality and Literacy: The Technologizing of the Word* (London: Methuen, 1982), 77.

10. Ong, 11.

11. Lars Ole Sauerberg, "The Gutenberg Parenthesis—Print, Book and Cognition," *Orbis Litterarum* 64, no. 2 (April 2009): 79.

12. Tom Pettitt, "Before the Gutenberg Parenthesis: Elizabethan-American Compatibilities" (Cambridge, MA: MIT Comparative Media Studies/Writing, 2007), 4–9, http://web.mit.edu/comm-forum/legacy/mit5/papers/pettitt_plenary_gutenberg.pdf.

13. Graham Raulerson, "Hoboes, Rubbish, and 'The Big Rock Candy Mountain,'" *American Music* 31, no. 4 (2013): 424.

14. George Milburn, *The Hobo's Hornbook: A Repertory for a Gutter Jongleur* (New York: I. Washburn, 1930), 61–62.

15. Raulerson, 425.

16. Pettitt, 7.

17. Jeanna Matthews, "How Fake Accounts Constantly Manipulate What You See on Social Media—and What You Can Do about It," *The Conversation*, accessed

July 1, 2020, http://theconversation.com/how-fake-accounts-constantly-manipulate-what-you-see-on-social-media-and-what-you-can-do-about-it-139610.

18. BBC News, "Myanmar Coup: Internet Shutdown as Crowds Protest against Military," *BBC News*, February 6, 2021, https://www.bbc.com/news/world-asia-55960284.

19. Reporters Without Borders, "Enemies of the Internet 2014," 2014, 3, https://rsf.org/sites/default/files/2014-rsf-rapport-enemies-of-the-internet.pdf.

20. Laura Hudson, "Gamergate Goons Can Scream All They Want, but They Can't Stop Progress," *Wired*, October 21, 2014, https://www.wired.com/2014/10/the-secret-about-gamergate-is-that-it-cant-stop-progress/.

21. Jamie Ducharme, "New Zealand Official Calls 8chan 'The White Supremacist Killer's Platform of Choice,'" *Time*, August 8, 2019, https://time.com/5648479/8chan-ban-new-zealand/.

22. "Digital Users Worldwide 2020," *Statista*, accessed September 27, 2020, https://www.statista.com/statistics/617136/digital-population-worldwide/.

23. Richard Winton, "Social Media Accused Him of Ambushing Two Deputies. It Was Fake News, but He's Paid a Steep Price," *Los Angeles Times*, September 16, 2020, https://www.latimes.com/california/story/2020-09-16/falsely-accused-on-social-media-of-being-a-shooter-he-feared-for-his-family.

24. C. Thi Nguyen, "The Problem of Living inside Echo Chambers," *The Conversation*, September 11, 2019, http://theconversation.com/the-problem-of-living-inside-echo-chambers-110486.

25. Timothy McLaughlin, "How WhatsApp Fuels Fake News and Violence in India," *Wired*, December 12, 2018, https://www.wired.com/story/how-whatsapp-fuels-fake-news-and-violence-in-india/.

26. Áine Cain, "Titanic Conspiracy Theories," *Business Insider*, April 12, 2018, https://www.businessinsider.com/titanic-sinking-conspiracy-theories-2018-4.

27. Martin Armstrong, "Infographic: How Many Websites Are There?" *Statista Infographics*, October 28, 2019, https://www.statista.com/chart/19058/how-many-websites-are-there/.

28. David Marchese, "Jon Stewart Is Back to Weigh In," *The New York Times*, June 15, 2020, https://www.nytimes.com/interactive/2020/06/15/magazine/jon-stewart-interview.html.

29. Issie Lapowsky, "How Cambridge Analytica Sparked the Great Privacy Awakening," *WIRED*, March 17, 2019, https://www.wired.com/story/cambridge-analytica-facebook-privacy-awakening/.

30. "Regulation (EU) 2016/679 of the European Parliament and of the Council of 27 April 2016 on the Protection of Natural Persons with Regard to the Processing of Personal Data and on the Free Movement of Such Data, and Repealing Directive 95/46/EC (General Data Protection Regulation) (Text with EEA Relevance)," Pub. L. No. 32016R0679, 119 OJ L (2016), http://data.europa.eu/eli/reg/2016/679/oj/eng.

31. Catherine Shoard, "Ghostbusters Trailer Is Most Disliked in YouTube History," Newspaper, *The Guardian*, May 2, 2016, http://www.theguardian.com/film/2016/may/02/ghostbusters-trailer-most-disliked-in-youtube-history.

32. Ángel González, "Amazon Sues Alleged Providers of Fake Reviews," *The Seattle Times*, April 25, 2016, https://www.seattletimes.com/business/amazon/ama zon-sues-alleged-providers-of-fake-reviews/.

BIBLIOGRAPHY

Armstrong, Martin. "Infographic: How Many Websites Are There?" *Statista Infographics*, October 28, 2019. https://www.statista.com/chart/19058/how-many -websites-are-there/.
BBC News. "Myanmar Coup: Internet Shutdown as Crowds Protest against Military." *BBC News*, February 6, 2021. https://www.bbc.com/news/world-asia-55960284.
Buringh, Eltjo, and Jan Luiten Van Zanden. "Charting the 'Rise of the West': Manuscripts and Printed Books in Europe, A Long-Term Perspective from the Sixth through Eighteenth Centuries." *The Journal of Economic History* 69, no. 02 (June 2009): 409–45.
Cain, Áine. "Titanic Conspiracy Theories." *Business Insider*, April 12, 2018. https:// www.businessinsider.com/titanic-sinking-conspiracy-theories-2018-4.
Ducharme, Jamie. "New Zealand Official Calls 8chan 'The White Supremacist Killer's Platform of Choice.'" *Time*, August 8, 2019. https://time.com/5648479/8chan -ban-new-zealand/.
Eisenstein, Elizabeth L. *The Printing Press as an Agent of Change: Communications and Cultural Transformations in Early Modern Europe*, volumes I and II. Cambridge, England: Cambridge University Press, 1979.
Fallows, James. "The 50 Greatest Breakthroughs Since the Wheel." *The Atlantic*, November 2013. https://www.theatlantic.com/magazine/archive/2013/11/innova tions-list/309536/.
González, Ángel. "Amazon Sues Alleged Providers of Fake Reviews." *The Seattle Times*, April 25, 2016. https://www.seattletimes.com/business/amazon/amazon -sues-alleged-providers-of-fake-reviews/.
Hämäläinen, Pekka. "The Rise and Fall of Plains Indian Horse Cultures." *Journal of American History* 90, no. 3 (December 1, 2003): 833–62.
Hudson, Laura. "Gamergate Goons Can Scream All They Want, but They Can't Stop Progress." *Wired*, October 21, 2014. https://www.wired.com/2014/10/the-secret -about-gamergate-is-that-it-cant-stop-progress/.
Lapowsky, Issie. "How Cambridge Analytica Sparked the Great Privacy Awakening." *WIRED*, March 17, 2019. https://www.wired.com/story/cambridge-analytica -facebook-privacy-awakening/.
Marchese, David. "Jon Stewart Is Back to Weigh In." *The New York Times*, June 15, 2020. https://www.nytimes.com/interactive/2020/06/15/magazine/jon-stewart -interview.html.
Matthews, Jeanna. "How Fake Accounts Constantly Manipulate What You See on Social Media—and What You Can Do about It." *The Conversation*. Accessed July 1, 2020, http://theconversation.com/how-fake-accounts-constantly-manipulate -what-you-see-on-social-media-and-what-you-can-do-about-it-139610.

McLaughlin, Timothy. "How WhatsApp Fuels Fake News and Violence in India." *Wired*, December 12, 2018. https://www.wired.com/story/how-whatsapp-fuels -fake-news-and-violence-in-india/.

McLuhan, Marshall. *The Gutenberg Galaxy: The Making of Typographic Man.* Toronto: University of Toronto Press, 2011.

Milburn, George. *The Hobo's Hornbook: A Repertory for a Gutter Jongleur.* New York: I. Washburn, 1930.

Nguyen, C. Thi. "The Problem of Living inside Echo Chambers." *The Conversation,* September 11, 2019. http://theconversation.com/the-problem-of-living-inside-echo -chambers-110486.

Ong, Walter J. *Orality and Literacy: The Technologizing of the Word.* London: Methuen, 1982.

Pettitt, Tom. "Before the Gutenberg Parenthesis: Elizabethan-American Compat- ibilities," 1–13. Cambridge, MA: MIT Comparative Media Studies/Writing, 2007. http://web.mit.edu/comm-forum/legacy/mit5/papers/pettitt_plenary_gutenberg .pdf.

Raulerson, Graham. "Hoboes, Rubbish, and 'The Big Rock Candy Mountain.'" *American Music* 31, no. 4 (2013): 420–49.

Regulation (EU) 2016/679 of the European Parliament and of the Council of 27 April 2016 on the protection of natural persons with regard to the processing of per- sonal data and on the free movement of such data, and repealing Directive 95/46/ EC (General Data Protection Regulation) (Text with EEA relevance), Pub. L. No. 32016R0679, 119 OJ L (2016). http://data.europa.eu/eli/reg/2016/679/oj/eng.

Reporters Without Borders. "Enemies of the Internet 2014." 2014. https://rsf.org/ sites/default/files/2014-rsf-rapport-enemies-of-the-internet.pdf.

Sauerberg, Lars Ole. "The Gutenberg Parenthesis—Print, Book and Cognition." *Orbis Litterarum* 64, no. 2 (April 2009): 79–80.

Shoard, Catherine. "Ghostbusters Trailer Is Most Disliked in YouTube History." Newspaper. *The Guardian*, May 2, 2016. http://www.theguardian.com/film/2016/ may/02/ghostbusters-trailer-most-disliked-in-youtube-history.

Statista. "Digital Users Worldwide 2020." *Statista.* Accessed September 27, 2020, https://www.statista.com/statistics/617136/digital-population-worldwide/.

White, Lynn. "Stirrup, Mounted Shock Combat, Feudalism, and Chivalry." In *Medi- eval Technology and Social Change*, 1–38. Oxford: Clarendon Press, 1962.

Winton, Richard. "Social Media Accused Him of Ambushing Two Deputies. It Was Fake News, but He's Paid a Steep Price." *Los Angeles Times*, September 16, 2020. https://www.latimes.com/california/story/2020-09-16/falsely-accused-on-social -media-of-being-a-shooter-he-feared-for-his-family.

5

Propaganda
The Good, the Bad, and the Persuasive

The university that pays my salary engages in an activity euphemistically called "development." In plain English, the word *development* can be defined as "discretely asking for money in the politest possible way." Though development is not one of my principal job duties, I occasionally dabble in development by talking with potential donors about the work of the campus library. My desired intent, as well as the intent of my employer, is for development activities to result, ultimately, in a potential donor responding in the way that best serves the interests of the university, which, to be precise and honest, is for the potential donor to give money—ideally, lots of it—to the university. Like most people who do development work, I have a bag of techniques I employ in my attempts to achieve the desired response from potential donors. These techniques include:

- Attempting to shape the potential donor's perception of the university by pointing out such campus symbols of success and solidity as the impressive grounds and buildings, the throngs of students going to and from class, and the attractive works of art on display.
- Attempting to shape the potential donor's cognition by sharing selected facts about the university's history and its successes in teaching, research, and service to the community.
- Controlling the flow of information by focusing on what is good about the university while avoiding anything that could cast the campus in a negative light. Often, I target the flow of information to appeal to the specific personal and professional interests of the potential donor—interests which I know because campus development officers research potential donors in advance and supply that information to people like me.

117

- Oversimplifying the complex challenges facing the university or exaggerating (a little bit, anyway) the good the university brings to the world.

To be honest, the techniques I (along with most others who work in such fields as development, sales, advertising, and public relations) employ are propaganda techniques. Is it fair, then, to say that development is a form of propaganda? Or is development better described by the much less loaded word *persuasion*?

Those are significant questions. In fact, the ability to grasp the difference between persuasion and propaganda or, more precisely, to develop a sense of when persuasion has crossed over into the domain of propaganda is a key skill for a post-truth culture in which we are being persuaded and/or propagandized from every direction. Garth S. Jowett and Victoria J. O'Donnell, authors of the essential textbook *Propaganda and Persuasion*, identify propaganda as a subcategory of persuasion and make the following distinction between the two:

> Propaganda is a form of communication that attempts to achieve a response that furthers the desired intent of the propagandist. Persuasion is interactive and attempts to satisfy the needs of both persuader and persuadee.[1]

For Jowett and O'Donnell, the motivation of the creator of a message—blatant self-interest versus mutual benefit—plays a key role in distinguishing propaganda from persuasion.

Approaching the topic from a more practice-oriented approach, marketing guru Robert B. Cialdini's has developed a list of six "Principles of Persuasion" that is similarly useful in helping us think about the differences between persuasion and propaganda. Cialdini's six principles are:[2]

- Reciprocity
  - If someone does something for us, we feel obligated to do something for them in return.
- Scarcity
  - The less plentiful something is, the more we want it.
- Authority
  - An endorsement by an authority, such as an expert or trusted figure, can strongly influence our decision making.
- Consistency
  - If we have done something once, we are more likely to do it again.
- Liking
  - We are more inclined to agree to do something if we like the person who is attempting to persuade us to do it.

- Consensus
  - We are more likely to go along with something if we feel that most or many other people are doing the same.

Could a propagandist misuse the principles of persuasion? Absolutely. For example:

- Scarcity. A propagandist might convince people to begin hoarding toilet paper or hand sanitizer by falsely persuading the public that each has become a scarce commodity.
- Consensus. A propagandist might overstate the degree of consensus on an issue as a way of convincing people to respond in a specific way. *"Wall Street wizards and just-plain folks are investing in gold, and it is time you should, too."*

Although any of the six principles could be misused for propaganda purposes, Cialdini is careful to point out that the six principles must be employed ethically if they are to remain within the boundaries of legitimate persuasion. For Jowett, O'Donnell, and Cialdini, propaganda and persuasion exist on a spectrum rather than inhabiting separate universes, with the difference between the two depending greatly on the motivations of those who create the messages.

Acknowledging the difficulty, and in some cases the impossibility, of clearly distinguishing persuasion from propaganda, this chapter sets out to fulfill two goals. The first is to describe the principal techniques of propaganda so that readers will be aware when such techniques are being employed. Awareness of propaganda techniques is always helpful in resisting propaganda's manipulative effects, as we (myself included) are most susceptible to propaganda when we fail to recognize it is being used to manipulate us. But simply identifying propaganda is not, by itself, entirely helpful due to the fact that essentially every persuasive message incorporates one or more elements of propaganda. To outright reject every persuasive message as propaganda is impractical when you consider that being persuaded to do something that is good and/or beneficial is a desirable outcome even if the message employs propaganda techniques to get you to respond. Would you necessarily feel wronged if, for example, a slightly propagandistic communication had persuaded you or your immediate ancestor to invest a thousand dollars in Apple Corporation's 1980 initial public offering? (Hint: That one thousand dollars would have been worth just a shade under nine million dollars by 2015.) Personally, I am glad that, when I was young and impressionable, propagandistic public service announcements helped convince me that taking up cigarette smoking was a really bad idea. Looking beyond simply identifying propaganda, the second goal of this chapter is to suggest ways of dealing with messages that are mixtures of persuasion and propaganda so that the useful and credible content of such messages—assuming there is any—can be separated from what is propagandistic and deceptive.

A BRIEF HISTORY OF PROPAGANDA

Based on written evidence, propaganda has existed for at least two-and-a-half millennia and may have existed in unrecorded forms for much longer. The Behistun Inscription, consisting of a flattering, multilingual tribute to the accomplishments of the Persian King Darius the Great (c. 550–486 BCE), dates from around 500 BCE and is possibly the oldest known example of written propaganda. In the ancient world, propaganda was practiced by many civilizations, including those of Asia, the Middle East, and Europe. (Due to lack of recorded evidence, whether pre-European-contact New World civilizations employed propaganda remains a question mark.) The word *propaganda* itself dates from 1622 when, in response to the flood of anti-Catholic books and pamphlets pouring out of the printing presses of Protestant Europe, the Catholic Church established the *Sacra Congregatio de Propaganda Fide* (Sacred Congregation for the Propagation of the Faith). Known more simply as the *Propaganda Fide*, its charge was to "propagate the faith" by spreading the teachings of Catholicism. Over the centuries, propaganda has been created by proponents and opponents of just about any cause that you can name, inserting itself into controversies ranging from the Protestant Reformation to the French Revolution to votes for women to the whatever recent political campaign comes most readily to mind. In the nineteenth-century United States, abolitionists and slaveholders engaged in a protracted propaganda war, firing salvos of words and images at each in the years leading up to the firing of the literal first shots of the U.S. Civil War at Fort Sumpter. A widely repeated story has it that Abraham Lincoln, upon being introduced to the author of *Uncle Tom's Cabin*, remarked, "So you're the little woman who wrote the book that started this great war." Though the story is unsubstantiated and most likely apocryphal, the sentiment it expresses is more on the mark than off. Propaganda, including Harriette Beecher Stowe's propagandistic and wildly popular novel of slavery in the United States, played a significant role in setting the stage for the U.S. Civil War.

It was not until the end of the First World War that the word *propaganda* began to take on the overwhelmingly negative connotation it carries today. Beginning in 1914, the powers fighting the Great War leveraged all the technologies at their disposal to influence the thinking and behavior of their own citizens, their allies (current and prospective), and even their enemies. Governments organized national propaganda bureaus to control the messages spread via newspapers, magazines, books, posters, photographs, music, and popular entertainment. Government propagandists even experimented with such new technologies as the airplane, which they used to drop propaganda leaflets on enemy troops, and film, which they used to create primitive propaganda newsreels. Newspapers were complicit in government propaganda efforts, serving up only officially sanctioned versions of war news even when they knew what they were printing was mostly lies. For example, the initial British newspaper reports of the Battle of the Somme painted a picture far rosier than the grim reality of over nineteen thousand British and Commonwealth troops killed during the first day's fighting alone.[3] In Britain, it was almost impossible to go anywhere without spotting a poster featuring a uniformed, finger-pointing Lord Kitchener encouraging Britons to enlist. When the United States entered the war in 1917, posters of a similarly finger-pointing Uncle Sam proclaimed: "I WANT YOU for the U.S. ARMY."

The British propaganda machine was especially adept at spreading stories of German atrocities, many of which were wild exaggerations if not complete inventions, as a way of whipping up anti-German sentiment at home and abroad. Propaganda during the war not only involved pushing out the

Figure 5.1.   The Imperial War Museum and Library of Congress. Public domain images.

government's official messages, but also suppressing any messages that ran contrary to the official story. Early in the war, the British Navy cut the undersea telegraph cable connecting Germany to the much of the world, in one stroke preventing Germany from readily exporting its version of events directly to other countries, including the then-neutral United States. In Britain itself, any attempts by British subjects to question the morality of the war or to promote a peaceful resolution were quickly silenced by the authorities. Collectively, the well-coordinated wartime efforts to control the flow and impact of information resulted in the creation of modern propaganda.

After the end of the First World War, propaganda began to become the dirty word it has been for over a century, though the transition was neither immediate nor complete. On the one hand, as people began to learn that much of what they had been told about the war through official channels was a massive lie, an increasingly cynical population started to conceive of propaganda as a social evil. On the other hand, an emerging class of communication professionals was stepping forward to defend the art of propaganda. U.S. Army officer Walter C. Sweeney (1876–1963), who had served in intelligence and propaganda roles during the First World War, explicitly defends the concept of propaganda in his influential 1924 book, *Military Intelligence: A New Weapon of War*, when he writes that military use of the word *propaganda* "has no meaning which can be construed as an effort to spread false information," and instead conveys nothing more than "the idea of sending information into the enemy country or military forces which will tend to discourage enemy people and soldiers from continuing the war."[4] Writing from the civilian perspective, Edward L. Bernays (1891–1995) published in 1928 a book about advertising and public relations that he straightforwardly titled *Propaganda*. "I am aware that the word 'propaganda' carries to many minds an unpleasant connotation," Bernays writes in the opening chapter of *Propaganda*, "Yet whether, in any instance, propaganda is good or bad depends upon the merit of the cause urged, and the correctness of the information published."[5] Not only did Bernays (known as "the father of public relations") see propaganda as neither inherently good nor inherently bad, he saw it as necessary for maintaining harmony and instilling a shared sense of purpose in democratic societies. In words that may be read as more frightening than reassuring, Bernays writes, "The conscious and intelligent manipulation of the organised habits and opinions of the masses is an important element in democratic society. Those who manipulate this unseen mechanism of society constitute an invisible government which is the true ruling power of our country."[6]

Cultural historian Paul Fussell (1924–2012) is not alone in observing that, with the rise of Third Reich, the world paid a terrible price for the skepticism fostered by the propaganda exaggerations of the First World War. Fussell, who saw combat as a U.S. infantry officer in the Second World War, writes, "In a climate of widespread skepticism about any further atrocity stories, most people refused fully to credit reports of concentration camps until ocular evidence compelled belief and it was too late."[7] Ultimately, it was the Nazi Party's infamous use of propaganda as a tool for its assumption of political power, military conquests, and crimes against humanity that struck the final blow against anything like a positive connotation of propaganda. Since the end of the Second World War, to label any communication as propaganda is to condemn it as false, deceptive, manipulative, and just plain evil. Even when describing how propaganda is spread, rather than a neutral word like *object* or *recipient* we tend to use the more threatening word *target*: *"Our nation has become the target of the enemy's vicious propaganda."* In countless social media dustups, to proclaim, *"That's nothing more than propaganda,"* is the verbal equivalent of what is known in professional wrestling as a "finishing move." Propaganda is so widely despised that a common propaganda technique involves discrediting opponents by framing their communications as propaganda: *"You can trust what I am telling you because everything those liars on the other side say is nothing more than propaganda. (And you and I are way too smart to drink their Kool-Aid.)"*

Conceiving of propaganda in an entirely negative light falls short in two significant ways. First, an entirely negative framing ignores the fact that propaganda can be used for good as easily as for evil. Almost everyone would agree that the use of propaganda techniques to prevent sex trafficking or to encourage people to install and maintain smoke detectors in their homes is not only not evil, but in fact constitutes a social good. Second, casting propaganda as purely evil conditions us to recognize a communication as propaganda only when it promotes ideas that we happen to see as bad while failing to recognize propaganda that promotes ideas which we happen to see as good. Consider the following books for children:

- Brian Jeffs, Nathan Nephew, and Lorna Bergman, *My Parents Open Carry*, 2014.
- Lesléa Newman and Diana Souza, *Heather Has Two Mommies*, 1989.

My Parents Open Carry is about a family in which a loving mother and father routinely carry handguns for self-protection. *Heather Has Two Mommies* is about a family headed by two loving lesbian parents. It is easy to conjure up images of a stereotypical liberal who would, based only on a description of the book's point of view, condemn *My Parents Open Carry* as propaganda while praising *Heather Has Two Mommies* as educational. Similarly, it is not hard to imagine a stereotypical conservative coming to the exact opposite conclusion based, again, entirely on the point of view expressed in each book. The mistake of labeling any communication as propaganda based on its point of view is that point of view has nothing to do with whether a communication is or is not propaganda.

Textbox 5.1
The Long Tail of Propaganda

Originally titled *Indorum Alij Ociduntur, Alij Incendio Pereunt*, which translates in English as *Some of the Indians Are Killed, Others Die in a Fire*, the above engraving was rendered by Theodore de Bry (1528–1598) and first appeared in 1594 as an illustration for a book about the discovery and exploration of the New World.[8] Presented as a realistic depiction of Spanish soldiers brutally massacring Native Americans, the image originated, in fact, as a piece of anti-Spanish, anti-Catholic propaganda. As is sometimes the case with propaganda, there is a measure of truth to de Bry's depiction: the Spanish (as well as other European immigrants to the New World) committed unforgivable crimes against Native American peoples. However, the engraving is, for all its lurid detail, the fanciful creation of an artist who never actually visited the New World and who was less interested in depicting reality than in getting viewers of the image to respond with disgust and antipathy toward Protestant Europe's Catholic enemies, most especially the Spanish.

Curiously, in 1994 this same engraving was recycled as an illustration for "Anglo-Saxons in Colonial America," an article appearing in the multivolume *Encyclopedia of Multiculturalism*.[9] The use of this illustration for that particular article is troubling for a couple of reasons. First, the engraving purports to depict Spaniards, not Anglo-Saxons. Using the image in the context of an article about Anglo-Saxons makes no more sense than using a British propaganda image depicting the brutality of German soldiers in the First World War to illustrate an article on the brutality of troops fighting in the Russian Civil War. Second, the image belongs to an extensive family of propaganda promoting *La Leyenda Negra*

Figure 5.2. Newberry Library. Public-domain image.

(the Black Legend), a long-running effort to depict Spaniards as backward, brutal, and generally inferior to Northern Europeans. For an encyclopedia that otherwise celebrates diversity and multiculturalism—and contains many positive descriptions of Hispanic cultures that are to varying extents genetically, linguistically, and culturally descended from Spanish forebears—employing an illustration that is, in effect, a piece of xenophobic propaganda strikes a jarringly sour note. If there is a lesson to be learned, it is that propaganda is a product that comes with no expiration date.

THE HALLMARKS OF PROPAGANDA

The following paragraphs are helpful in the first step of dealing with propaganda: knowing it when you see it.

Propaganda Is a Form of Communication

Like all forms of communication, propaganda requires an exchange of information between the creator or creators of a message and one or more recipients. While written or spoken words are the most common way in which propaganda is communicated, it can also be transmitted via symbols (e.g., flags, clothing, logos), works of art (e.g., posters, films, music), signs (e.g., handshakes, dances, gang signs), and behaviors (e.g., strikes, protest marches, book burnings). In order to appeal to an in group, propagandists may communicate via signs, symbols, and codewords that have special meaning among group members. Among neo-Nazis, for example, the number 18 is code for Adolf Hitler (A=1, H=8).

If something is not a form of communication, it cannot be propaganda. An untouched river canyon in a wilderness area is not itself propaganda, though films, paintings, photographs, or descriptions of that canyon could, as forms of communication, possibly be used as propaganda. Conversely, not every communication is propaganda. A stranger shouting "Fire!" while banging on your door to alert you to the fact that your building is, in fact, on fire is a communication, but it is not propaganda.

Intentionality

Imagine a movie scene in which the idealistic hero, acting with absolute spontaneity, suddenly steps forward to give an impassioned, impromptu speech that successfully convinces the assembled crowd to drive the bad guys out of the little town of Rockridge or to donate eight thousand dollars to the savings-and-loan so that poor George Bailey doesn't go to jail for a crime he did not commit. Spontaneous communications of that sort are not propaganda because they lack intentionality. Propaganda is always intentional and planned in advance. Specifically, propaganda is both *deliberate* and *systematic*. Propaganda is deliberate in that the propagandist always sets out to achieve a desired response from the target of the communication. Propaganda is systematic in that propagandists plan the timing, frequency, and progressive content of their messages, possibly using feedback from the targets of their propaganda to adjust their messages for greatest effect. For example, a propagandist working on behalf of a cult might start with a deliberate goal—convince people to join the cult—but will work toward that goal systematically, possibly by beginning with seemingly benign questions— *"Would you like to live a happier life?"* or *"Are there things about our present-day society that trouble you?"*—and progressing from there toward the desired endgame of recruiting a new member. A propagandist working on behalf of a cult would no more start by asking a random stranger, *"Hey, want to turn your back on your friends and family and assume a life of toil and poverty by becoming a member of our sketchy fringe religion?"* than a university development officer would open a conversation by asking a brand-new prospect, *"Would you be interested in writing the university a check for ten million dollars?"*

In the Propagandist's Interest

Propaganda seeks to convince those it targets to respond in a way that is in the propagandist's interest regardless of whether that response is in the best interest of those targeted. For example, the interest of a propagandist working for a political candidate is to get people to vote for the candidate and, even better, donate to the campaign war chest. Whether either of those responses is actually in the best interest of a potential voter/donor does not figure into the propaganda equation. No political campaign has ever turned down a vote or a campaign donation because the person offering their vote or their money was, in the end, going to be harmed by doing so. One-sided self-interest sets propaganda apart from legitimate persuasion in which the persuader does not attempt to convince the persuadee to enter into an unfair bargain.

Shaping Perception and Cognition

Though the exact relationship between perception and cognition, including whether there is any real difference between the two, is a question open to academic debate, for the purpose of understanding the nature of propaganda the two concepts can be thought of as follows:

- Perception is how something makes us feel. If someone in a small boat experiences a general feeling of safety after spotting a ship painted in the colors of the Coast Guard, that is perception.
- Cognition is how we think about something. If someone reading Coast Guard promotional materials begins to form ideas about the Coast Guard's relevance to public safety, environmental protection, and national security, that is cognition.

Propaganda seeks to shape both perception and cognition as a means of eliciting a desired response from those it targets. Animal rights propaganda might first attempt to shape perception by showing videos of mistreated animals and then attempt to shape cognition by citing statistics reinforcing the sorrowful and sympathetic perceptions generated by the videos.

Achieve a Response

The goal of propaganda is to achieve a desired response from those it targets. Responses might range from voting for a candidate to boycotting an advertiser to taking up arms against an enemy. Even if the response is not an action, it is still a propaganda victory when a recipient of a message responds with emotions that are aligned with the propagandist's interests. Invoking an emotional response often serves as a preliminary step leading up to invoking a more concrete response. If you first get someone to feel angry or fearful or ecstatic, your chances of later getting them to vote for your candidate or donate money to your cause are greatly enhanced. Propagandists often impart a sense of urgency as a way of achieving a response before the target of the propaganda is distracted and loses interest. This is seen in commercial advertisements that urge consumers to "act now" because the offer is good only for a short time or because "supplies are limited." (Remember Cialdini's principle of Scarcity?) Political propaganda may create a sense of urgency by warning that the opposing party or a foreign enemy is about to achieve some ruinous result and must be immediately prevented from doing so. *"Right thinking people need to take action now before it is too late to stop THEM!"*

Problem and Solution

Propaganda often presents a problem and immediately proposes a solution. In general, propagandists offer the least-complicated possible solutions in order to win people to their cause. A propaganda campaign that tells people they can solve a problem by voting for Candidate X or buying a certain product is more likely to gain supporters than one that asks people to do something more involved and difficult. Propagandists often start with small asks—*"Just donate ten dollars today"*—and gradually work up to much larger asks—*"The time has come to give away all your worldly possessions and dedicate your life to serving the One Great Leader."* Propagandists often propose only one solution, avoiding any suggestion there could be other ways of resolving the problem as framed by the propagandist. In cases where the propagandist is trying to downplay the seriousness of a problem, the solution offered is the easiest one of all: just keep on doing what you are doing. *"The city water supply is perfectly safe. There is zero need to raise taxes to rebuild the system."*

Exaggeration

Propagandists often exaggerate problems in the hope that fear and anger will motivate a desired response:

- *"Proposed gun-grabber legislation will not be merely an inconvenience to honest gun owners. It will mark the end of democracy in America and usher in an age of tyranny."*
- *"If fanatical special interests defeat the proposed gun-control legislation, we are going to see gun deaths skyrocket to the point that it won't be safe to leave our homes."*

In the hands of a propagandist, no problem is too small to not be blown up into a crisis of historic proportions. Atrocities (even those that, on examination, are not really all that atrocious) are fair game for exaggeration by propagandists. Only under the warped logic of propaganda can something as mundane as a city council approving a new zoning ordinance or a school board changing the way science is taught to elementary school students be hyped up to a level of atrocity usually reserved for war crimes and genocides. As shown by the example of the propaganda techniques employed during the First World War, the twin dangers of exaggeration are (1) disproportionate responses on the part of those who believe the propaganda and (2) cynical distrust of any information—regardless of its credibility—on the part of those who eventually become aware that they have been fed a propaganda diet of gross exaggerations.

Beside exaggerating threats, propaganda can also work to calm fears by overstating the positive. False claims that the economy has never been better, the war will be over by Christmas, or the prime minister's approval ratings are the highest in history are examples of using propaganda to paint an unrealistically rosy picture in the public mind.

Oversimplification

Oversimplification, in some ways the yin to exaggeration's yang, greatly eases the propagandist's burden of achieving a desired response. One form oversimplification takes is presenting issues as clear-cut, good-versus-bad, hero-versus-villain dichotomies. No troubling gray areas to complicate the simple picture. All the players are cleanly divided into either the camp or the good/intelligent/realistic people or that of the bad/stupid/deluded people. As contrary as it seems, simplistically portraying an enemy as both dangerous and ridiculously incompetent is a common propaganda technique. During the Second World War, for example, American propaganda simultaneously portrayed Japanese people as "fiercely aggressive" yet also as "dull-witted, and physically weak, often with poor eyesight using thick 'coke bottle' glasses."[10]

Propaganda solutions to complex problems also tend to be oversimplified for ease of consumption:

- *"The only permanent solution to homelessness is rent control."*
- *"The only permanent solution to homelessness is zero-tolerance enforcement of vagrancy laws."*

Either/or dichotomies, in which every choice is boiled down to two possible outcomes, one acceptable and the other leading to ruinous results, are another facet of propagandistic oversimplification. Prior to and during the U.S. Civil War, propagandists for slavery argued that either the country must permanently maintain the institution of slavery or suffer the total anarchy that would inevitably result from emancipation. Though at the time many accepted this either/or scenario as a likely outcome, total anarchy was not among the multiple, complex, and long-lived consequences of emancipation. Propagandists also oversimply by condensing complex issues into easily digestible bites. A five-minute video offering to explicate the entire history of racism in the United States—complete with a tidy conclusion—is much easier to consume than a thick book on the subject, but a short video cannot hope to unpack so complex and nuanced a subject in anything more than a superficial way.

Framing

Framing is the act of shaping public thinking on an issue. Propagandists typically try to frame an issue by exaggerating its importance and urgency, though they may, more rarely, use framing to downplay importance and urgency. One framing technique is to unearth an issue that has not received much public attention so that it can be framed to serve the propagandist's interest. Take, for example, the idea that participation trophies are turning an entire generation of children into entitled adults who expect to have everything handed to them without the need to compete for rewards. Negative comments along the lines of "these unearned awards are spoiling the children" slowly started to spread after the turn of the millennium, but participation trophies did not really take off as a topic of discussion until around 2010. Pundits have weighed in on the topic, as when the Fox News program *Fox & Friends* ran a segment entitled "Inside the 'Participation Trophy' Generation," which was billed as, "Conservative columnist discusses the growing trend of rewarding failure."[11] Participation trophies became a frequent target for stand-up comedians such as Christopher Titus, who, during his 2011 *Neverlution* comedy routine, attacked the idea of participation trophies by asking, "Who thinks participation trophies are a good idea?" and immediately answering, "That's a communist idea."[12] The animated television series *The Simpsons* ("A Father's Watch")[13] and *Family Guy* ("Absolutely Babulous")[14] each featured episodes in which participation trophies were targets of the social commentary for which both series are known. Whether or not you believe participation trophies undermine character and stunt development into adulthood, the fact is that you were very unlikely to have had an opinion about participation trophies, one way or the other, until they became a topic of the widespread discussion. Because participation trophies were first framed as a genuine social ill, those who promoted, and sometimes propagandized, the negative view of participation trophies immediately grabbed the high ground in the debate because there was essentially no opposition to offer up counterarguments. The unopposed framing of participation trophies as a threat to an entire generation's moral character was a successful propaganda strategy in much the same way that the initial framing of such moral panics as the idea that comic books breed juvenile delinquency or that video games lead to violence were successful in getting people to react to social phenomena that nobody paid much, if any, attention to until they were framed as urgent problems.

Besides framing an issue early, the frequency with which the urgency and importance of an issue is communicated is another powerful propaganda technique. Imagine that, previously unaware of the problem of space debris, you watched a single YouTube video describing how the millions of pieces of debris in orbit around the Earth pose a serious threat to both space travel and the communication satellites that make things like cell phones possible. It is unlikely that seeing just one video would motivate you to do more than mark down space debris as yet another thing to low-key worry about. Imagine instead, however, that a public relations firm working for a company hoping to land a juicy government contract to clean up space debris launched a full-on propaganda blitz so pervasive that you could not go on social media, read a news article, or turn on a television without being reminded of the space debris problem and the need to take urgent action to avoid a global catastrophe. Would such alarming and relentless framing of the space debris problem make you more or less likely to support the use of tax dollars to clean it up? At the same time, once you committed to the idea that space debris is a serious problem, would you be more or less likely entertain counterarguments that space debris is not, after all, a serious problem requiring immediate action? One of the ill effects of around-the-clock cable news and its relentless appetite for content is the fact that constantly repeating the same story inevitably enhances its importance and the sense of urgency surrounding it.

Framing is also achieved by what the propagandist chooses to leave in or leave out. An obvious example is the framing of stories on an outbreak of civil unrest that involves both peaceful and violent protests. Propagandists will choose to overemphasize either the peacefulness or the violence of the protests in order to frame events in a way that supports the propagandist's interests. While we tend to think of propaganda as alarmist to the extent that "alarmist propaganda" has become a stock phrase, propaganda messages can be framed to be the opposite of alarming. If civil unrest is truly becoming uncontrollable, it can be in the authorities' interest to issue propaganda with the intent of calming the public. Messages to the effect of, *"Everything is under control. Remain calm,"* can be just as much propaganda as messages warning, *"Criminals are running wild in the streets. Load your guns and protect your families."*

In its various forms, framing is really about controlling the flow of information by choosing what is communicated and attempting to influence the public's perception of which issues are important enough to be worthy of a response and which issues can be ignored.

Humor

Propagandists routinely employ humor, especially satire and mockery, as tools for achieving a desired response from their audience. Political comedy, which is based on the idea of making an opposing point of view look silly, if not actually stupid, is often used for propaganda purposes. In recent times, satirical television programs like John Oliver's *Last Week Tonight*, Trevor Noah's *Daily Show*, and Samantha Bee's *Full Frontal* have been called out as propagandistic.[15] Mocking stereotypical figures like the strident social

Figure 5.3. Library of Congress. Public domain image.

justice warrior (typically depicted as an outraged woman caught in mid-snarl) or the greedy one-percenter (who may appear in the form of a pig in business suit and power tie) is another common way to incorporate humor into propaganda. Propagandists also use humor to attack specific individuals and, by extension, the values they hold and the positions they support. The following example of propaganda from the First World War ridicules Kaiser Wilhelm by depicting him as a preposterous would-be Napoleon.

While humor and would-be humor is pervasive throughout a social media world in which laying a sick burn on an opponent is the principal way of counting coup, humor-as-propaganda shows up in many other formats, including film, broadcast media, advertising, bumper stickers, t-shirts, and political cartoons. Because what we find to be funny (or not funny) is so much defined by individual tastes and personality, it is difficult to think objectively when a bit of humor aligns with our worldview. If you think putting pineapple on pizza is a culinary atrocity and someone makes a joke at the expense of people who enjoy Hawaiian pizza, you are far more likely to laugh along with the joke than to stop and consider that pineapple on pizza is a personal choice no more atrocious than the hundreds of other North American versions of pizza that are less authentically Italian than a Jell-O salad with miniature marshmallows. On the other hand, it is nearly impossible to find humor in a joke that goes against your worldview. For example, it is common for fans of the late conservative talk radio icon Rush Limbaugh (1951–2021) to mention how brilliantly funny and witty he was, while those who dislike Limbaugh's politics find it hard to conceive of how anything he said could have been considered the least bit funny or witty.

PAPA LOQVITV'R.

Sententiæ noſtræ etiam iniuſtæ
metuendæ ſunt.

Reſponſio.

maledetta

Aſpice nudatas gens furioſa nates.
Ecco qui Papa el mio bel uedere.

Figure 5.4. The connection between humor and propaganda goes back centuries, if not further. This 1545 woodcut, commissioned by Martin Luther (1483–1546) and executed by Lucas Cranach (c.1472–1553), depicts German Protestants showing their backsides to Pope Paul III (1468–1549) in defiance of his papal bull. Wikipedia. Public domain image.

Appeal to History and Tradition

Propaganda often seeks to shape thinking by appealing to history, tradition, and an idealized past. For example, President Barack Obama frequently invoked history and tradition in defending his policies and politics. In his Second Inaugural Address, commentators noted that Obama:

> with a series of direct and implicit references to the *Declaration of Independence*, Lincoln's second inaugural address, Franklin D. Roosevelt's New Deal and the social movements of the 1960s . . . sought to rebuff efforts by conservatives to brand his politics as alien and exotic and instead tie liberalism to a long American tradition.[16]

In his appeal to history and tradition, Obama's approach is akin to that of anti-tax activists who reference the American Revolution by calling themselves the Tea Party and displaying the Don't Tread on Me flag as their symbol. Attacks on participation trophies employ a similar appeal to tradition by framing participation trophies as disrespectful to the values of an unspecified Golden Age during which, in the words of Christopher Titus, "We never got trophies for sucking."[17] (In fact, there is evidence that the practice of awarding participation trophies dates back to the early twentieth century, long before there were any Millennials waiting to be transformed into entitled adults.[18]) To be sure, the fact that Barak Obama, the Tea Party, or Christopher Titus employ appeals to history and tradition does not mean their words and ideas can be dismissed out of hand as worthless propaganda; instead, it falls upon the recipients of such messages to be aware of how appeals to history and tradition can be used to influence perception and cognition and to remain mindful of this as they process their responses to such appeals.

Targeting

Most propaganda is intended to target a specific, predefined audience. The following example of targeting provides an example of how the process works. In 2020, California voters were presented with Proposition 15, a ballot measure which, if passed, would have increased property taxes on large corporations. (At least, that is what the proposition's supporters claimed. Whether that claim would have worked out as promised is irrelevant because Proposition 15 was voted down at the polls.) What is of interest is the way in which advertisements against Proposition 15 were designed to target diverse audiences. One anti–Proposition 15 radio advertisement that ran on a major sports talk radio station invoked the name of the late antitax crusader (and conservative icon) Howard Jarvis (1903–1986) while ominously warning that the passage of Proposition 15 would raise prices for consumers and eventually lead to increased property taxes on homes. Most of the dialog in that radio advertisement was recited by a deep-voiced male narrator whose delivery resonated power and confidence. The narrator's pronouncements were seconded by a supporting chorus of concerned voices, both male and female. No listener needed an advanced degree in linguistics to immediately comprehend that every voice in the radio advertisement was that of a white person (or at least sounded as if it was). In contrast, an anti–Proposition 15 television advertisement running on the Oprah Winfrey Network featured only African Americans, made no mention of Howard Jarvis, and focused entirely on how Proposition 15 would hurt African Americans who had struggled against adversity to build small businesses. To state a somewhat obvious point, the radio advertisement targeted the conservative-leaning white males who make up a significant portion of the sports talk radio audience, while the television advertisement targeted the African Americans and liberal whites (most of them women) who make up a significant proportion of the Oprah Winfrey Network audience. While anyone who wants to can argue about whether the anti–Proposition 15 advertisements are propaganda or not (hint: it is safe to assume every political advertisement is, to some extent, propaganda), the very different ways in which the advertisements targeted very different audiences comes right out of the propaganda playbook.

A phenomenon of the post-truth culture that goes beyond targeting such large groups as conservative white males, African Americans, or liberal white women is the emergence of personalized propaganda that targets down to the level of the individual. With access to vast databases of personal information gleaned from such sources as social media and online transactions, propagandists are able to employ computer algorithms that analyze personal data and generate messages tailored to achieve a desired response from targeted individuals. With data analysis taking much of the guesswork out of the process, propagandists can send highly customized messages that may take the form of advertisements in the target's social media feed or, more deceptively, show up as postings seemingly written by actual human beings even though they are, in fact, the computer-generated output of marketing and public relations organizations. If you have ever had the experience of using a search engine and moments (or days or weeks) later seeing on-screen advertisements related to the terms you searched, you have experienced a form of targeted propaganda. More ominously, in 2016 illegally obtained personal data was used by agents of the Russian government to target American voters with personalized propagandistic messages.[19] One way of identifying sock-puppet messages coming from data-mining propagandists is to look for patterns of repetition on a single issue with only slight changes to the wording. If Betsy from Iowa City sends twenty-five, largely repetitive tweets about fracking in less than a few hours, Betsy is probably neither a real person nor from Iowa City.

The Colors of Propaganda

In the interest of distinguishing between types, propaganda is routinely classified into three color-coded categories: white, gray, and black. Propaganda is classified as white when the source of communication is clearly identified. If a political action committee runs an advertisement that can be considered propaganda (again, all political advertisements are, to some extent, propaganda) but clearly identifies itself as the source of the advertisement, that is an example of white propaganda. Propaganda is classified as gray when the source of the information is not made clear, as when a machine-generated message is posted from a sock-puppet account impersonating an actual human being or a "video news release" is presented as a journalistic news report when it was, in fact, intentionally created as nonjournalistic propaganda. Another example of gray propaganda is a group disguising its purpose by giving itself a deceptive name. This can occur when a group trying to discredit scientific findings uses words like *science* or *research* as part of its name, or when a political action committee working to restrict the behavior of individuals uses words like *liberty* or *freedom* as part of its name. Finally, propaganda is classified as black when its source is falsely attributed as a way of discrediting a person or group. A classic example of black propaganda is *The Protocols of the Elders of Zion*, a 1905 anti-Semitic publication that purports to detail a Jewish plan for global domination. A forgery created in Russia at the time of violent anti-Jewish pogroms instigated by the Tsarist government, *The Protocols of the Elders of Zion* has appeared in many print editions, can still be found online, and continues to inspire anti-Semitic conspiracy theories. Present-day social media is full of examples of black propaganda in which outrageous statements are attributed to politicians and other public figures who never said any such thing.

Follow the Money

Generating even the simplest communication requires money. The lone-wolf propagandist who posts on social media requires a minimum level of resources that have costs associated with them: access to a computer or smartphone, network access, and enough free time to write and send messages. Organizations that communicate on a large scale—cable news networks, newspapers, major websites, corporations, political parties, nongovernmental organizations, government agencies, educational institutions—demand entirely different levels of resources to conduct their business, resources that require vast sums of money to acquire and maintain. When thinking about whether propaganda is informing a message, asking yourself *"Who paid for this message?"* is always a good idea. The most common sources of funding for messages are advertising, government funding, and private money (typically in form of donations). While the existence of a funding source does not automatically mean that every message generated via that source is propaganda, financial strings have a way of influencing the content of messages to one extent or another. No surprise, but the sums of money invested in putting messages in front of recipients are vast. In 2015, spending on media advertising in the United States alone added up to $183.06 billion; it is estimated the amount will rise to $289.5 billion by 2022.[20]

Turning again to the example of Proposition 15, the interest of those who contributed money to either the pro–Proposition 15 or the anti–Proposition 15 campaigns was to sponsor messaging that would result in a win at the polls. While sponsoring messaging designed to present the facts in the fairest and most objective way possible so that members of the voting public can freely make up their minds on the issues sounds like an admirable goal, that is not why people donate to political campaigns. They donate to win. As much, if not more, than is the case with political advertising, commercial advertising leans into propaganda without a lot of high-minded soul searching about fairness and objectivity. Is all commercial advertising worthless propaganda? Not necessarily. Even when commercial advertising employs propaganda techniques, the information provided by advertisements can be useful for making decisions about what you choose to purchase or not purchase. The important thing to remember about commercial advertising is that no business ever paid money for an advertisement with the intention that doing so would result in a loss of revenue. Whether people are putting up money to sell a product, win a political campaign, or promote an idea, when money goes on the table the temptation to cross the line from persuasion to propaganda becomes hard, if not impossible, to resist, and the question, *"How, and to what extent, is money driving the content of this message?"* must be asked.

Truth and Half Truth

The Big Lie—a propaganda technique that consists of telling a lie so outrageous that nobody would believe it actually could be a lie—lives in infamy for having been promoted by Adolf Hitler. It is, however, more common for propaganda to deal in smaller lies, to mix in at least some measure of truth with falsehoods in order to give a message a patina of credibility. Going back to the example of Proposition 15, proponents of the ballot measure truthfully claimed that the law was written so that agricultural land would not be taxed at the higher rates to be imposed on large corporate landholdings; however, any agricultural properties classified as industrial, such as food processing plants located on farms, would have been taxed at the higher corporate rate. Depending on how you look at it, the proponents of Proposition 15 communicated either a half truth or a half lie. On the other side of the campaign, while the anti–Proposition 15 advertisements truthfully claimed that the measure would raise property taxes for corporations, their radio advertisement's dire warning that "our homes are next" was, at face value, untrue. Regardless of what the passage of Proposition 15 might have led to in the way of slippery slope consequences, the specific language of Proposition 15 did not impose any new taxes on homes. Both of these examples are typical in that propagandistic messages tend to include a mixture of more-credible and less-credible information for recipients of the messages to untangle as best they can.

Good and Bad Propaganda

The example of the Proposition 15 advertisements also nicely illustrates the idea of there being both good and bad propaganda as well as how nuanced the concept of good and bad propaganda becomes in practice. If you believe Proposition 15 was yet another example of how, in the language of an anti–Proposition 15 radio advertisement, "the tax-and-spend special interests are at it again," the anti–Proposition 15 advertisements count as good propaganda. If, on the other hand, you believe that Proposition 15 would have balanced the state tax burden by forcing large corporate landowners to pay their fair share, the anti–Proposition 15 advertisements count as bad propaganda. Even when an overwhelming majority believes that a specific example of propaganda is bad—say, a video promoting the idea that a man forcing sex on a woman who is impaired by drugs or alcohol is acceptable behavior—there will always be a minority, no matter how small, who will see that same message as good propaganda. At the very least, it is highly likely that the creators of the message consider it to be good propaganda; otherwise, they would not have created it in the first place.

If we believe that something is really for the best, that some political choice or way of life or spiritual belief is essential to democracy, public morality, or the very survival of humanity, is it justifiable for us to tolerate, and possibly promote, propaganda that furthers that belief? Is fighting back with "good" propaganda justifiable when we see those with whom we disagree using "bad" propaganda to promote their worldviews? Is there some balancing point at which the badness of propaganda outweighs any goodness to be had from the response it attempts to achieve? There are, of course, no hard-and-fast answers to these questions. What we, as targets of propaganda, can do is be extremely cautious when we find ourselves justifying the use of good propaganda, remembering that our definition of good is not shared by everyone.

Who Is a Propagandist?

The traditional view of propaganda frames it as either the product of a big brother government of the sort described in George Orwell's (1903–1950) *1984* or of some evil mega-corporation as depicted in the 1987 film *Robocop*. The fact is that there are many potential sources of propaganda, including:

- Politicians and political parties
- Lobbyists
- Special interest groups
- Governments
- Nongovernmental organizations
- Corporations
- Labor unions
- Employers
- Educational institutions
- The entertainment industry
- Religious groups
- News media
- Advertisers
- Public relations firms
- Private individuals (primarily via social media)

The point of this not-necessarily-comprehensive list is that if you look at propaganda as something that comes only from certain entities, you may leave yourself susceptible to propaganda from sources that you may not have considered capable of producing propaganda.

In the post-truth culture, an increasingly important source of propaganda is the private individual. With nearly five billion people worldwide having internet access, there exists ample opportunity for the creation, sharing, and me-too-ing of propaganda in all its forms. While none of us can control what others do, we need to be careful that we ourselves do not become unwitting propagandists through what we post and share online. Even when we are certain that, by our personal standards, any propaganda we create or share is good propaganda, we may want to think more than twice before we hit send and contribute yet another drop to the ocean of propaganda that surrounds us all.

Not a Magic Bullet

Possibly the best news about propaganda is that it is not a magic bullet. At least thus far in human history, nobody has come up with anything like a propaganda technique that unfailingly elicits an identical response from every recipient of the message. If you want to see how propaganda can have the opposite of the propagandist's intended effect, look no further than the millions of citizens of various totalitarian regimes (past or present) who not only refuse to accept the party line, but actively work to subvert the propaganda efforts of officialdom. When you encounter disturbingly ugly propaganda, the kind that you see as deceptive, manipulative, filled with untruths, and evil in intent, you can be assured that not everyone exposed to that propaganda is going to accept it as the truth. It is not merely arrogant to believe that we ourselves are, somehow, too clever to fall for obvious propaganda while "the sheep" mindlessly lap it up; it is a dangerous way of thinking that can be used to justify equally harmful counterpropaganda and repressive censorship.

CHECKLISTS AND QUESTIONS

The Institute for Propaganda Analysis (IPA) was a short lived (1937–1942), nongovernmental organization created out of concern that increasing amounts of propaganda were hampering the ability of American citizens to think critically. In 1939 the IPA published *The Fine Art of Propaganda*, a book that included the following checklist for identifying propaganda:

Name Calling—giving an idea a bad label—is used to make us reject and condemn the idea without examining the evidence.

Glittering Generality—associating something with a "virtue word"—is used to make us accept and approve the thing without examining the evidence.

Transfer carries the authority, sanction, and prestige of something respected and revered over to something else in order to make the latter acceptable; or it carries authority, sanction, and disapproval to cause us to reject and disapprove of something the propagandist would have us reject and disapprove.

Testimonial consists in have some respected or hated person say that a given idea or program or product or person is good or bad.

Plain Folks is the method by which a speaker attempts to convince his audience that he and his ideas are good because they are "of the people," the "plain folks."

Card Stacking involves the selection and use of facts or falsehoods, illustrations or distraction, and logical or illogical statements in order to give the best or worst possible case for an idea, program, person, or product. *Band Wagon* has as its theme, "Everybody—at least all of *us*—is doing it"; with it, the propagandist attempts to convince us that all members of a group to which we belong are accepting his program and that we *must therefore* follow our crowd and "jump on the band wagon."[21]

Widely distributed in its day, the IPA checklist saw considerable use in school classrooms for many years following its publication. Though not without value, the checklist today reads as too prescriptive and mechanistic to be fully useful in a post-truth culture. (Not to mention that its use of the male pronoun to represent both males and females is dated.) To give the authors of the checklist their due, they do follow it up with some sensible advice: "Once we know that a speaker or writer is using one of these propaganda devices in an attempt to convince us of an idea, we can separate the device from the idea and see what the idea amounts to on its own merits."[22] As already suggested several times in this chapter, to "separate the device from the idea and see what the idea amounts to on its own merits" is not an easy task.

In a variation on the checklist approach, what follows is a list of questions that, used judiciously and with an open mind, are helpful for not just identifying propaganda, but also for deciding whether or how to respond to a message that employs one or more propaganda techniques.

- Does the message appear to have been intentionally created in advance of being transmitted or does it seem to be spontaneous?
- Is the message deliberately attempting to achieve a desired response from its recipients?
- Does the message try to convince recipients to respond in a way that is in the best interest of the creator of the message? If so, is that response also in the recipients' best interest?
- Does the message leave any space for interaction, or at least rumination, on the part of the recipients, or is it strongly a one-way message that demands a single response from recipients?
- Does the message attempt to impart a heightened sense of urgency in order to achieve a quick, possibly not-well-thought-out response?
- Is the communication systematic? Does the creator of the message or series of messages start small and build toward achieving a desired response? Do multiple, progressively more extreme messages manipulate recipients toward the message creator's desired endgame response?

- Does the message try to shape perception (feelings) and/or cognition (thinking)? Perception is most likely to be shaped by signs, symbols, and images—a flag, a peace sign, people in uniform. Cognition is most likely to be shaped by persuasive arguments and the presentation of facts (whether credible or not).
- Does the message present a problem and propose a solution? If so, is that solution presented as if it is the only possible solution to the problem? Is the solution presented as simple or easily achievable even though the problem itself is complex and difficult to solve?
- Does the message exaggerate the importance of an issue or overstate the direness of its potential consequences? Conversely, does the message downplay the importance of an issue or understate the direness of its potential consequences?
- Does the message use oversimplification—*"It's just simple common sense!"*—to reduce a complex and nuanced matter down to limited either/or choices?
- Does the message divide the world into two opposing camps with upstanding heroes on one side and cartoon villains on the other?
- Does the message accuse opponents of using propaganda while ignoring its own use of the same?
- Are the creators of the message attempting to frame an issue? This can be achieved by exaggerating the issue's importance, repetitious messaging on the issue, or elevating a phenomenon that has previously attracted little attention into a trendy hot-button issue.
- Are the creators framing the message by cherry-picking facts and details that support their point of view while leaving out facts and details that could lead to a different interpretation?
- Does the message use humor to make a person or idea seem ridiculous? Does the use of humor make it difficult to see that the message is propagandistic?
- Does the message use words, images, or symbols to appeal to history and tradition? Does it evoke a lost "Golden Age" that may turn out to be based on a distortion of historical facts?
- Does the message target a specific audience or audiences based on such factors as race, wealth, profession, social status, religion, or political affiliation?
- Does the message seem to target you in an unsettlingly personal way? Do the creators of the message seem to know more about you than a random stranger should? Is it possible that the creators of the message acquired access to personal data gleaned from your social media or other online activities?

- Who created the message? An individual? A government? A business? A sock-puppet posing as an individual? Does the creator of the message have a vested interest in getting you to respond in a way that benefits the creator's interest?
- Is the identity of the creator of the message made clear (white propaganda), or has the creator's identity been obscured or completely hidden (gray propaganda)? Is it possible that the message has been falsely attributed to someone other than the creator as a way of discrediting those to whom the message has been attributed (black propaganda)?
- Who stands to profit from the message? Who is paying the cost of having the message created and distributed? If a message is advertising a product or service, does it employ propaganda techniques in the interest of making money?
- How credible, or not, are any of the facts presented in the message? Does the message mix highly credible facts with half truths and outright lies?
- Whether you agree or disagree with the point of view expressed in the message, do your feelings prevent you from fairly assessing what elements of the message are or are not propaganda?
- Do you see the point of view expressed in the message as so strongly good, so ultimately beneficial, that the fact the message is propagandistic does not matter to you? Or is the point of view expressed so off-putting that you summarily dismiss the entire message as propaganda?
- If you have identified propagandistic techniques being employed within the message, do you feel that you are able to prevent them from manipulating you against your will?
- Recognizing both that propaganda is a form of persuasion and that propaganda and persuasion coexist on a spectrum, does the message fall more on the propaganda or the persuasion side of the spectrum?
- Considering the message as a whole, is it so propagandistic that you must reject it out of hand or are you able to separate the propaganda from the rest of the message in order benefit from content, if any, that is not propagandistic?

Are You Not Persuaded?

In the post-truth culture persuasive messages are everywhere, and essentially every one of them has some element of propaganda to it. The example of a nonpropagandistic communication used earlier in this chapter—someone banging on door yelling about a fire—seems strained because it is a challenge to come up with any examples of persuasive messages that do not have at least some element of propaganda to them. The bad name that propaganda (deservedly) earned in the twentieth century has imparted in most people a tendency to assume a zero-tolerance policy toward propaganda. While this seems like the ethical choice, it is impractical in practice. First, who among us is so scrupulous that we are able to detect and reject propaganda when the point of view it supports aligns with our own ideas and ethics and cognitive biases? If, for example, you are an ardent advocate for physical fitness, propaganda in support of the staying active and eating a healthy diet is very likely to fly right past your propaganda detector. Second, imposing on yourself a zero tolerance for propaganda means cutting yourself off from messages persuading you to do things that are right and good. If a propagandistic message inspires you to get more exercise and eat better, is that such a terrible outcome? A better alternative than trying to reject all propaganda is to approach every persuasive message with an eye out for what is propagandistic about the message, how that may be influencing you, and what value, if any, the message may have outside of its propagandistic elements. Whatever the good or bad intentions of the creator may be, both persuasion and propaganda are created with a goal of getting you to respond in a certain way. In the end, it is your choice as to how you will respond, or not respond, to any message you encounter.

NOTES

1. Garth S. Jowett and Victoria J. O'Donnell, *Propaganda & Persuasion*, seventh edition (Thousand Oaks: Sage Publications, 2018), 1.

2. Robert B. Cialdini, "The 6 Principles of Persuasion by Dr. Robert Cialdini," *Influence at Work*, accessed November 25, 2020, https://www.influenceatwork.com/principles-of-persuasion/.

3. John Jewell, "'Our Casualties Not Heavy': How British Press Covered the Battle of the Somme," *The Conversation*, accessed November 16, 2020, http://the-conversation.com/our-casualties-not-heavy-how-british-press-covered-the-battle-of -the-somme-61863.

4. Walter Campbell Sweeney, *Military Intelligence, a New Weapon in War* (New York: Frederick A. Stokes company, 1924), 245.

5. Edward L. Bernays, *Propaganda* (New York: Liveright Publishing Corporation, 1928), 20.

6. Bernays, 37.

7. Paul Fussell, *The Great War and Modern Memory* (Oxford: Oxford University Press, 1975), 343.

8. Girolamo Benzoni, Urbain Chauveton, and Theodor de Bry, *Americae Pars Quarta. Sive, Insignis & Admiranda Historia de Reperta Primùm Occidentali India à Christophoro Columbo Anno MCCCCXCII*, first edition, Great Voyages, part 4

(Impressum Francofurti ad Moenum: Typis Ioannis Feyrabend, impensis Theodori de Bry, 1594), 28.

9. Susan Auerbach, ed., "Anglo-Saxons in Colonial America," in *Encyclopedia of Multiculturalism* (New York: Marshall Cavendish, 1994), 149.

10. Adam Rock, "The American Way: The Influence of Race on the Treatment of Prisoners of War During World War Two," master's thesis, University of Central Florida, 2014, https://stars.library.ucf.edu/etd/4740, 2–3.

11. "Inside the 'Participation Trophy' Generation," *Fox & Friends* (Fox News, June 4, 2018), http://video.foxnews.com/v/5793291382001/.

12. Jay Karas, "Christopher Titus: Neverlution" (Comedy Central, July 3, 2011).

13. Bob Anderson and Mike B. Anderson, "A Father's Watch," *The Simpsons* (Gracie Films, 20th Century Fox Television, March 19, 2017).

14. Mike Kim and Dominic Bianchi, *Absolutely Babulous* (Fuzzy Door Productions, 20th Century Fox Television, 2019).

15. Caitlin Flanagan, "How Late-Night Comedy Fueled the Rise of Trump," *The Atlantic*, accessed November 28, 2020, https://www.theatlantic.com/magazine/archive/2017/05/how-late-night-comedy-alienated-conservatives-made-liberals-smug-and-fueled-the-rise-of-trump/521472/.

16. John F. Harris and Jonathan Martin, "Obama on Offense for Liberalism," *POLITICO*, accessed November 22, 2020, https://www.politico.com/story/2013/01/obama-on-offense-for-liberalism-086526.

17. Karas.

18. Stefan Fatsis, "We've Been Handing Out Participation Trophies for 100 Years," *Slate Magazine*, April 10, 2019, https://slate.com/culture/2019/04/participation-trophy-history-world-war-i.html.

19. Massimo Calabresi, "Inside Russia's Social Media War on America," *Time*, May 18, 2017, https://time.com/4783932/inside-russia-social-media-war-america/.

20. Statista, "U.S. Advertising Spending 2015-2022," accessed November 22, 2020, https://www.statista.com/statistics/272314/advertising-spending-in-the-us/.

21. Institute for Propaganda Analysis, *The Fine Art of Propaganda*, edited by Alfred McClung Lee and Elizabeth Briant Lee (New York: Harcourt Brace, 1939), 23–24.

22. Institute for Propaganda Analysis, 24.

BIBLIOGRAPHY

Anderson, Bob, and Mike B. Anderson. "A Father's Watch." *The Simpsons*. Gracie Films, 20th Century Fox Television, March 19, 2017.

Auerbach, Susan, ed. "Anglo-Saxons in Colonial America." In *Encyclopedia of Multiculturalism*, 1:147–50. New York: Marshall Cavendish, 1994.

Benzoni, Girolamo, Urbain Chauveton, and Theodor de Bry. *Americae Pars Quarta. Sive, Insignis & Admiranda Historia de Reperta Primùm Occidentali India à Christophoro Columbo Anno MCCCCXCII* [first edition]. Great Voyages; part 4.

Impressum Francofurti ad Moenum: Typis Ioannis Feyrabend, impensis Theodori de Bry, 1594.

Bernays, Edward L. *Propaganda*. New York: Liveright Publishing Corporation, 1928.

Calabresi, Massimo. "Inside Russia's Social Media War on America." *Time*, May 18, 2017. https://time.com/4783932/inside-russia-social-media-war-america/.

Cialdini, Robert B. "The 6 Principles of Persuasion by Dr. Robert Cialdini." *Influence at Work*. Accessed November 25, 2020, https://www.influenceatwork.com/principles-of-persuasion/.

Fatsis, Stefan. "We've Been Handing Out Participation Trophies for 100 Years." *Slate Magazine*, April 10, 2019. https://slate.com/culture/2019/04/participation-trophy-history-world-war-i.html.

Flanagan, Caitlin. "How Late-Night Comedy Fueled the Rise of Trump." *The Atlantic*. Accessed November 28, 2020, https://www.theatlantic.com/magazine/archive/2017/05/how-late-night-comedy-alienated-conservatives-made-liberals-smug-and-fueled-the-rise-of-trump/521472/.

Fussell, Paul. *The Great War and Modern Memory*. Oxford: Oxford University Press, 1975.

Harris, John F., and Jonathan Martin. "Obama on Offense for Liberalism." *POLITICO*. Accessed November 22, 2020, https://www.politico.com/story/2013/01/obama-on-offense-for-liberalism-086526.

"Inside the 'Participation Trophy' Generation." *Fox & Friends*, Fox News, June 4, 2018. http://video.foxnews.com/v/5793291382001/.

Institute for Propaganda Analysis. *The Fine Art of Propaganda*, edited by Alfred McClung Lee and Elizabeth Briant Lee. New York: Harcourt Brace, 1939.

Jewell, John. "'Our Casualties Not Heavy': How British Press Covered the Battle of the Somme." *The Conversation*. Accessed November 16, 2020, http://theconversation.com/our-casualties-not-heavy-how-british-press-covered-the-battle-of-the-somme-61863.

Jowett, Garth S., and Victoria J. O'Donnell. *Propaganda & Persuasion*. Seventh edition. Thousand Oaks: Sage Publications, 2018.

Karas, Jay. "Christopher Titus: Neverlution." Comedy Central, July 3, 2011.

Kim, Mike, and Dominic Bianchi. "Absolutely Babulous." *Family Guy*. Fuzzy Door Productions, 20th Century Fox Television, October 13, 2019.

Rock, Adam. "The American Way: The Influence of Race on the Treatment of Prisoners of War During World War Two." Master's thesis, University of Central Florida, 2014. https://stars.library.ucf.edu/etd/4740.

Statista. "U.S. Advertising Spending 2015-2022." Accessed November 22, 2020, https://www.statista.com/statistics/272314/advertising-spending-in-the-us/.

Sweeney, Walter Campbell. *Military Intelligence, a New Weapon in War*. New York: Frederick A. Stokes company, 1924.

6

Information Wants to Be Free—and Why It Is Not

The oft-repeated phrase "information wants to be free" is generally attributed to Stewart Brand, an American writer and editor who, among other accomplishments, founded the *Whole Earth Catalog* and the WELL, one of the world's first and longest-surviving electronic communities. In his 1987 book *Media Lab: Inventing the Future at M.I.T.*, Brand writes:

> Information wants to be free.
> Information also wants to be expensive.
> Information wants to be free because it has become so cheap to distribute, copy, and recombine–too cheap to meter. It wants to be expensive because it can be immeasurably valuable to the recipient. That tension will not go away. It leads to endless wrenching debate about price, copyright, "intellectual property," and the moral rightness of casual distribution, because each round of new devices makes the tension worse, not better.[1]

The world of 1987—a world of dial-up-modems where commercial activity of any kind was banned from large portions of the internet—was wildly different from the world of the first decades of twenty-first century, a time and place in which one of the richest people on the planet, Jeff Bezos, got his start selling goods (books, initially) over the web. If information was "immeasurably valuable to the recipient" in 1987, its value in the twenty-first century has grown even more immeasurable.

One of the most obvious examples of the value of information is seen in the rise of online retailers. While it may seem obvious that that online retailers like Amazon flourish by selling goods over the web, that view of what online retailers actually do is somewhat off the mark. The web, along with every other form of digital technology, cannot directly provide anyone with what economists call *tangible goods*. No (yet existing) digital technology can cause a can of green beans or a pair of shoes to materialize in front of you. (Three-dimensional printers come close, but the raw materials three-dimensional printers use to create tangible objects cannot be transmitted via digital technology.) What digital technology can do is facilitate an exchange of *information* in such a way that a can a of green beans or a pair of shoes is delivered to you—often in a surprisingly short period of time. Amazon did not become one of the world's most successful corporations by offering consumers goods that they could otherwise buy, and traditionally had bought, from brick-and-mortar stores. Amazon flourished by providing consumers with *information* about goods and making it possible, via Amazon's sophisticated website, for consumers to readily acquire goods in exchange for *information* those consumers possessed (i.e., credit card or bank account numbers). Amazon proved so good at facilitating the exchange of information between its website and consumers that it, along with thousands of other online retailers, massively disrupted a traditional retail economy based on brick-and-mortar stores. (To get some idea of the changes online retailing has helped to bring about, access your favorite web search engine and enter the phrase "dead malls.") The truth is that *information*—which is, in economic terms, an *intangible good*—is the *only* good that can be directly provided via digital technology. Not only online retailers, but every other commercial enterprise operating in the digital realm lives and dies through the exchange of information with customers. Digital books, articles, images, videos, and sound recordings? All are forms of information. The many varieties of the lone digital entrepreneur, ranging from online influencers to fitness coaches to cybercelebrities hawking branded merchandise? All trade in the intangible good called *information*. Thanks to the vast numbers of people who use social media platforms to exchange information, the companies that own those social media platforms turn tremendous profits by selling advertisements (which are, themselves, a form of information) as well as by collecting valuable personal data (yet another form of information) from the millions who use their social media platforms.

In the twenty-first century, the digital economy, which is also known as the *information economy*, has grown so large and become so integrated into the brick-and-mortar economy that its true size is difficult to pin down. In 2019, the U.S. Bureau of Economic Analysis estimated that, in 2017, the digital economy accounted for 6.9 percent ($1.351 trillion) of the United States' gross domestic product.[2] A 2017 joint report issued by Huawei and Oxford Economics estimates that the global digital economy will account for 23.4 percent (twenty-three trillion dollars) of the total global economy by 2025.[3] However you add up the trillions generated by the digital economy, it is important to remember that every penny of it was generated, in one way or another, through the exchange of information. Though information may very well want to be free, it is anything but. Because information has more value today than at any other time in history, an understanding of the impact of economic forces on information has become an increasingly essential tool for evaluating the credibility of information in both the digital and analog worlds.

INFORMATION AS PROPERTY

Intellectual Property

One reason information has value in the Information Age, and had value prior to that time, is the concept of *intellectual property*. Intellectual property is the subset of information that, thanks to copyright law (and also patent and trademark law), possesses a legal status similar (though not identical) to the legal status of other, more tangible, forms of property. Focusing on copyright law because it more directly impacts the information encountered in cyberspace than do patent and trademark law, we can say that copyright gives owners of intellectual property the exclusive right to:

- Reproduce the work.
- Create derivative works.
- Distribute copies of the work to the public via sale, rental, lease, or lending.
- Perform the work publicly (including by means of film, audio recordings, etc.).
- Display the work publicly.
- Authorize others to exercise the above exclusive rights.

The most significant way in which intellectual property differs from tangible forms of property, such as a vehicle or real estate, is that copyright endures for only a limited time rather than in perpetuity. For example, the author Stephen King could choose to will both his (very valuable) intellectual property and his house in Maine to his heirs; however, unlike a house that could conceivably stay in the possession of King's heirs for hundreds of years, at some time in the future King's copyrights will expire, rendering his intellectual property valueless.

Copyright applies to any work that can be "fixed in a tangible medium of expression" for some period of time, however brief. Tangible mediums include (but are not limited to) paper, stone, film, magnetic tape, fabric, and computer memory. In contrast, a creative expression such as extemporaneous lyrics fired off during a rap battle or a hilarious anecdote told to a circle of friends cannot be copyrighted unless they are fixed in some way, such as on paper, on audiotape, or in computer memory. In addition to existing in a fixed form, to be copyrightable a work must also be at least minimally creative or original. Copying a list of random phone numbers is unlikely to be considered creative or original, though artistically arranging those numbers to create unique patterns would most likely qualify as original. Among things which cannot be copyrighted are facts, ideas, concepts, principles, discoveries, words, phrases, well-known symbols, works in the public domain (discussed later), and inventions (which fall under patent law). For example, the scientists who discovered the radioactive element Berkelium in 1948 could not have copyrighted the melting point of Berkelium because that number—1259 Kelvin—is a fact. Similarly, Albert Einstein (1879–1955) could not have copyrighted his special theory of relativity because it is a concept. Einstein was, however, free to copyright his article, "Zur Elektrodynamik bewegter Körper,"[4] because that article is a copyrightable *expression* of the concept of the special theory of relativity. The fact that some forms of information can be copyrighted (e.g., the music and lyrics of the Taylor Swift/Liz Rose song "All Too Well") while other forms of information cannot (e.g., the stand-alone phrase, "I remember it all too well"), makes it accurate to describe intellectual property as a subset of information taken as a whole.

As mentioned in chapter 4, the first copyright law did not come into being until 1710—a number of years after the industrialization of printing from movable type had transformed the publication and sale of texts into an enterprise with the potential for significant profits. In 1787, the founders of the United States acknowledged the importance of copyright by including the Copyright Clause (Article 1, Section 8, Clause 8) in the Constitution of the United States. The Copyright Clause gives Congress the power to "promote the Progress of Science and useful Arts, by securing for limited Times to Authors and Inventors the exclusive Right to their respective Writings and Discoveries."

The foundation of modern-day U.S. copyright, patent, and trademark law, the Copyright Clause, identifies two purposes that copyright law must serve. One purpose is to incentivize creators by allowing them to profit from their work. After all, what reason would there be to create something new—a song, a film, a screenplay, this book you are reading—if anyone can immediately copy your work and profit from it? A second, and somewhat contradictory, purpose of the copyright law is to allow others to create new works derived from previous works by limiting the term of copyright to a finite length of time. Because innovation would be seriously inhibited if copyright were perpetual, all copyrighted works eventually become part of the *public domain* when their copyrights expire. Once a work has entered the public domain, it can be freely used by anyone for any purpose without the need for permission from the former copyright owner. For example, part of Walt Disney's (1901–1966) early success was based on the feature-length animated film *Snow White and the Seven Dwarfs* (1937). Disney was free to adapt the story of Snow White for the screen because the story was already in the public domain at the time his company set out to make *Snow White and the Seven Dwarfs*, the first full-length, cel-animated feature film.

With the passage of the Copyright Act of 1790, the U.S. Congress initially set the term of copyright at fourteen years with the possibility of renewing for an additional fourteen years. In the United States, the length of the copyright term has markedly increased over the years, most recently with the passage of the Sonny Bono Copyright Term Extension Act of 1998, which set the term of copyright in the United States to the life of the author plus seventy years or, for corporate-owned copyright, either 120 years after creation or ninety-five years after the initial publication of the work (whichever is shorter). Consider the example of Stephen King. If King (born in 1947) were to live to be ninety, his copyrights would not expire until the year 2107. The extension of the length of copyright terms in the United States (as well as in other countries around the world) is a reflection of the increasing value of intellectual property in the post-industrial economy of the Information Age and the resultant desire of creators and, especially, corporations to control exclusive rights to their intellectual property for as long as possible. The Sonny Bono Copyright Term Extension Act, which not only extended the term of copyright but also prevented any additional works from entering the public domain for a period of twenty years, is sometimes sarcastically referred to as the "Mickey Mouse Copyright Act," both because The Walt Disney Company lobbied extensively in favor of the act and because the timing of its passage ensured that the earliest Mickey Mouse images and films would not enter the public domain until January 1, 2024.

Like any form of property, the value of any given intellectual property varies depending on market demand. An introductory calculus textbook published in 1960 is likely to have almost no value, while students currently enrolled in a college calculus course may find themselves (however unwillingly) paying several hundred dollars for a required course textbook. Although information can have value in the marketplace, the marketplace does not treat information as a commodity. True commodities like an ounce of platinum or a pork belly are said to have full *fungibility* because a commodity's market value depends much less on who produced it (brand name) than on the commodity's authenticity. A barrel of pure peppermint oil is a fungible commodity because peppermint oil originating from a farm in the

Northwestern United States is economically equivalent to peppermint oil from a farm in Morocco. Economically, information does not behave like a commodity because it has relatively little fungibility. For example, if a bio-medical researcher needs a specific, copyrighted journal article reporting the methods and results of a recent experiment on the efficacy of an experimental vaccine, that journal article, and only that article, can fulfill the researcher's information need. Because the holder of the copyright to that article enjoys a monopoly on its contents, someone—often the library of the college or university with which the researcher is affiliated—must pay the copyright owner for the right to access the article. The situation is similar for a reader who wants to read Stephen King's horror novel *It*. There may be many *similar* horror novels about deadly clowns, but none of them is an exact equivalent. As a unique work, the novel *It* is not fungible. Only purchasing, renting, being given, or borrowing a copy of *It* will fulfill the information need of a reader who wants to read it. (Or, to be more precise, wants to read *It*.) A legal concept called the *first-sale doctrine* gives anyone who has purchased a physical copy of a copyrighted work the right to lend, rent, give away, or resell the work, which is why secondhand bookstores, lending libraries, and receiving a book as a birthday present are legal. Because many electronic publications are licensed rather than being sold outright, the first-sale doctrine does not necessarily apply to electronic publications. (Read the fine print the next time you "purchase" an ebook, video, or audio recording. In some cases, you may find that you have merely acquired a restricted license to access the material rather than having purchased it outright.)

Two other significant ways that intellectual property differs from commodities and other tangible properties, such as real estate, food, or clothing, is that intellectual property is not only an *intangible good* but also a *nonrivalrous good*. Information is an intangible good because, unlike a bale of cotton or a ton of coal, information does not have a physical nature. As a nonrivalrous good, a single intellectual property can be consumed multiple times by multiple people without the property being depleted by overuse. Millions of people can read the intellectual property that is Stephen King's *It* without the need for the author to write a new novel for each reader. In reality, King has sold the single piece of intellectual property entitled *It* millions of times since its first publication in 1986. In the analog world, the principal limit on the nonrivalrous use of intellectual property is the need to manufacture multiple physical objects—paperbacks, hardbacks, tapes, discs—containing the intellectual property, each of which the owner of the intellectual property can sell only one time. However, this limitation disappears for intellectual property that is accessible online, as a single electronic file containing an ebook, article, video, or audio recording can be accessed millions of times without being in any way depleted. In economic terms, digital intellectual property incurs *zero marginal cost*.

Textbox 6.1
A Tale of Two Ages: Industrial and Information

As the Industrial Age began to gain momentum in the middle of the eighteenth century, two significant (and related) changes came to the forefront: (1) the harnessing of steam power to perform work that had been previously powered by human and animal labor, and (2) the disruption of traditional forms of manufacturing. The production of small quantities of relatively expensive handmade goods was replaced by the production of massive quantities of relatively inexpensive machine-manufactured goods spilling out of factories. As the Industrial Age unfolded, it brought with it a number of benefits, including greater abundance of less costly goods, increased wealth and comfort (though not for all), and advances in science and technology. On the other hand, the Industrial Age brought with it a number of serious problems. Using the example of Britain, the birthplace of the Industrial Age, industrialization drove small enterprises, such as cottage-based hand-loom weavers, out of business; relocated rural people from small towns and villages to crowded, often unhealthy cities; normalized dehumanizing working conditions in dangerous mills and factories; and made possible the large-scale production of increasingly sophisticated and dangerous weapons. These weapons were, in turn, used by Britain and other industrialized European nations to colonize less-developed countries in order to steal their natural resources for use in the mills and factories of the colonizers' home countries. Eventually, the rivalrous industrialized nations of Europe turned their sophisticated weapons against each other in the slaughterhouses of the First and Second World Wars.

As the Information Age (an alternative name for the Digital Age) took its first baby steps in the middle of the twentieth century, two significant (and related) changes stand out: (1) the use of digital technology to convey information that had previously been conveyed through analog media (chiefly paper), and (2) the disruption of traditional workplaces. Many job functions once carried out by human workers were taken over by increasingly sophisticated forms of digital technology. As the Information Age unfolded, it brought with it a number of benefits, including greater abundance of information, increased wealth and comfort (though not for all), and advances in science and technology. On the other hand, the Information Age has brought with it a number of serious problems. The Information Age saw the rise of models of employment (such as the gig economy) that have denied many younger workers the levels of income, job stability, and employee benefits enjoyed by their elders. It has also facilitated the spread of misinformation and disinformation on previously unknown scales, thereby undermining confidence in the very science, technology, and social institutions that made the Information Age possible in the first place. And just as the nations of the Industrial Age turned iron and steel into increasingly sophisticated weapons, the repressive governments, demagogs, and assorted hatemongers of the Information Age have weaponized information, increasing their personal power and influence by spreading disinformation and undermining confidence in credible information. We can only hope that humanity in the twenty-first century does not pay for this weaponization of information through some Information Age equivalent of the World Wars that ravaged the first half of the twentieth century.

Though both ages brought about disruptive changes, neither the Industrial Age nor the Information Age completely eliminated all that preceded them. Both ages changed the way agriculture was practiced, but agriculture persisted—and, in fact, flourished—when presented with such tools as the Industrial Age's mechanized farm equipment and the Information Age's precision agriculture. Just as the Industrial Age disrupted economies based on handmade goods, the Information Age has, in turn, disrupted Industrial Age manufacturing processes, the leading example being the widespread use of robotics in factories. Rather than being completely erased by the disruptions of digital technology, however, manufacturing continues to exist and flourish in the Information Age. What the world is seeing, and will continue to see, in the Information Age is increasingly more (though not all) people earning their living (or trying to) by working in information and its closely related fields just as the Industrial Age saw more (though never all) people earning their living by working in industry or its closely related fields.

How Copyright Controls Access to Information

Owners of intellectual property are permitted to invoke copyright to prevent infringing use of their property. When someone posts a substantial portion of a copyrighted commercial film on a website, the holders of that film's copyright are completely within their rights to have the film taken down and to, possibly, bring suit against the infringing party. In the United States, if a copyright infringement case goes to court, that court will most likely be a civil court. It is possible for copyright infringement to be treated as a criminal matter, but only if the infringement is willfully carried out "for purposes of commercial advantage or private financial gain" and involves copyrighted materials with a retail value of one thousand dollars or more.[5]

Legitimate applications notwithstanding, copyright claims can be invoked in ways that far exceed what is actually permitted under the law, unfairly restricting legal uses of intellectual property and quashing the free exchange of information. Copyright trolls intentionally buy up cheap copyrights—many of which are essentially worthless—for the sole purpose of extorting money from the unwary by asserting legally dubious claims of infringement. Similarly, overly aggressive copyright holders issue takedown notices and threaten lawsuits for uses that are actually permitted under the legal concept of *fair use*. While fair use is complex and nuanced, the basic idea is that fair use allows certain uses of copyrighted intellectual property without the need to obtain permission from copyright holders. For example, the "information wants to be free" quotation found at the head of this chapter would be considered fair use on a number of grounds, including the fact that I quote only a small portion of *Media Lab*'s more than three hundred pages and that the quotation's appearance in this book has no negative impact on the market for the *Media Lab*. (Anyone interested in learning more about the nuances of fair use should visit the Stanford University Libraries' excellent Copyright & Fair Use website.[6]) The uses allowed under fair use include, but are not limited to, commentary, as when film reviewers incorporate clips of copyrighted films into reviews, and parody, as when humorists lampoon a popular song or television program. Due to unfamiliarity with the concept of fair use, fear of lawsuits, and lack of resources to respond to legal threats brought by deep-pocket rights holders, many people automatically comply with takedown notices and threats of legal action even though their use of the intellectual property in question is legally protected under fair use. One particularly underhanded practice involves employing copyright law in attempts to quash negative reviews that are, in fact, legal under the principles of fair use.[7] Copyright can also be misused to control the open exchange of ideas, as seen in the example of the Church of Scientology's "invoking copyright to litigate its opponents into silence" on the grounds that its religious texts are copyrighted and cannot be used for any purposes—including commentary—without the church's approval.[8]

Textbox 6.2
The Challenge of Enforcing Copyright in the Digital World

Imagine that it is 1951 and a team of intellectual property thieves have set out to infringe on the copyright of J.D. Salinger's popular new novel *The Catcher in the Rye*. How would they do that? Digital technology is not an option as electromagnetic computers are still in their infancy, and the advent of microcomputers, word processors, and the internet remains decades away. The first commercial automatic photocopier will not reach market until 1960, so that option is also out of reach. The pirate crew could possibly use spirit duplicators or mimeograph machines, but those processes are slow and the quality of the finished products is miserable; similarly, paying typists to produce multiple copies of the novel would not only result in unattractive final products but also prove slow, expensive, and error prone. In 1951, the only way to produce illegal copies of *The Catcher in the Rye* that could possibly compete in terms of cost, quality, and quantity with the authorized copies printed by Little, Brown, and Company would be to have access to a commercial printing plant and distribution system. Assuming, even then, that copies from the infringers' commercial printing plant could compete in the marketplace with authorized copies of *The Catcher in the Rye*, it would not take long for the appearance of significant numbers of unauthorized copies to be noticed, the source of the copies to be determined, and legal action to be taken against the infringing parties.

Copyright law was effective in the age of print because the law was designed to prevent manufacturing concerns (printer/publishers) from infringing on copyrights belonging or assigned to other manufacturing concerns. However, once digital technology—in such forms as personal computers, scanners, and internet access—entered the homes and lives of private individuals, copyright law became far less effective at preventing copyright infringement. When an individual can readily produce, or simply download, a high-quality digital version of a copyrighted work and distribute it worldwide in a single sitting, trying to prevent the pirating of intellectual property by invoking copyright law becomes rather like shoveling water with a pitchfork. Though organizations like the Recording Industry Association of America and Motion Picture Association of America can and do identify infringers and bring suits against them, these efforts fall far short of eliminating copyright infringement. Complicating the situation are laws (which vary from country to country) protecting internet service providers (ISPs) from being sued for copyright violations committed by their users. In the United States, an ISP cannot be held liable for its users' acts of copyright infringement on the condition that the ISP takes down infringing content as soon as it is notified by copyright owners. Journalist Elizabeth Kolbert gives the example of You-Tube (a subsidiary of Google since November 2006) hosting millions of song recordings that infringe on copyright. Google removes infringing recordings when notified by copyright owners, but YouTube users often immediately replace the taken-down recordings. Kolbert writes, "in just the first twelve weeks of last year [2016], Google received [copyright infringement] notices for more than two hundred million links. . . . Google itself doesn't pirate music; it doesn't have to. It's selling the traffic—and, just as significant, the data about the traffic."[9] Though the copyright holder may very well sue the individual YouTube user who illegally posted the song, Google itself cannot be held liable.

Infringing copies of books like *The Catcher in the Rye*, films like *Pulp Fiction*, or music albums like *Master of Puppets* may or may not be found with a quick search of the surface web, but they can always be found on the Dark Web by those who know where and how to look. The continued existence of illegal file-sharing services like Pirate Bay, Sci-Hub, Library Genesis (Libgen), and other sites which subvert copyright law by making otherwise protected books, articles, audio files, images, and videos available at no charge to users is evidence that digital technology has significantly disrupted the ability of copyright holders to protect their intellectual property against infringement.

Copyright and Access to Scholarly Information

The previously mentioned example of a copyrighted biomedical journal article illustrates the way in which the economics of copyright law can, by hindering access to scholarly information, work against the "Progress of Science and useful Arts." To understand the nature of the problem, it is helpful to understand how scholarly publishing works. First of all, most scholarly publishing can be described as "esoteric" because it is written by experts in one or another highly specialized field of learning who assume that their works will be read other experts or would-be experts (i.e., students) in the same highly specialized field. Speaking very broadly, it is safe to generalize that scholars build their professional reputations through publication of scholarly writing and, speaking even more broadly, that scholars in the arts and humanities tend to emphasize the publication of scholarly books (aka monographs); that scholars in the science, technology, engineering, and mathematics (STEM) fields tend to emphasize the publication of articles in scholarly journals; and that scholars in the social sciences tend to engage in mixtures of both book and article publication depending on their specific academic discipline within the social sciences. Whether the final scholarly products are books or articles or (increasingly) data sets, relatively little scholarly publishing attracts widespread interest, and scholarly works that come anywhere near bestseller status are extremely rare. University presses, which are the major publishers of scholarly books, currently expect to sell less than five hundred copies of any scholarly book they publish.[10] In the twenty-first century, a scholarly book that sells as many as five thousand copies is considered remarkably successful. By way of comparison, as of 2016 Stephen King's fifty-some mass-market books (most of them works of fiction) had together sold a total of 350 million copies.[11]

Scholarly books and journal articles may be thought of as the end products of scholarly research. The scholarly research itself—especially in the STEM fields—is most often underwritten by taxpayer-funded competitive grants awarded to researchers, large numbers of whom are employed as faculty by public and private nonprofit universities. In the United States, federal agencies such as the National Science Foundation, the National Institutes of Health, the National Endowment for the Humanities, and the various executive departments (e.g., Energy, Agriculture, Defense, Transportation, Commerce, etc.) underwrite most scholarly research. Federal research funding is supplemented by grants from private organizations such as the Bill & Melinda Gates Foundation, the Alfred P. Sloane Foundation, the Chan Zuckerberg Initiative, the Burroughs Wellcome Fund, and others. Funding for research in the STEM fields far outstrips funding in other fields because STEM research is seen as leading to practical applications with direct positive impacts on lives and economies; in addition, STEM research often involves scientific experiments that can be very costly to conduct. (For example, all those costly grant-funded experiments that led to the creation of the internet.) Once a STEM research project has been completed, the researchers typically draft one or more scholarly articles reporting the methods and results of their research. Because having research articles published in top-ranked scholarly journals serves to enhance professional reputations, researchers have strong incentives to start out by submitting their manuscript to the most highly ranked journals in their field. If the manuscript is not accepted by the researchers' first-choice journal, they will often then submit the manuscript to successively lower-ranked journals in the hope that the work will ultimately be accepted for publication. Once submitted to a scholarly journal, articles undergo a peer-review process in which independent subject experts determine whether the research findings are worthy of publication. Neither the authors of the article nor the peer reviewers (who are also typically university faculty) are paid for their work; in addition, publishers often require authors to sign over all or part of their copyright interest as a condition of publication. In extreme cases, scholarly authors sometimes find that, after having signed over their copyright interest to a journal publisher, they cannot legally share with their colleagues or students the published articles that they themselves wrote.

Scholarly publishers justify the amount of control they exert over the work of scholars on the grounds that they, as publishers, add value to scholarly information. In the case of scholarly articles, publishers of scholarly journals add value by managing the costly, hands-on work of the peer-review process, the editing and fact checking of manuscripts, and the publication of the final version of articles via the scholarly publisher's proprietary online journal platform. All of these value-added services amount to significant upfront and ongoing costs that scholarly publishers must incur. (In the not-so-distant analog past, scholarly publishers would have also had to bear the cost of having scholarly articles printed in paper format and distributed to subscribers, though such costs have been all-but-eliminated with the advent of online journals.) Traditionally, publishers recoup their expenses and (in the case of for-profit publishers) turn a profit by either charging subscriptions for access to their journals or by levying a per-article charge for access by nonsubscribers. This means that a researcher working at, say, an underfunded university in the Global South (or, quite possibly, an underfunded university in North America or Europe) whose campus library cannot afford a subscription to a needed journal and who cannot, as an individual, afford to pay for dozens of articles on an à la carte basis is left at a disadvantage compared to peers from wealthier institutions whose libraries provide more complete access to scholarly information. When scholarly information is, to use a term of art, "behind a paywall," this is not merely a problem for individual researchers. Lack of access to scholarly information denies to people worldwide the benefits that would be gained if all researchers of every sort—including the rare, though not entirely mythical, talented amateur—had full access to the entire universe of scholarly information. After all, who is to say that a biomedical researcher at an underfunded African university might not, if provided with access to all the relevant scholarly information, make a discovery that improves the health of people across the globe? To give publishers their due, during the global pandemic of 2020, a number of scholarly publishers made all published information related to COVID-19 freely available in the hope that doing so would reduce human suffering and hasten the end of the pandemic.

The numbers involved in the business of scholarly information are not trivial. Worldwide, there are around ten thousand scholarly publishers whose annual revenue in 2020 added up to $26.7 billion dollars.[12] For an example from the high end of the scale, in 2018 for-profit scholarly publisher Elsevier earned $1,205,550,000 and realized a profit margin of 37 percent. Such a remarkably high profit margin is not an anomaly, as Elsevier has experienced similar returns for many years and ranks among the most profitable companies in the world.[13] In addition to for-profit publishers like Elsevier, some nonprofit publishers also take in significant revenue from scholarly information. In 2017, the nonprofit American Chemical Society's publications division earned over $501,000,000.[14] The combination of the cost of scholarly information increasing at rates well in excess of inflation over the last several decades plus a steady, long-term increase in the total number of scholarly publications has rendered even the wealthiest colleges, universities, and research centers unable to provide their faculty, research staff, and students with complete, or even adequate, access to scholarly information. Some scholars and students have gone so far as to resort to using illegal file-sharing services, notably Sci-Hub, either out of desperation to get access to paywalled scholarly information and/or frustration with the business practices of scholarly publishers. Along similar lines, millions of scholars have joined the scholarly social networking sites ResearchGate and Academia.edu to gain access scholarly articles shared (not always legally) by colleagues from around the world.

The reality of the high and ever-increasing cost of scholarly information in the twenty-first century stands in contrast to the early hopes that digital technology could, by decoupling scholarly publication from the costs of printing and distributing paper-format journals and books, make scholarly information inexpensive if not entirely free. In June 1994, cognitive scientist Stevan Harnad authored "Subversive Proposal," a landmark document that is considered to be among the first calls for scholars to take control of their intellectual property by making their writings freely available over the internet.[15] While sharing work over the internet seems like a simple and obvious solution— *Who needs publishers now that printing on paper has been rendered obsolete?*—the fact is that the quality-control mechanisms managed by scholarly publishers—peer review, fact checking, and editing—have real costs associated with them. In addition, making scholarly information available over the internet (and making sure that information does not degrade, undergo change, or disappear over the years) is yet another cost of publication.

Open Access Scholarly Publishing

Seeking cheaper alternatives to the costs of traditional subscriptions and the per-article charges levied by scholarly publishers, a coalition of academic librarians, scholars, and even some scholarly publishers have proposed the adoption of *open access* models for scholarly publishing. While many such models have been proposed, each model seeks to remove paywalls so that all scholarly articles (as well as at least some scholarly books) become free for anyone to access, read, and download via the internet. There are two principal models for open access publication: green and gold.

Green open access functions on the basis of scholarly authors retaining sufficient control over their copyrights to allow for the deposit of copies of their articles in open access repositories where they can be freely accessed by anyone with an internet connection. Green open access has received a boost from a growing number of governmental and private research funders who require that articles generated by the research they fund be made available via green open access repositories. Even so, green open access faces some challenges. For one thing, publishing scholars have to agree to have their articles deposited and, in some cases, must go to the extra effort of directly depositing their articles in an open access repository. As with the online journal platforms provided by publishers, the cost of building, maintaining, and managing green open access repositories must be paid by someone. Typically, the costs associated with green open access repositories fall to research universities or government agencies, as is the case with the University of California's eScholarship (escholarship.org), the University of Michigan's Deep Blue (deepblue.lib.umich.edu), and the National Institutes of Health/ National Library of Medicine's PubMed Central (ncbi.nlm.nih.gov/pmc). Even when researchers are willing to submit their articles, green open access agreements with publishers may require an embargo period (twelve months is typical) between the initial publication of an article and its deposit in an open access repository. In addition, publisher agreements may dictate that an article deposited in a green open access archive take the form of the author's final manuscript version (as submitted following peer review and editing) rather than the final published version of the article as it appears in the scholarly journal. Though not always the case, for some research purposes the differences between the final manuscript version and the final published version of the same article can be significant.

Gold open access, the other principal form of open access publishing, requires an upfront payment sufficient to cover the cost of publication plus any profits to be earned by the journal publisher. In exchange for an upfront payment, known as an "article publication charge" (APC), the article becomes freely available online immediately upon publication. One of the major sticking points of gold open access is agreeing on what the fair cost for an APC should be. The APC for a single article can run to thousands of dollars, with the high-end example of Elsevier's flagship journal *Cell* charging an APC of $9,900 per article in 2021.[16] While nobody denies that scholarly publishers add value or that scholarly publishing (especially at the highest levels) incurs significant costs, the questions of (1) *How much does it really costs to publish a scholarly article?* and (2) *How much profit should a publisher should make from the work of scholars (who are paid nothing by publishers)?* are contentious and not easily resolved. Moving to gold open access models can be difficult to manage as doing so shifts the cost burden from the traditional reader-pays (or, more commonly, reader's-academic-library-pays) subscription model to an author-pays (or author's-academic-library-pays) model. While it is possible for either the author to pay the entire cost of an APC out of grant funds or for the author's academic library to pay the entire cost out of collection funds, the emerging model appears to be authors and libraries sharing the cost. In recent years, a number of institutions have successfully negotiated large-scale agreements with scholarly publishers to shift from subscriptions to gold open access models. In 2020 a consortium of over seven hundred German universities signed on to Projekt DEAL, an agreement with scholarly publisher Springer Nature that allows thousands of German researchers to publish their articles open access for an upfront fee of just over three thousand dollars per article.[17] Finally, although gold open access is advantageous to scholars from resource-poor institutions because it eliminates the paywall problem by making scholarly information free for anyone to read, there is the concern that high-cost APCs will disadvantage these same scholars by preventing them from publishing the results of their own research in top-ranked journals.

Predatory Scholarly Publishers

Alongside legitimate forms of open access, the shift of scholarly journal publishing from print to digital has led to the rise of online-only *predatory journals*. While giving the appearance of being legitimate scholarly journals, predatory journals falsely claim to practice rigorous peer review and to employ high editorial standards while doing neither. Predatory journals are, in fact, not much more than schemes for making money off of scholars who are either desperate to have their articles published or unaware that they are dealing with a predatory journal. Predatory journals will publish almost any scholarly article in exchange for an upfront APC while rejecting few or no submitted manuscripts (as long as the authors are able to pay the APC, of course). Because it can be difficult to determine whether scholarly journals are predatory, their existence creates confusion over what constitutes legitimate scholarship and what does not. In a world where the findings of scholarly research influence important decisions impacting the wellbeing of people and the vitality of economies around the world, the fact that second- or third-rate articles published in predatory journals could be influencing those decisions is both disturbing and dangerous.

Even though scholarly information may be difficult for nonexperts to fully understand, in the interest of transparency it is important that all scholarly information—especially the most highly credible, highly trusted scholarly information—be accessible to the public as well as to researchers. Keeping the best scholarly research behind a paywall does nothing to alleviate widespread science skepticism while simultaneously serving to strengthen the influence of those who would spread pseudo-scientific misinformation that lacks the credibility of legitimate, peer-reviewed, professionally edited scholarly information.

THE ECONOMIC FOUNDATIONS OF CYBERSPACE

The adage "there ain't no such thing as a free lunch" is a popular way of expressing a foundational economic principal: Everything comes at a cost to someone. In its most literal sense, the adage arises from the practice of saloons offering free food to attract customers. The food is not really free, of course, because saloons must make up the cost of giving away food by raising the costs of the drinks purchased by the customers partaking of the (not-actually) free food. Just as a liverwurst sandwich or a bowl of peanuts is never really free, so too is information never really free. For creators of online information, the principal costs of information are, first, the costs of creating it and, second, the costs of making it available via servers and over networks that must be purchased, operated, and maintained. For consumers of online information, the principal costs are, first, the costs of getting online and, second, the costs associated with accessing any given piece of online content. Because information is never free (even if it wants to be), the economics of information will always have, to greater or lesser extents, influence not only on our access to information, but also on the credibility of the information itself. This makes an understanding of how economics influences information an essential tool for anyone trying to evaluate the trustworthiness of information in the chaos of the post-truth culture.

The Economics of Access to Cyberspace

As discussed in chapter 3, what would become the internet started as a collection of taxpayer-funded research projects conducted by university-based scientists and engineers. As the experimental internet backbone began expanding during the mid-1980s, private internet service providers (ISPs) such as America Online, Prodigy, and CompuServe emerged to provide limited suites of internet services to their paid subscribers. With the flourishing of the world wide web in the mid-1990s, large telecom companies began to get into the ISP business, offering subscription-based access to the full breadth of internet services. In the twenty-first century, the extent to which internet infrastructure and access are provided by governments instead of, or in addition to, commercial and nonprofit entities vary among countries and, in some cases, within countries.

Internet infrastructure consists of all the parts and pieces required to move information around computer networks: communications satellites, fiberoptic cables, routers, microwave links, email servers, the domain name system, and so on. If you go online in the United States, the infrastructure may be commercially owned, community owned, or nonprofit owned. On the other hand, if you go online in China, it is likely the infrastructure will be provided by one of two government-owned companies: China Telcom or China Netcom. While the Chinese government is well known for tightly controlling what online content its citizens can access, such countries as Iran, North Korea, Myanmar, and Cuba have gone one step further by creating insulated national intranets that are entirely closed off to traffic from other countries. Quite obviously, governments that use their economic and political power to tightly control essential online infrastructure also have the power to severely limit their citizens' access to information.

Textbox 6.3
Big Brother and Tech Giants

One of the lead characters from the HBO dark-comedy series *Succession* is business executive Kendall Roy, the son of the founder of the Waystar Royco media empire (the in-universe stand-in for Fox News). In the second season episode "DC," Kendall Roy is called to testify before Congress where liberal U.S. Senator Gil Eavis (the in-universe stand-in for Senator Bernie Sanders) accuses Waystar Royco of "using news as your own personal ATM." Roy scores major debate points when he responds: "I think you might be under a misapprehension, Senator. In this country, all news, from the *Times* to the supermarket tabloid, is for profit, sir. We don't have a state media. As I'm sure you know, you'd have to go to China or Russia for that."[18]

Roy's response strikes at least two familiar chords. First, in the United States almost all media, whether news media or entertainment media, is created on a for-profit basis. Second, the mere suggestion of state-run media is anathema to most Americans, conjuring up Orwellian images of a tyrannical, antidemocratic government attempting to control independent thought and behavior through pervasive campaigns of lies and propaganda.

By emphasizing the private, for-profit nature of American media, Roy speaks to the notion that every media product—news program, television series, magazine article, theatrical film, song, and podcast—must compete against every other media product in what may be the most rough-and-tumble, purely capitalistic marketplace in the country, if not the world. Within such a ruthlessly competitive system, consumers vote with their dollars and with their attention (which has its own economic value) to decide which media products succeed and which do not. Ultimately, consumers have the power to exercise total control over for-profit media. In theory, consumers acting collectively could terminate any media phenomenon regardless of size—*The New York Times*, *Fox News*, *Dr. Who*, *Hamilton: An American Musical*, the entire Marvel Cinematic Universe, YouTube—simply by closing their wallets and turning their attention elsewhere.

What Kendal Roy's glib response fails to acknowledge, however, are the ways in which the economic model of for-profit media holds the potential to engender lies and propaganda equal to anything emanating from the party headquarters of a tyrannical government. When artists, journalists, cable news executives, and tech billionaires become entirely focused on chasing consumer attentions and dollars, inconveniences like facts, integrity, and the greater good can fall victim to the lure of fame and money.

- For much of the twentieth century, smoking was extremely popular and manufacturing cigarettes profitable. Did that justify Big Tobacco saturating every form of media with advertisements normalizing and encouraging cigarette smoking?
- Millions of people accept unfounded conspiracy theories as fact. Does that make it okay for a television network to profit from this phenomenon by airing pseudo-documentary programs that employ exaggerations and outright lies in ways that reinforce belief in unfounded conspiracies?
- There is a large online audience for videos depicting incredibly dangerous stunts. Is it therefore acceptable for a podcaster to encourage viewers to make and submit homemade videos of their own foolhardy stunts if doing so increases the number of followers and boosts advertising income?

The answer is that, ultimately, popularity and profit do not justify every result. There are limits, though not everyone agrees what those limits should be.

In addition to any detrimental effects the pursuit of profits may have on the integrity and credibility of media products, there is the irony of the economic competitions in the great free market of cyberspace having resulted in the winners of those competitions doing everything in their considerable power to make sure the competitive free market remains anything but competitive or free. Antitrust investigations launched in both the United States and Europe demonstrate the seriousness of the concern that a small number of tech giants—most notably Google, Amazon, Facebook, and Apple—have tilted the playing field of the online free market so entirely in their favor that emerging competitors are left with no chance of succeeding against the entrenched tech giants. Tech giants that likely would not have survived to grow so large and become so dominant if the playing field had been tilted against them when they were getting their starts.

The point here is not that, when it comes to media, the for-profit economic model is all bad. Nor is the point that rigid government control of media is ever good. Rather, the point is the importance of being as aware that, in combination, the dominant forces within a for-profit marketplace—personified as the Tech Giants—as well as the forces of government—personified as Big Brother—can and do impact the integrity and credibility of the information that passes through their distorting filters.

For average individual users in nontotalitarian countries, more important than who ultimately owns the online infrastructure is the matter getting online in the first place—the so-called last-mile problem. Employees and students are often provided with onsite network access by their workplace or school, though in return their activities on school or workplace networks may be restricted and/or monitored. Many customer service businesses (such as coffee shops and stores) and cultural institutions (such as museums and zoos) offer free Wi-Fi to their customers and visitors. Such far-flung cities as Geneva, Switzerland; Taipei, Taiwan; and Harrisburg, North Carolina are among the municipalities offering free internet access via city-wide Wi-Fi networks. Even more common are municipalities offering free Wi-Fi access to certain districts within their city boundaries, such as downtown corridors and popular tourist destinations like parks and historic districts. While free access is nice, the most common means of obtaining internet access is through payment to an ISP or cellular provider. Obtaining internet access in rural regions or within less-developed countries remains challenging. In such settings, satellite-based commercial ISPs, such as HughesNet, are an option for those who can afford the monthly fees, while grassroots wireless community networks can provide free or lower-cost options in areas that are too sparsely populated to be attractive to commercial providers. There are trade-offs with each model of infrastructure and access. Commercial models work well for those who can afford to pay, but they often prove to be prohibitively expensive for many, especially those living in the developing world. City, community, and nonprofit models are an option for those who cannot afford commercial services, but such models may not offer the fastest connections and keeping noncommercial services funded via taxes, grants, and donations is always a challenge. Government models can provide free or low-cost connectivity, but the trade-off may be various levels of government control over what information can or cannot be accessed. For billions of people around the world, economic factors play the role of the ultimate censor of online information: Cyberspace, with all its wealth of information, might as well not exist for those who cannot afford the entry fee of hardware, software, and network access.

The Economics of Content

As previously discussed, the only good that can be directly provided via digital technology is the intangible good of information, which in the online environment is often referred to as *content*. At the micro level, content can be thought of as text, images, sounds, and video. At a more macro level, content is the stuff that entices people to enter cyberspace in the first place: entertainment, news, educational materials, social media, shopping, and a host of online services. Regardless of the form it takes, for any content to exist there is a cost and so, one way or another, revenue must be generated to pay that cost. For nonprofits operating in cyberspace, the need is to generate sufficient revenue to cover the basic costs of their operations. For-profit entities must generate sufficient revenue to cover operating cost plus enough additional revenue to return a profit. While the fact that some individuals, businesses, or nonprofits generate revenue from online content does not invariably mean the content itself is tainted, it is crucial to recognize that money always holds the potential to influence the credibility of the information. The principal means for generating the revenue required to create content, keep it online, and (in some cases) turn a profit include:

- Retail sales
- Access fees
- Advertising
- Personal data
- Government funding
- Online services
- Online education
- Celebrity
- Fundraising
- Criminal activities

Retail Sales

Retail sales are, by far, the biggest business in cyberspace. In 2019, retail ecommerce spending amounted to $3.535 trillion, a sum that was over one thousand times greater than the amount spent on digital advertising in that same year.[19] Whether the online retailer is a born-online behemoth like Amazon, a long-established retailer like Macy's or Dillard's doing business in both the physical and online word, or a small operation offering its wares via a modest website, the content provided by online retailers consists mostly of information about the products they sell along with varying amounts of information regarding the retailer's reliability and sales policies. Online retailers often also provide customer reviews of their goods and services, though such reviews are not always objective or authentic. As is true of almost any sales situation, the potential for exaggeration, if not complete falsehoods, is always a possibility. The ancient adage "let the buyer beware" applies to any information provided to potential customers by anyone looking to make a sale or close a deal.

Access Fees

Access fees, which may take the form of one-time payments or ongoing subscriptions, are a very old model for funding the cost of (and generating profits from) content. For hundreds of years, anyone who wanted access to a printed book, newspaper, or magazine had little choice other than purchasing a copy or paying for a subscription. The only practical alternatives were either being given or borrowing a printed item previously purchased by someone else. In the online world, many analog-legacy entities such as newspapers, magazines, and scholarly journals have adopted business models based on charging traditional monthly or annual subscriptions for access to their content. If whisked into the twenty-first century from the year 1920, a time traveler might be confused by the sight of an online newspaper, but that traveler would understand the concept of paying a monthly subscription fee to read that newspaper. Subscription fees are also the model for acquiring internet access from an ISP as well as for engaging in such online activities as establishing a website via a hosting service or storing large amounts of data on cloud servers. Among many providers of online content, a common alternative to traditional subscriptions is to offer part of their content for free as a way of attracting visitors while requiring payment (subscription or one-time) for access to the provider's most desirable "premium" content. Similarly, many newspapers and magazines allow a visitor to access a fixed number of free articles every month before prompting the visitor to acquire a subscription in order to access additional content. Another variation on the subscription model are sites that provide all of their content—with advertisements—for free while offering advertisement-free access for anyone willing to pay for a subscription.

Looking back at the time before radio and television, access to most forms of entertainment historically required the purchase of an admission ticket to a theater, stadium, concert hall, cinema, or other venue. In the online world, audio and video recordings, theatrical films, webcasts of live performances, collections of images, and electronic books—all of which are analog-legacy forms of content—may require a one-time fee either for temporary access or permanent ownership, though content providers such as Netflix, Disney+, Getty Images, Apple Music, and others employ all-you-can-eat subscription models that allow subscribers to pick and choose from large collections of content for a flat fee that is usually charged on a monthly or yearly basis. Fan-supported sites like Patreon and OnlyFans require monthly or one-time fees to access content provided by creators who operate as independent contractors. While access fees are a time-proven method for funding content, convincing potential customers that even the most prized content is worth paying for is a challenge in an online world so filled with free content that paying for access has become a foreign concept to many consumers. The challenge of getting potential customers to pay for online content is further complicated by the availability of illegally hosted content accessible to anyone who is willing to seek it out and is undeterred by the ethical issues or potential penalties associated with copyright infringement. Somewhat relatedly, consumers may balk at paying for content that they see as being grossly overpriced by copyright holders taking unfair advantage of their monopoly status—a common and long-standing complaint in the world of scholarly information.

One type of online content that, in most cases, does not require an access fee is content that has entered the public domain. Thousands of libraries, museums, and other cultural institutions have digitized large amounts public domain content—including, books, periodicals, manuscripts, government documents, photographs, maps, artwork, and videos—and made it freely available via the internet. Initiatives such as Google Books, HathiTrust, and Internet Archive offer millions of public domain books and other content at no cost to users.

Advertising

> United States Senator Orrin Hatch: "So, how do you sustain a business model in which users don't pay for your services?"
> Facebook Chief Executive Officer Mark Zuckerberg: "Senator, we run ads."[20]

Advertising has been partially underwriting the cost of content for hundreds of years, though it was not until the early nineteenth century that it became a major factor in the economics of information, a status advertising achieved by simultaneously lowering the cost of print newspapers and magazines to consumers while increasing the profits of publishers. With the advent of broadcast radio and, later, television, advertising by itself proved so profitable as to make content entirely free to listeners and viewers—an arrangement made possible because broadcast radio and television are, unlike printed matter, nonconsumptive goods with zero marginal costs. (The cost of broadcasting a radio or television program if one person tunes in is equal to the cost of broadcasting that same program if forty million people tune in.) The practice of using advertising to underwrite the cost of free online content closely follows the free-content-with-advertisements model pioneered by radio and television. Whether advertising is used to underwrite free online content or free broadcast media, the adjective *free* is somewhat deceptive in that, while no money changes hands between content consumers and content providers, consumers pay for their ostensibly free content through exposure to advertisements. Consumers may consider the advertisements to which they are exposed a waste of time, propaganda, a form of entertainment (as with many Super Bowl advertisements), or useful sources information for making decisions about everything from pet food to health care to political candidates.

When an advertiser pays to place an advertisement in a media outlet—whether it is a newspaper, magazine, television channel, radio station, social media platform, website, or roadside billboard—the advertiser judges the success of the advertisement on the response it generates in terms of sales or engagement. Media outlets base their *ad rates*, the amount they charge to place an advertisement, on the amount of exposure the advertisement will receive. In general, the more people exposed to an advertisement on any given media outlet, the higher the ad rate (though such factors as the age, sex, and incomes of those exposed may also influence ad rates to varying degrees). In the online environment, the number of people who visit any given destination is known as *traffic*. Successful online destinations like Google and Facebook are highly profitable because the heavy traffic they receive positions them to charge a premium for the advertisements run on their sites. In 2020, Google earned $181.69 billion in advertising revenues, whereas Facebook earned eighty-six billion dollars.[21] Less popular online destinations charge proportionally less to run advertisements and do not pull in advertising revenues anywhere near those of the tech giants. Lightly trafficked sites that earn revenue from advertisers are typically paid very small amounts, perhaps only a fraction of a cent, every time a visitor clicks a link on a page displaying an advertisement. This model of generating advertising revenue is responsible for the existence of click-bait sites that first attract visitors with alluring photos and teaser headlines and then require visitors to click link after link to read a single article or view a series of images.

Since long before the Digital Age advertising-funded media outlets have had to negotiate the tension between the need to earn money from advertising and the desire of advertisers to influence content. If, for example, a magazine that reaps significant revenues from advertisements placed by a major oil company publishes an article accusing executives of that company of lying about the environmental impacts of fracking, the magazine runs the risk of lost revenues if the oil company pulls its advertisements. Conversely, a magazine might intentionally court oil company advertising dollars by running an article disputing the environmental impacts of fracking.

Besides the danger of content that dives away advertisers, advertising-funded media outlets also run the risk of lost revenue if they drive away traffic. That same magazine article that criticizes fracking might drive away readers (traffic) who believe that any environmental problems caused by fracking are overstated and a small price to pay for increasing the domestic oil supply. Similarly, if a social media site bans a controversial-but-popular

figure for violating its terms of use, any boycotting of the site by that figure's loyal followers equals less traffic, which in turn equals lower ad rates.
Illustrations of the tension between profits and the limits of free expression
are seen in social media sites that allow users to post hateful messages,
repeat unfounded conspiracy theories, and spread blatantly false information because banning those posters—especially those with large followings—would lower advertising revenues. While there is truth in the claims
that banning users stifles free expression, the fact remains that advertising
revenue influences decisions about who is, or is not, allowed a voice in much
the same way that advertising revenue influences what content gets published
and what does not. The most notable example of the last few years is the
case former U.S. President Donald Trump, whose trademark Twitter posts
were often called out as both inflammatory and filled with untrue statements.
Twitter persisted in allowing Trump to post on the grounds that Trump had
a right to speak his mind and his millions of avid followers had the right to
hear what the president of the United States had to say. Principled defense
of free expression aside, the corporate leadership of Twitter also knew very
well that banning Trump would cost their company millions in lost advertising revenue. For anyone, justifying an action (or a nonaction) as the right
thing to do becomes much easier when doing the right thing increases your
wealth rather than reduces it. In the end, it was only the violent January 6,
2021 takeover of the U.S. Capitol Building by several hundred angry Trump
supporters that finally caused Twitter, as well as other social media platforms,
to ban Trump along with other, less-prominent users with histories of promoting hatred, unfounded conspiracy theories, and violence. In the immediate
aftermath of the banning of Trump, Twitter's stock dropped 6.4 percent while
Facebook, which imposed an indefinite ban on Trump around the same time,
saw its stock drop by 4 percent.[22] However, on June 7, 2021, six months after
the takeover and following Facebook's extension of its ban on Trump to full
two years, Facebook's opening stock price was $331.26, an increase of 24.58
percent over its opening price ($265.90) on January 7, 2021.[23]

Yet another example of the influence of advertising dollars on content is
seen in product placement, a form of stealth advertising. In a theatrical film,
the fact that the camera lingers on a brand name can of soda or the logo of a
flashy sports car may be the result of the director's artistic vision; on the other
hand, those goods may appear on screen only because manufacturers have
paid considerable sums to have their products exposed to filmgoers. Because
filmmakers are human, it becomes much easier to rationalize the inclusion
of a closeup on a branded smartphone in the hand of the film's attractive
star when that small sacrifice of artistic integrity is rewarded by a hefty payment from the makers of the smartphone. While product placement is most

commonly associated with theatrical films and television programs, examples of product placement in the online world include:

- Influencers giving positive reviews of products or using products in front of the camera without disclosing that they are being compensated to do so.
- Creators of online content inserting references to products into articles, photos, and videos in ways that seem organic when, in fact, the creators have accepted payment to reference those products.
- Search engine algorithms prioritizing results in ways that favor the interests of advertisers.

For media outlets that, first, wish to operate as independent sources of credible information and/or uphold high standards of artistic integrity (not all outlets do) and, second, depend on advertising for revenue, the battle between the content side of the house, whose mission is to provide authentic content that is as free as possible from the influence of money, and the business side of the house, whose mission is to generate as much advertising revenue as possible, is an old and ongoing conflict. For consumers of content, the questions they must always ask when content and advertising appear side-by-side, are:

- Has advertising revenue influenced this content?
- If so, how, and to what extent, has advertising revenue influenced this content?

Such questions are not always easy to answer. Suppose an article posted on an alternative-health website extolls the benefits of elderberry extract while, at the same time, a banner across the top of the screen advertises River/Valley Farms Elderberry Extract. Was the synchronicity between content and advertisement the result of a blatant money-making collusion between the owners of the website and River/Valley Farms? Or was the article written without any outside influence and, by lucky coincidence, its contents happened to appeal to the advertiser? Or was the truth somewhere in between? *"A freelancer is pitching an article on the benefits of elderberry extract. If we run it, we can sell an ad to River Valley Farms in a heartbeat."* While it is always good to be alert to possible advertiser influence on content, in the end the focus should be on establishing the essential credibility of the content itself. Advertising revenue may (and often enough does) influence content, but advertising does not invariably corrupt content.

In addition to commercial advertising that is intended to sell products and services, there is the related phenomenon of public relations. Public relations, which involves creating and distributing messages that shape public opinion about nonprofits, governments, businesses, or individuals may at times employ the same focused, hard-sell techniques as commercial advertising, though practitioners of public relations tend to employ softer approaches than their commercial advertising counterparts. The website of almost any university will provide a good example of public relations at work. University websites typically use combinations of upbeat stories, photos of smiling students and faculty, and attractive images of campus grounds, buildings, and activities for the purpose of making students, parents, alumni, and prospective donors want to be part of the institution. Political advertising can also edge over into the realm of public relations. The highly successful political advertising campaign popularly known as "Morning in America" (though officially titled "Prouder, Stronger, Better") supported the reelection of sitting President Ronald Reagan (1911–2004) by taking the public-relations-based approach of invoking good feelings about life in America. Aired during the runup to the 1984 U.S. presidential election, "Morning in America" mostly steered clear of deeply contentious political issues, instead featuring cinematic-quality scenes of average-looking people happily heading off to work. The intention was not to make anyone think critically about Reagan's actual accomplishments or failures during his first four years in office, but to instead make people feel good about the country and themselves and to associate those feelings with Regan. Whether you consider "Morning in America" to be a brilliant piece of public relations or sentimentalist propaganda, the fact remains that the campaign contributed to Reagan winning reelection in a historic landslide.

While not every advertisement (or public relations campaign) is a hit, as a whole advertising is successful at influencing human behavior; after all, if advertising did not work, businesses, politicians, and nonprofits would not spend billions of dollars on it, year in and year out. In 2019, worldwide spending on digital advertising amounted to $325.02 billion and is estimated to rise to $526.17 billion by 2024.[24] As pointed out in chapter 5, because advertising and public relations present persuasive messages, they have elements of propaganda to them and need to be evaluated with appropriate levels of skepticism. Advertising and public relations both have the goal of influencing the way you think, though not always in ways that are in your best interest.

Personal Data

In the field of advertising, the biggest difference between the analog and online worlds is the ability of online advertisers to collect and analyze massive amounts of personal data in order to persuasively target individuals in ways that are simply not possible using traditional advertising techniques. One example of targeted online advertising is *contextual advertising*, which takes the form of advertisements that directly relate to the topic of the page on which they appear. If you are reading an online article defending the right to bear arms, you may well see contextual advertisements for firearms and ammunition sales or for politicians who strongly support Second Amendment rights. Similarly, if you are reading an article about ice hockey, you might see a contextual advertisement for tickets to an upcoming NHL game in your area. (Your technology reveals your location to online marketers unless you take steps to ensure it does not.) Another example of targeted online advertising is *remarketing advertising*, which are advertisements based on visitors' previous online behavior. Remarketing is the reason you will continue to see advertisements for automobile tires for several days following a visit to a website of a tire store or be bombarded with advertisements for flowers for several days after doing an online search for "one dozen red roses."

According to Asunción Esteve, a professor of law at the University of Barcelona, "Contextual and remarketing advertising are Google and Facebook's core business. Both companies constantly track certain information about their individual users in order to tailor advertisements."[25] The tracking, storing, and reselling of individual users' personal data by technology-sector companies, including large and well-known companies like Google and Facebook as well as thousands of smaller and lesser-known companies, has become a key business model (and source of contention) in the online world. Companies like Google and Facebook justify their collection of personal data on the grounds that they use the data to improve the quality of their services (as well as to earn advertising revenue). We, as inhabitants of cyberspace, are complicit in that we enjoy fast, efficient, and entertaining online services that we can use at no cost (at least at no upfront monetary costs). As consumers, one way in which we pay for free services is by voluntarily entering our names, email addresses, genders, ages, and other personal data when signing up for online services such as social media accounts or retail rewards programs. We get to use the services, but at the same time we are building huge databases of personal information that businesses can exploit for profit. While individuals have the option of not volunteering personal data, the cost for opting out is exclusion from full participation in the social, business, and other opportunities available in cyberspace. *"Look, I value my privacy, but free shipping is free shipping." "I don't really want to be on Facebook, but it's the best way to stay in touch with my grandparents."*

A second, and more controversial, way in which tech companies collect personal data is by tracking users' online behavior, including what we post online, our online purchases, the sites we visit, the searches we conduct, the online petitions we sign, what we like and dislike, the things we retweet, the online groups we join, the individuals and groups with whom we communicate, and even the silly little quizzes we take: *"What flavor of ice cream are you? Take this fun quiz to find out!"* Essentially everything an individual does online has the potential to generate personal data that can be captured, stored, and analyzed by a business of one sort or another. Consumer protections against appropriation and misuse of personal data vary from country to country. As mentioned in chapter 4, the European Union's groundbreaking General Data Protection Regulation (GDPR) controls how the personal data of residents of the European Union may be processed and transferred.[26] As of 2021, the United States has no national legislative equivalent to the GDPR, though a few states have enacted online privacy laws. For example, on January 1, 2020, the California Consumer Privacy Act went into effect with the goal of providing stronger online privacy rights and consumer protections for state residents.

Whether personal data is voluntarily surrendered or is surreptitiously gathered without users' direct knowledge, businesses combine and analyze personal data to create detailed (some would say intrusive) profiles of billions of individual users; profiles that, in turn, make possible the highly profitable sale of contextual, remarketing, and other targeted advertisements. In addition, it is possible for businesses to earn revenue by selling the personal data they collect to third parties, opening up the possibility that data will be used in ways to which the individuals from whom it was collected did not consent. The annual economic value of personal data is not easy to quantify, though it certainly runs into the billions of dollars. The data-broker industry, which consists of "firms that specialize in gathering people's personal information from public and private sources, and making it available to other companies for marketing, employment, financial and other purposes" is estimated to be worth two hundred billion dollars.[27] The results of a study published in *The Washington Monthly* in the summer of 2019 estimate that the value of Americans' personal data will hit $127.9 billion by 2022, which works out to an average $434 per American expected to be online by that date.[28] More conservatively, an earlier (2013) analysis of online users in Spain estimated "our personal data has the value of a Big Mac."[29] While a Big Mac costs nowhere near $434, when you multiply the value of a Big Mac times the number of people in cyberspace, the total value of that data becomes enormous.

Economic value and privacy issues aside, what may be most troubling about the amassing of vast amounts of personal data is that the algorithms for mining that data, along with the techniques for exploiting it, are still in their infancy. In a worst-case scenario, the world could see data-driven advertising and/or propaganda become increasingly adept at shaping the thinking of those exposed to it. If that were to happen, the great irony would be that our very own, quite valuable personal data would end up funding our downfall. In the words of Anahiby Anyel Becerril of Mexico's Centro de Investigación e Innovación en Tecnologías de la Información y Comunicación: "As users of Facebook, Twitter, Instagram, Pinterest and other types of content online, we not only consume this 'free' content, but we have become the intangible asset of companies. . . . Facebook and Google, do not sell anything to Internet users, instead they sell billions of users to advertisers."[30]

Government Funding

As previously mentioned, government funding supported the initial creation of what would become the internet and continues to support the infrastructure of cyberspace to varying extents. Government funding of content, on the other hand, is more problematic than is government funding of infrastructure. In totalitarian countries, government-funded content deserves the highest level of skepticism. When it comes to the official government content produced by totalitarian regimes like North Korea or corrupt oligarchies like Russia, the naïveté of anyone who fully trusts such information is too great to measure with conventional instruments. But even in democratic countries, government funding can influence information in a number of ways.

Most obviously, there is the information that appears on the official, government-funded websites of elected officials. While any information found on the official website of any elected national, state, or local official may vary between the extremes of the credibility scale, such information is invariably influenced by politics and is always designed to serve the public relations goal of enhancing the voting public's opinion the elected official whose name appears on the website.

The information provided by agencies that fall under the administrations of high-level leaders—prime ministers, presidents, governors—can be a mixed bag. Statistical, scientific, technological, economic, and other essential decision-making information on such sites would not, in a perfect world, be tainted by politics. In the imperfect world in which we live, however, it is easy to find examples of politicians exerting their influence to compel state or federal agencies to present information in a way that furthers partisan political agendas. For one notable example, when Florida Governor Rick Scott was elected in 2011, employees of the Florida Department of Environmental Protection were forbidden from using the phrases "climate change" or "global warming" in any official documents.[31] Besides simply silencing any mention of an issue, another way in which politics influence official government information sources occurs when elected official forbid agencies from conducting research on controversial topics. Without research, there can be no (sometimes discomforting) scientific information to report in the first place. For example, out of political concern that government research into firearms violence could be used to support more stringent gun control legislation, the Dickey Amendment effectively prevented the Centers for Disease Control and Prevention (CDC) from funding any research on firearms violence from the amendment's passage in 1996 until 2018, when Congress allowed CDC to conduct research on firearms violence as part of the CDC's broader charge to conduct research into the prevention of violence and injury.[32]

Rather than being blindly accepted or cynically dismissed, the credibility of government-supported information must be evaluated on its own merits. While partisan politics can adversely influence the credibility of government information in a democracy, even the most controlling, propaganda-prone governments in the world may be capable of, at least once in a while, providing information that turns out to be credible.

Online Services

Just as online sales have disrupted retail businesses, online services have disrupted the service industry. In the business world, the growth of online services has allowed businesses to outsource such functions as customer service, payroll and accounting, and information technology. For the average person, online services may take the form of coaching and mentoring services in such areas as fitness, life coaching, and personal finance. In some ways, the biggest generator of online revenue, retail sales, can be thought of as an online shopping service that connects consumers with goods. Other major online services include online dating platforms, which generate millions of dollars in annual revenue, and online gambling services, which reliably generate billions of dollars in revenue year after year. The last decade has also seen growth in telemedicine services that allow individuals to connect with physicians and other health care providers, including nurses and mental health counselors. Online services, such as telemedicine, in which confidentiality is a consideration, often operate on a one-to-one basis. Other services may operate on a one-to-many basis, as when a single fitness coach is connected in real time to multiple users of the service. Online services may also follow a self-service model, as is the case with dating services in which users of the service fill out a questionnaire, are connected to likely matches, and are then left to their own devices to make contact and possibly initiate an in-person meeting.

Money can impact the integrity of online services when providers entice customers by overstating the effectiveness and potential benefits of the services provided. Are you really as likely to meet your soulmate as the providers of an online dating service claim? Are the hot tips provided by a sports-betting advisor really going to put you in the money every time? Is that online financial advisor (who also happens to sell gold coins) being entirely truthful about the wisdom of investing in precious metals?

Online Education

Because the internet was, to a large extent, the creation of university academics, it should be no surprise that the users of the internet have long explored and leveraged its potential as an educational tool or that, as soon as people began using the internet as a way to earn money, education was near the front of the pack. Online education takes many forms. It may be synchronous or asynchronous; led by an instructor who appears live (synchronous) or on video (asynchronous); presented via such digital learning object as videos, tutorials, simulations, quizzes, and exams; or involve combinations of all of these. While many online educational institutions and initiatives are nonprofit, for-profit education also has a strong presence in cyberspace. While online education has been gaining momentum for decades, the COVID-19 pandemic strikingly demonstrated to millions who had never before experienced online education both its value as well as the challenges that can hinder its effectiveness.

The leading ways in which education is used to generate revenue online include:

- Instruction leading to traditional certifications, diplomas, and degrees of the sort typically offered by public and private educational institutions at all levels—schools, colleges, and universities.
- Born-digital educational endeavors. A few leading examples include Wikipedia, Kahn Academy, and Coursera.
- Professional certification and continuing education courses covering a wide variety of fields, including engineering, computer science, teaching, medicine, etc.
- How-to articles and videos on topics ranging from hobbies to arts and crafts to the repair and maintenance of everything from computers to automobiles to homes and buildings.

The many forms of online education are funded in a variety of ways, with any one form of online education likely to be funded in multiple ways. Examples include taxpayer funding (as with public education), student tuition or fees, advertising revenue, donations of money, and volunteer efforts. The quality and legitimacy of education (online or in person) can be strongly impacted by the ways in which it is funded. In both the online and physical worlds, public schools may find themselves making educational compromises in order to appease local taxpayers just as colleges and universities may make compromises in order to prevent angry legislators from enacting funding cuts. Any educational endeavor that is supported by advertising may face conflicts between educational integrity and keeping advertisers happy. Volunteer efforts can create amazing learning opportunities—as exemplified by thousands of helpful how-to videos created by enthusiasts and the millions of Wikipedia articles created by volunteer writers and editors—but there is always the concern that volunteers may not really know as much as they think they do, are not good at teaching what they do know, or are unrestrainedly pushing agendas that have little to do with actual learning.

Celebrity

In cyberspace, celebrity has become a valuable commodity capable of generating large amounts of revenue. Some cybercelebrities are crossovers from such traditional generators of fame as film, television, and music, while others are digital natives who earned their celebrity via the likes of YouTube, Instagram, podcasts, TikTok, and Twitch. Successful cybercelebrities typically earn income from various combinations of advertising, endorsements, sales of branded goods, and direct contributions from fans. Regardless of the source of income, the formula for financial success adds up to more followers equaling more money. And the money that comes with large online followings can be significant. A *Forbes* article published in August 2020 lists twelve young TikTok stars who had each earned at least one million dollars in the previous twelve months.[33] As with any endeavor based on appealing to a mass audience, the temptation to pander to audience tastes in pursuit of wealth is always there. While the artistic integrity of a professional gamer who streams his Minecraft skills on Twitch or a teenager who dances on TikTok is, in the grand scheme of things, a matter of small concern, the circumstances become quite different when, say, political podcasters with large followings find that their followings and incomes both grow when they manufacture urgency and conflict through such techniques as repeating unfounded conspiracy theories, passing along fake news, exaggerating wrongs suffered by and/or threats to their followers, and, most dangerously, urging followers to commit acts of violence.

Fundraising

Independent creators of online content range from the likes of Kate Wagner, whose Patreon-based *McMansion Hell* educates readers on what makes good architecture good and bad architecture bad; to Rex Parker, who maintains a daily blog focused on the *New York Times* crossword puzzle; to an entire galaxy of online sex workers. What these varied content creators have in common is that they routinely ask fans to support their work through voluntary monetary contributions. On a much larger scale, major nonprofit information providers, such as Wikipedia, rely on tax-exempt foundations and sophisticated fundraising campaigns to support their efforts. Crowdfunding platforms like GoFundMe facilitate the funding of everything from new inventions to theatrical films to life-saving surgeries. What all forms of fundraising have in common, whether online or not, is that fundraising involves telling compelling stories (a form of information) that inspire people to donate to a cause. When presented with a compelling fundraising story, it is always wise to ask just how truthful that story is, as fundraisers always face the temptation to stretch the truth, if not actually lie, in order to keep the good cause for which they work alive and flourishing.

Criminal Activities

The use of digital technologies to commit criminal acts is well documented and pervasive. Content created to abet online crimes includes such ploys as the scam emails of Nigerian princes and their like, the false romantic promises of online gold diggers, virtual snares laid by human traffickers, and the mansion-and-automobile bedecked websites of self-proclaimed financial geniuses whose actual genius does not extend beyond running Ponzi schemes. To state the obvious, any information provided by someone who would commit a cybercrime is not to be trusted.

MONEY CHANGES EVERYTHING

Money changes everything it touches, and it touches almost everything, including online information that we are tempted to think of as free. As consumers of information, it is always appropriate for us to ask the following questions:

- "Who *really* paid for the creation and distribution of this information?"
- "Who benefits (*cui bono*) from the creation and distribution of this information?"
- "To what extent, if any, has the funding source impacted the credibility of this information?"

More broadly, we can also consider the questions, *"What information is unavailable to me because economic factors have put the information behind a paywall that I cannot afford to breach?"* as well as *"What economic factors have precluded the creation of information that would be of use to me?"* The latter question is, of course, so speculative that it can ultimately lead to conspiracy-minded thinking along the lines of, *"Yes, but what are they not telling us?"* And while there is nothing wrong with asking that question—it may very likely be the case that there are things *they* are not telling us—the question turns into a mental ant trap when the askers of that question start supplying answers based on a large portion of paranoia and zero actual evidence. This very circumstance will be considered in depth in the next chapter.

NOTES

1. Stewart Brand, *The Media Lab: Inventing the Future at MIT* (New York, NY: Viking, 1987), 202.

2. Kevin Barefoot et al., "Measuring the Digital Economy, Survey of Current Business, May 2019," Government, *Survey of Current Business: The Journal of the U.S. Bureau of Economic Analysis*, May 2019, https://apps.bea.gov/scb/2019/05-may/0519-digital-economy.htm.

3. William Xu and Adrian Cooper, "Digital Spillover: Measuring the True Impact of the Digital Economy," Huawei and Oxford Economics, 2017, https://www.huawei.com/minisite/gci/en/digital-spillover/files/gci_digital_spillover.pdf, 6.

4. Albert Einstein, "Zur Elektrodynamik Bewegter Körper," *Annalen Der Physik* 322, no. 10 (1905): 891–921.

5. "17 U.S. Code § 506–Criminal Offenses," 17 § 506 U.S. Code §, accessed January 27, 2021, https://www.law.cornell.edu/uscode/text/17/506.

6. Stanford University Libraries, "Copyright & Fair Use," *Stanford Copyright and Fair Use Center*, April 2, 2013, https://fairuse.stanford.edu/.

7. Kit Walsh, "Copyright Isn't a Tool for Removing Negative Reviews," *Electronic Frontier Foundation*, October 12, 2017, https://www.eff.org/deeplinks/2017/10/copyright-isnt-tool-removing-negative-reviews-1.

8. Wired Staff, "Scientology: The Web's First Copyright-Wielding Nemesis," *Wired*, September 21, 2009, https://www.wired.com/2009/09/mf-chanology-sidebar/.

9. Elizabeth Kolbert, "Who Owns the Internet: What Big Tech's Monopoly Powers Mean for Our Culture," *The New Yorker*, August 28, 2017, https://www.newyorker.com/magazine/2017/08/28/who-owns-the-internet.

10. Margaret Stieg Dalton, "The Publishing Experiences of Historians," *Journal of Scholarly Publishing* 39, no. 3 (April 2008): 211.

11. Karen Heller, "Meet the Writers Who still Sell Millions of Books. Actually, Hundreds of Millions," *Washington Post*, December 20, 2016, https://www.washingtonpost.com/lifestyle/style/meet-the-elite-group-of-authors-who-sell-100-million

-books-or-350-million/2016/12/20/db3c6a66-bb0f-11e6-94ac-3d324840106c_story
.html.

12. International Association of Scientific, Technical and Medical Publishers
(STM), "About the Industry," *STM*, accessed December 23, 2020, https://www.stm
-assoc.org/about-stm/about-the-industry/.

13. Relex, "Results for the Year to 31 December 2018," February 21, 2019, https://
www.relx.com/~/media/Files/R/RELX-Group/documents/press-releases/2019/relx
-results-2018-pressrelease.pdf.

14. Mike Tigas, Sisi Wei, Ken Schwencke, Brandon Roberts, and Alec Glassford,
"American Chemical Society, Full Filing–Nonprofit Explorer," *ProPublica*, accessed
December 31, 2020, https://projects.propublica.org/nonprofits/organizations/530196
572/201843129349300709/full, 10.

15. Stevan Harnad, "Subversive Proposal," June 28, 2004, https://groups.google
.com/g/bit.listserv.vpiej-l/c/BoKENhK0_00.

16. "Elsevier Expands Open Access Options for Cell Press Journals from January 2021," Elsevier, December 18, 2020, https://www.elsevier.com/about/press
-releases/corporate/elsevier-expands-open-access-options-for-cell-press-journals
-from-january-2021.

17. Lindsay McKenzie, "A Big Open-Access Deal for Germany," *Inside
Higher Ed*, accessed December 31, 2020, https://www.insidehighered.com/quick
takes/2020/01/10/big-open-access-deal-germany.

18. Mark Mylod, "DC," *Succession* (HBO, October 6, 2019), https://transcripts
.thedealr.net/script.php/succession-2018-W8w6/s2/e9.

19. Tugba Sabanoglu, "Global Retail E-Commerce Market Size 2014-2023,"
Statista, November 30, 2020, https://www.statista.com/statistics/379046/worldwide
-retail-e-commerce-sales/.

20. Facebook, Social Media Privacy, and the Use and Abuse of Data, § Senate Hearing 115-683, Committee on Commerce, Science, and Transportation
United States Senate and the Committee on the Judiciary United States Senate
(2018), 21, https://www.govinfo.gov/content/pkg/CHRG-115shrg37801/html/CHRG
-115shrg37801.htm.

21. Keach Hagey, "Facebook, Google and Publishers Are Fighting Over News.
What You Need to Know. Australia Showdown Is Seen as Test Case for Rest of
World," *Wall Street Journal (Online)*, February 24, 2021, https://search.proquest
.com/wallstreetjournal/docview/2492456377/citation/9F080F51C13343A8PQ/3.

22. Telford Taylor, "Wall Street Retreats from Record Highs amid Virus, Political
Uncertainty," *The Washington Post (Online)*, January 11, 2021, https://search.proquest
.com/washingtonpost/docview/2476743139/citation/24F1A18B89934A1EPQ/4.

23. "Facebook, Inc. (FB) Stock Historical Prices & Data," *Yahoo Finance*,
accessed June 13, 2021, https://finance.yahoo.com/quote/FB/history/.

24. A. Guttman, "Global Digital Advertising Market 2023," *Statista*, November 17, 2020, https://www.statista.com/statistics/237974/online-advertising-spending
-worldwide/.

25. Asunción Esteve, "The Business of Personal Data: Google, Facebook, and Privacy Issues in the EU and the USA," *International Data Privacy Law* 7, no. 1 (February 2017): 40.

26. "Fundamental Texts on European Private Law," Regulation (EU) 2016/679 of the European Parliament and of The Council, Official Journal of the European Union § (2016).

27. David Lazarus, "Shadowy Data Brokers Make the Most of Their Invisibility Cloak," *Los Angeles Times*, November 5, 2019, https://www.latimes.com/business/story/2019-11-05/column-data-brokers.

28. Eric Cortellessa and Robert J. Shapiro, "What Your Data Is Really Worth to Facebook: And Why You Deserve a Cut," *Washington Monthly*, July 13, 2019, https://washingtonmonthly.com/magazine/july-august-2019/what-your-data-is-really-worth-to-facebook/.

29. Anahiby Anyel Becerril, "The Value of Our Personal Data in the Big Data and the Internet of All Things Era," *ADCAIJ: Advances in Distributed Computing and Artificial Intelligence Journal* 7, no. 2 (June 30, 2018): 71.

30. Becerril, 72.

31. Tristam Korten, "In Florida, Officials Ban Term 'Climate Change,'" *Miami Herald*, March 8, 2015, https://www.miamiherald.com/news/state/florida/article12983720.html.

32. "An Act Making Omnibus Consolidated Appropriations for the Fiscal Year Ending September 30, 1997, and for Other Purposes," Public Law 208, *U.S. Statutes at Large* 104 (1996).

33. Abram Brown, "TikTok's 7 Highest-Earning Stars: New Forbes List Led by Teen Queens Addison Rae And Charli D'Amelio," *Forbes*, accessed January 29, 2021, https://www.forbes.com/sites/abrambrown/2020/08/06/tiktoks-highest-earning-stars-teen-queens-addison-rae-and-charli-damelio-rule/.

BIBLIOGRAPHY

17 U.S. Code § 506–Criminal offenses, 17 § 506 U.S. Code §. Accessed January 27, 2021, https://www.law.cornell.edu/uscode/text/17/506.

"An Act Making Omnibus Consolidated Appropriations for the Fiscal Year Ending September 30, 1997, and for Other Purposes." Public Law 208, *U.S. Statutes at Large* 104 (1996).

Barefoot, Kevin, Dave Curtis, William A. Jolliff, Jessica R. Nicholson, and Robert Omohundro. "Measuring the Digital Economy, Survey of Current Business, May 2019." *Survey of Current Business: The Journal of the U.S. Bureau of Economic Analysis*, May 2019. https://apps.bea.gov/scb/2019/05-may/0519-digital-economy.htm.

Becerril, Anahiby Anyel. "The Value of Our Personal Data in the Big Data and the Internet of All Things Era." *ADCAIJ: Advances in Distributed Computing and Artificial Intelligence Journal* 7, no. 2 (June 30, 2018): 71.

Brand, Stewart. *The Media Lab: Inventing the Future at MIT.* New York, NY: Viking, 1987.

Brown, Abram. "TikTok's 7 Highest-Earning Stars: New Forbes List Led by Teen Queens Addison Rae and Charli D'Amelio." *Forbes.* Accessed January 29, 2021, https://www.forbes.com/sites/abrambrown/2020/08/06/tiktoks-highest-earning-stars-teen-queens-addison-rae-and-charli-damelio-rule/.

Cortellessa, Eric, and Robert J. Shapiro. "What Your Data Is Really Worth to Face-book: And Why You Deserve a Cut." *Washington Monthly,* July 13, 2019. https://washingtonmonthly.com/magazine/july-august-2019/what-your-data-is-really-worth-to-facebook/.

Dalton, Margaret Stieg. "The Publishing Experiences of Historians." *Journal of Scholarly Publishing* 39, no. 3 (April 2008): 197–240.

Einstein, Albert. "Zur Elektrodynamik Bewegter Körper." *Annalen Der Physik* 322, no. 10 (1905): 891–921.

"Elsevier Expands Open Access Options for Cell Press Journals from January 2021," Elsevier, December 18, 2020. https://www.elsevier.com/about/press-releases/corporate/elsevier-expands-open-access-options-for-cell-press-journals-from-january-2021.

Esteve, Asunción. "The Business of Personal Data: Google, Facebook, and Privacy Issues in the EU and the USA." *International Data Privacy Law* 7, no. 1 (February 2017): 36–47.

Facebook, Social Media Privacy, and the Use and Abuse of Data, § Senate Hearing 115-683, Committee on Commerce, Science, and Transportation United States Senate and the Committee on the Judiciary United States Senate (2018). https://www.govinfo.gov/content/pkg/CHRG-115shrg37801/html/CHRG-115shrg37801.htm.

"Facebook, Inc. (FB) Stock Historical Prices & Data." *Yahoo Finance.* Accessed June 13, 2021, https://finance.yahoo.com/quote/FB/history/.

"Fundamental Texts on European Private Law," Regulation (EU) 2016/679 of the European Parliament and of The Council, Official Journal of the European Union § (2016).

Guttman, A. "Global Digital Advertising Market 2023." *Statista,* November 17, 2020. https://www.statista.com/statistics/237974/online-advertising-spending-worldwide/.

Hagey, Keach. "Facebook, Google and Publishers Are Fighting Over News. What You Need to Know. Australia Showdown Is Seen as Test Case for Rest of World." *Wall Street Journal (Online),* February 24, 2021. https://search.proquest.com/wallstreetjournal/docview/2492456377/citation/9F080F51C13343A8PQ/3.

Heller, Karen. "Meet the Writers Who still Sell Millions of Books. Actually, Hundreds of Millions." *Washington Post,* December 20, 2016. https://www.washingtonpost.com/lifestyle/style/meet-the-elite-group-of-authors-who-sell-100-million-books-or-350-million/2016/12/20/db3c6a66-bb0f-11e6-94ac-3d324840106c_story.html.

Harnad, Stevan. "Subversive Proposal." June 28, 2004. https://groups.google.com/g/bit.listserv.vpiej-l/c/BoKENhK0_00.

International Association of Scientific, Technical and Medical Publishers (STM). "About the Industry." *STM*. Accessed December 23, 2020, https://www.stm-assoc .org/about-stm/about-the-industry/.

Kolbert, Elizabeth. "Who Owns the Internet: What Big Tech's Monopoly Powers Mean for Our Culture." *The New Yorker*, August 28, 2017. https://www.newyorker .com/magazine/2017/08/28/who-owns-the-internet.

Korten, Tristam. "In Florida, Officials Ban Term 'Climate Change.'" *Miami Herald*, March 8, 2015. https://www.miamiherald.com/news/state/florida/article12983720. html.

Lazarus, David. "Shadowy Data Brokers Make the Most of Their Invisibility Cloak." *Los Angeles Times*, November 5, 2019. https://www.latimes.com/business/ story/2019-11-05/column-data-brokers.

McKenzie, Lindsay. "A Big Open-Access Deal for Germany." *Inside Higher Ed*. Accessed December 31, 2020, https://www.insidehighered.com/quick-takes/2020/01/10/big-open-access-deal-germany.

Mylod, Mark. "DC." *Succession*. HBO, October 6, 2019. https://transcripts.thedealr .net/script.php/succession-2018-W8w6/s2/e9.

Relex. "Results for the Year to 31 December 2018." February 21, 2019. https:// www.relx.com/~/media/Files/R/RELX-Group/documents/press-releases/2019/relx -results-2018-pressrelease.pdf.

Sabanoglu, Tugba. "Global Retail E-Commerce Market Size 2014-2023." *Statista*, November 30, 2020. https://www.statista.com/statistics/379046/worldwide-retail -e-commerce-sales/.

Stanford University Libraries. "Copyright & Fair Use." *Stanford Copyright and Fair Use Center*, April 2, 2013. https://fairuse.stanford.edu/.

Taylor, Telford. "Wall Street Retreats from Record Highs amid Virus, Political Uncertainty." *The Washington Post (Online)*. January 11, 2021. https://search.proquest .com/washingtonpost/docview/2476743139/citation/24F1A18B89934A1EPQ/4.

Tigas, Mike, Sisi Wei, Ken Schwencke, Brandon Roberts, and Alec Glassford. "American Chemical Society, Full Filing–Nonprofit Explorer." *ProPublica*. Accessed December 31, 2020, https://projects.propublica.org/nonprofits/ organizations/530196572/201843129349300709/full.

Walsh, Kit. "Copyright Isn't a Tool for Removing Negative Reviews." *Electronic Frontier Foundation*, October 12, 2017. https://www.eff.org/deeplinks/2017/10/ copyright-isnt-tool-removing-negative-reviews-1.

Wired Staff. "Scientology: The Web's First Copyright-Wielding Nemesis." *Wired*, September 21, 2009. https://www.wired.com/2009/09/mf-chanology-sidebar/.

Xu, William, and Adrian Cooper. "Digital Spillover: Measuring the True Impact of the Digital Economy." Huawei and Oxford Economics, 2017. https://www.huawei .com/minisite/gci/en/digital-spillover/files/gci_digital_spillover.pdf.

Conspiracy Theories in the Post-Truth Culture

TWA 800: A THEORY IN SEARCH OF A CONSPIRACY

On July 17, 1996, a massive explosion tore apart Trans World Airlines (TWA) Flight 800 twelve minutes after the Boeing 747 took off from New York's John F. Kennedy International Airport, killing all 230 passengers and crew on board. Although the authorities initially suspected terrorism, a four-year investigation by aviation and law enforcement professionals concluded that the explosion was accidental, the result of a simple-but-fatal short circuit in the aircraft's central fuel tank.[1] Not surprisingly, conspiracy theories about what *really* caused TWA 800 to plunge into the sea a few miles off the coast of Long Island began circulating almost before any of the wreckage had begun to be recovered. Though certainly not the first rumors to be spread via the internet, the TWA 800 conspiracy theories were among the earliest to emerge and propagate at the time when internet use was becoming increasingly widespread among the general public. (In September 1997, one month and a year after the tragedy of TWA 800, the untimely death of Diana, Princess of Wales, would emphatically demonstrate the ability of the rapidly growing internet masses to not only take control of the narrative surrounding a major news event, but also to propagate multiple related rumors and conspiracy theories.) One popular TWA 800 conspiracy theory, championed by former Kennedy and Johnson administration press secretary Pierre Salinger (1925–2004), held that TWA 800 was accidentally downed by missiles fired by the American guided-missile cruiser USS *Normandy* during a training exercise. This conspiracy theory flourished for several years despite the absence of any credible evidence to support it.

THE HOUSTON MASS MURDERS:
A CONSPIRACY HIDDEN AMONG THE THEORIES

Over the course of the first three years of 1970s, in the then down-at-its-heels Houston, Texas, neighborhood of The Heights, teenage boys began turning up missing at an alarming rate. Though repeatedly confronted by distraught parents insisting their sons would have never left home without so much as a word, police refused to conduct more than the most cursory of investigations, in every case dismissing the vanished youths as thrill-seeking runaways.[2] Lacking the money or political influence to get action from the authorities, working-class parents taped flyers to telephone poles and searched on their own as best they could, hoping and praying that their wayward sons would return of their own accord. The grim truth was that none of their sons had run away and none would return home. A local power company employee and his two teenaged accomplices had been carrying out a sadistic criminal conspiracy that ultimately resulted in the torture-murders of at least twenty-eight boys and young men. These horrific crimes were finally revealed not as a result of any police investigations, but only after a deadly confrontation among two of the conspirators prompted the survivor to confess. Police might have investigated sooner, and possibly have prevented at least some of the murders, if they had not been blinded by the then-current flood of rumors and conspiracy theories concerning the bizarre, mysterious, and threatening world of hippies. Members of the establishment simply took it for granted that shadowy hippie cults—like the one led by the very real, though anomalous, Charles Manson (1934–2017)—were conspiring to lure naïve young people away from family, school, and church with promises of plentiful drugs and uninhibited sex. *Of course* the boys had run away to become hippies. After all, everyone knew that was what all the kids were doing because it was what the everyone said all the kids were doing.

As easy as it was in the days of the Nixon administration for rumors and conspiracy theories to conceal the existence actual crimes, the situation is much worse in a post-truth culture in which the spreading of conspiracy theories is orders of magnitude easier than it was in the analog 1970s.

CONSPIRACY THEORIES VERSUS CONSPIRACIES

The TWA 800-USS *Normandy* fable has been largely forgotten, long replaced in the popular imagination by thousands of fresher conspiracy theories vying for popular attention. I chose to start with this somewhat obscure conspiracy theory in order to alienate the fewest possible readers before this chapter even gets under way. So powerful is the psychological pull of conspiracy theories that deeply invested conspiracists will simply tune out if a favorite conspiracy theory is challenged. A second reason I chose the TWA 800-*Normandy* conspiracy theory is so I could share the following story. Years ago, I worked with a colleague who had served as an enlisted sailor aboard the USS *Normandy* during the Gulf War of 1990–1991. Though my colleague had left the Navy prior to the TWA 800 incident, he had heard of the USS *Normandy* conspiracy theory and was strongly skeptical of it. He explained his reasoning as follows: During the time of the Gulf War, one of the duties assigned to the *Normandy* was to serve as a communications relay station patching telephone calls from the Persian Gulf Region through to the United States. My colleague, who held the naval rating of Electronics Technician, explained how one time *Normandy* had patched through a call from the actress Brooke Shields, then visiting the region as part of a U.S.O. tour, to her home in the United States. According to my colleague, within an hour of that call every sailor and Marine aboard the *Normandy* was privy to Brooke Shields' home phone number. If the *Normandy* had fired a missile at the time TWA 800 went down, my colleague reasoned, every one of the over three hundred personnel aboard would have known. And, sooner or later, some of them would have talked. (Unlike patching through a phone call, launching a ship-to-air missile is a noisy and specular event of which every single person on board would be immediately aware.)

Conspiracies, which are not the same as conspiracy theories, are both quite real and quite common. History is filled with examples of verified conspiracies, such as the following:

- The Gunpowder Plot of 1605 was an elaborate religious/political conspiracy among a group of English Catholics to blow up the House of Lords, kill King James the First (a Protestant), and place a Catholic ruler on the throne. An anonymous letter from a whistleblower tipped off the Royal authorities before the conspirators were able to follow through with their plans, resulting in, respectively, a series of gruesome executions, the British tradition of celebrating Guy Fawkes Day every November 5, and the eventual adoption of the Guy Fawkes mask as an iconic symbol of antiestablishment sympathies.
- The Gleiwitz Incident was a military/political conspiracy in which German operatives disguised as members of the Polish military attacked a German radio station on the night of August 31, 1939. Even though most of the world saw through the staged attack as a false-flag operation, the incident was used by the leaders of Nazi Germany as a justification for the German invasion of Poland, which commenced the following day, September 1, 1939, thereby launching the Second World War.

- The Tuskegee Syphilis Experiment, which ran from 1932 to 1972, was a scientific/medical conspiracy that allowed African American men suffering from syphilis to go untreated without their knowledge while under the impression they were being provided with health care by the U.S. Federal Government. Over the years, several medical doctors objected to the unethical nature of the experiment, though the conspiracy did not finally end until a U.S. Public Health Service whistleblower took the story to the press.
- The November 2015 Paris Attacks were a coordinated series of bombings and shootings carried out in and around Pairs, France. Later investigations determined the attacks were the result of a conspiracy planned in Syria and carried out by terrorists affiliated with the Islamic State of Iraq and the Levant (ISIL).

A *conspiracy*, which requires an agreement, oral or in writing, between two or more persons to commit a wrongful act, can be exposed by the testimony of whistleblowers (who may themselves be involved in, or witnesses to, the conspiracy) or through the work of investigators such as journalists, law enforcement officials, intelligence agents, or private citizens. Proving the existence of an actual conspiracy requires more than testimony and finger pointing—it requires credible, factual evidence of the sort that might be presented in a court trial. In the case of the Gunpowder Plot, tipped-off British officials discovered Guy Fawkes (1570–1606) guarding dozens of barrels of gunpowder concealed in a cellar beneath the House of Lords. In the case of the Houston Mass Murders, the two surviving conspirators led initially skeptical police to the bodies of the murdered youths. A *conspiracy theory*, on the other hand, is like magic in *Peter Pan*. Believing so makes it real. No credible evidence required. Those who tend to adhere to conspiracy theories are said to have a *conspiracist ideation*, a mindset in which conspiracy theories serve to make sense of a reality that may seem ambiguous, arbitrary, unfair, or frightening. Writing before the advent of social media or the upheavals brought about by the 9/11 attacks, scholar Timothy Melley makes the still-pertinent observation that conspiratorial ideation can be a reaction to "agency panic," a term which he defines as "intense anxiety about apparent loss of autonomy or self-control—the conviction that one's actions are being controlled by someone else, that one has been 'constructed' by powerful external agents."[3] Taken to its extreme, conspiracist ideation can be so psychologically damaging that highly invested believers lash out against perceived enemies with hatred and violence. It is quite likely the terrorists who carried out November 15 Paris Attacks accepted as true any number of the anti-Western conspiracy theories regularly circulating throughout the Middle East. In much the same way, the operatives who perpetrated the Gleiwitz Incident almost certainly accepted as fact the anti-Jewish conspiracy theories that contributed to the German Nazi Party's rise to power.

But wait a minute. If there are real conspiracies taking place, doesn't that mean that some conspiracy theories are correct? In fact, no. It does not. The phrase *conspiracy theory* implies, and always has implied, an imaginary, rather than a factual, conclusion. That, by definition, conspiracy theories never turn out to be correct may be somewhat a matter of semantics, but semantics actually do matter in this case. Of fairly recent coinage, the earliest written example of the phrase *conspiracy theory* cited by the *Oxford English Dictionary* dates only from 1909.[4] The spread of the phrase *conspiracy theory* into the popular consciousness (via the channel of academia) may be most accurately attributed to Austrian-British philosopher Karl Popper (1902–1994). Writing during a time, the Second World War, when people were quite literally dying by the millions due, in part, to the powerful allure of conspiracy theories, Popper coined the phrase "conspiracy theory of society," which he defines as:

> the view that an explanation of a social phenomenon consists in the discovery of the men or group who are interested in the occurrence of this phenomenon (sometimes it is a hidden interest which has first to be revealed), and who have planned and conspired to bring it about.[5]

From the start, the popular understanding of the phrase *conspiracy theory* carried with it a connotation of thinking disconnected from factual reality, of being more about how distraught human minds imagine the world than how the world actually is. Popper himself skewers the conspiracy theory mindset on the grounds that it:

> arises, of course, from the mistaken theory that, whatever happens in society—especially happenings such as war, unemployment, poverty, shortages, which people as a rule dislike—is the result of the direct design by some powerful individuals and groups. . . . Conspiracies occur, it must be admitted. But the striking fact which, in spite of their occurrence, disproves the conspiracy theory is that few of them are ultimately successful. *Conspirators rarely consummate their conspiracy.*[6]

That last statement is not merely Popper's opinion. Recent mathematical modeling has demonstrated the impossibility of keeping a large conspiracy secret for long.[7] In the case of TWA 800, covering up the alleged conspiracy would have required not only the complicity of the entire crew of the USS *Normandy*, but also the willingness of dozens of investigators and technical experts to jeopardize their professional reputations by lying about the facts.

The idea simply does not make any sense. Imagine, for example, a Federal Bureau of Investigation (FBI) agent or a National Transportation Safety Board expert discovering evidence of a missile strike and *not* coming forward to take credit for solving the mystery and exposing an actual crime. It is about as likely as people who have devoted decades of their lives to medical research developing a highly effective treatment for pancreatic cancer and then, as part of some grand medical conspiracy, completely burying their discovery even though making that discovery public would have garnered public admiration, professional recognition, and, quite possibly, a Nobel Prize in medicine.

The disconnect between an actual conspiracy and a conspiracy theory which Popper addresses plays out with predictable regularity. On the one hand, there are real conspiracies that can be proven through verifiable facts. For yet another example of an actual conspiracy, it is well established that, starting in 1956, the U.S. government's COINTELPRO (COunter INTELigence PROgram) spied on and interfered with the legitimate political activities of American citizens, including nonviolent civil rights, environmental, and antiwar groups. And while perpetrators of COINTELPRO chalked up some successes, the program failed to thwart the social and political movements it deemed a danger to the state, confirming Popper's statement: "*Conspirators rarely consummate their conspiracy.*" So, yes, governments really do conspire against their citizens. Scientists can be wrong, at times intentionally so. Some manufacturers knowingly make and sell dangerous products. Corporations sometimes engage in criminal conspiracies that end up costing ordinary people dearly. Religious and charitable institutions can be used as covers for terrible crimes. Calling out and objecting to actual conspiracies is neither a form of madness nor a delusion—as long as there is credible evidence to support such responses.

In contrast to verifiable conspiracies are unverifiable conspiracy theories—the latter by definition are fantasies based on no credible evidence. For example, there is credible evidence that environmental extremists in fact drove metal spikes into trees as part of a conspiracy to discouraging logging. In 1987, a California sawmill worker was injured as a result of tree spiking by environmental extremists.[8] Concrete evidence equals a real conspiracy. In 2010, following the Deepwater Horizon explosion and oil spill which killed eleven oil rig workers and devastated large swaths of the Gulf of Mexico, unfounded conspiracy theories, including one given airtime by popular radio personality Rush Limbaugh (1951–2021), claimed that the disaster was caused by environmental extremists out to discredit the oil industry.[9] Unfounded speculation equals a conspiracy theory. The confounding of conspiracies (real) with conspiracy theories (fictional) can have the unfortunate effect, as in the case of the Houston Mass Murders, of making it easier for credible evidence of actual wrongdoing to simply get lost in all the noise generated by conspiracy theories. The phenomenon of real wrongdoing being obscured by made-up conspiracy theories resembles the military technology known as *chaff*—a radar countermeasure in which a military aircraft releases a cloud of tiny metal strips in order to create so cluttered a radar picture that it becomes difficult, if not impossible, for an opposing force to target the actual aircraft among all the false echoes. Even if conspiracies rarely succeed (and even less often work out as the conspirators intended) the chaff of thousands of fanciful conspiracy theories—along with their close cousins, rumors—makes it that much easier for actual conspiracies to avoid detection.

In addition to their chaff effect, conspiracy theories undermine confidence in institutions and facts to the extent that individuals and organizations can take advantage of conspiracy theories to sway public opinion in their favor. Accused white-collar criminals are especially prone to positioning themselves as victims of government-led conspiracies as a way of gaining sympathy and, possibly, avoiding conviction. For a current example, legal observers anticipate that in the fraud and conspiracy trials of Elizabeth Holmes and Ramesh Balwani, respectively the founder and the president of the discredited medical science company Theranos, "The defense will undoubtedly fight back vigorously and likely will try to 'flip the conspiracy script' by putting the government on trial and asking the jury to see the case as a 'government/press conspiracy' against the company and the defendants."[10] If the defense prevails on the argument that the accused white-collar defendants are themselves victims of a conspiracy, it will not represent a legal precedent.

CONSPIRACY THEORIES, FALSIFIABILITY, AND CIRCULAR REASONING

In addition to his writing on conspiracy theories, Karl Popper also developed the concept of *falsifiability* (aka *refutability*). It is Popper's contention that a statement, hypothesis, or theory can be considered empirical only if its truthfulness is capable of being subjected to examination via a negative test (i.e., is *falsifiable*). It is important to understand that just because a statement is falsifiable does not mean it *is* false, only that it has the *potential* to be proven false. Every empirical statement is falsifiable even if it is, in fact, as true as any statement can possibly be. Popper provides the statement, "It will rain here tomorrow," as an example of an empirical statement that is falsifiable; conversely, Popper provides the statement, "It will rain or not rain here tomorrow," as an example of a nonempirical statement that is not falsifiable.[11] Falsifiability is essential to scientific studies. If a herpetologist were to hypothesize that a certain subspecies of lizard has become extinct, yet afterwards specimens of that subspecies are discovered living in the wild, the extinction hypothesis would have been falsified and no longer be considered scientifically valid. Falsifiability also applies outside of science. The true statement, "In August 2007, NASA Mission Specialist Barbara R. Morgan flew to the International Space Station on board the space shuttle *Endeavour*" is empirical because it is falsifiable. Unlike empirical statements, conspiracy theories are nonfalsifiable because they are constructed on a foundation of *circular reasoning*, a type of logical fallacy based on the idea that an argument begins with a conclusion rather ending with one. The application of circular reasoning in defense of a conspiracy theory plays out as follows:

- The conspiracy theory is, a priori, true.
- Evidence that supports the conspiracy theory, therefore, must also be true.
- Evidence that contradicts the conspiracy theory must, therefore, be false.
- Furthermore, evidence that appears to contradict the conspiracy theory is disinformation created by the actual conspirators to hide their involvement and, as a result, constitutes further evidence that the conspiracy is real.

Going back to the TWA 800-*Normandy* conspiracy theory, the Navy's official response was to say that the *Normandy* was not conducting missile tests at the time of the disaster and, even if it had been, TWA 800 was at a distance of over twice the maximum the range of the *Normandy*'s ship-to-air missiles when it went down.[12] By the laws of physics and ballistics, the *Normandy* could not have shot down TWA 800 if it had tried, much less have done so accidentally. For the conspiratorially minded, however, the fact that the Navy responded at all is itself evidence of a cover up: *"Why would they be they denying it if they didn't have something to hide?"* Of course, if the Navy had said nothing, that, too, would have been evidence of a cover up. The situation is a bit like investigators concluding that a criminal suspect must be guilty on that grounds that the suspect demonstrated either (1) a suspicious lack of emotion or (2) a suspicious excess of emotion. Either way, guilt is assumed. Operating with the same certainty shown by an investigator who has settled on the guilt of a suspect without regard for the weight of all the evidence, a conspiratorial state of mind enables a conspiracist to confidently dismiss any and all contradictory facts:

- *The Navy lied about where the* Normandy *actually was.*

- *The Navy had to have lied about the actual range of their ship-to-air missiles—that's obviously a military secret they would never reveal.*
- *None of the crew of the* Normandy *talked because the Navy threatened them into silence.*
- *Any competing conspiracy theories about TWA 800 were dreamed up to cast doubt on the real conspiracy.*

The existence of competing conspiracy theories surrounding a single event is actually quite common. In the case of TWA 800, a competing conspiracy theory holds that, instead of a wayward Navy missile, the Boeing 747 was brought down by a surface-to-air missile fired by terrorists. The facts, so this rival conspiracy theory goes, were covered up by the Clinton administration out of fear that a successful terrorist attack in American airspace would have been used against President Clinton in the upcoming election. Of course, if the terrorist conspiracy theory were true, then the *Normandy* conspiracy theory could not also be true. TWA 800 could not have been shot out of the sky by both terrorists *and* the U.S. Navy any more than, for a notable example, President John F. Kennedy could have been assassinated by pro-Castro Cubans *and* anti-Castro Cuban exiles *and* organized crime *and* the Central Intelligence Agency *and* the right-wing military-industrial complex *and* the Soviet Union *and* the Secret Service *and* the FBI *and* Vice President Lyndon Johnson *and* . . . the list goes on. Confoundingly, the existence of multiple conspiracy theories about the same event can spur on, rather than deter, conspiratorial thinking. *"Something fishy has to be going on. With so many conspiracy theories floating around, what are the chances that none of them are true?"*

IS THE CURRENT POPULARITY OF CONSPIRACY THEORIES A PRODUCT OF THE DIGITAL AGE?

If any feature of the post-truth culture deserves the title of "Hallmark of the Age," conspiracy theories have to be a leading contender. In their book *Propaganda and Persuasion*, Garth S. Jowett and Victoria J. O'Donnell note, "Coupling conspiracy theories with the viral nature of social media has become an important component of contemporary cyber propaganda and an impressive platform for disinformation."[13] If it is true that the "viral nature of social media" is the source of the problem, it is worth asking if the world is looking at a problem that will never get better, and possibly get much worse, or if it is looking at a problem that may go away as the newness of social media wears off and people generally get better at managing their use and consumption of social media messages? Going beyond blaming digital technology for being a too-efficient medium for the spreading of conspiracy theories, political scientist Thomas Milan Konda contends:

> there is also something new that has transformed the conspiratorial landscape: conspiracism—a mental framework, a belief system, a worldview that leads people to look for conspiracies, to anticipate them, to link them together into a grander overarching conspiracy. Conspiracism has been building for some time, and by now it appears to have emerged as the belief system of the twenty-first century.[14]

Transformed landscape or not, it seems like every new day reveals at least one new, often seemingly unhinged from reality, conspiracy theory. Totaling up the number of conspiracy theories circulating in twenty-first-century cyberspace would be an impossible task, not only because they are so numerous, but also because they appear in so many languages and across so many cultures. The United States may see itself as the world hotbed of conspiracy theories, but conspiracy theories are very much an international phenomenon, surfacing on every continent and finding adherents in every nation. And while it may be convenient to think of conspiracist ideation as a phenomenon of a certain type or class of person, that is not the case. Adherents to conspiracy theories can be liberal or conservative, rich or poor, powerful or disenfranchised, religious or nonbelievers. Along with anonymous unknowns seeking to establish a distinctive identity through adherence to conspiracy theories, it is not hard to find famous politicians, entertainers, sports figures, or online celebrities flamboyantly pledging allegiance to one conspiracy or another (or several at once). Nor is the popular image of a conspiracist as an uneducated bumpkin anything more than a stereotype. Conspiracy theories can circulate among university faculty as well as among migrant farmworkers. And even though the rise of extremist political movements in the United States during the first decades of the twenty-first century shines the conspiracy theory spotlight on white, right-wing populists, other communities in the United States also share conspiracy theories that speak to their fears. One example selected from among a number of conspiracy theories that circulate almost exclusively among African Americans is the long-standing accusation that the Church's Fried Chicken fast-food chain is both owned by the Ku Klux Klan and adds a secret ingredient to their chicken that renders Black men sexually impotent.[15]

Just as there are examples of actual conspiracies that predate the Digital Age, invented conspiracy theories also date far back into the past. Paranoid fears of the alleged dangers posed by such outsiders as Jews and witches were reflected in conspiracy theories that circulated widely among Christians in Medieval Europe. Since the eighteenth century (and into the present day) both the Illuminati and the Freemasons have been the object of conspiracy theories. From the earliest European settlers through the westward expansion, conspiracy theories about Native Americans were common in, first, the American colonies and, later, the United States; far too often, these conspiracy theories led to atrocities carried out in the name of foiling alleged Native American plots that existed only in the minds of paranoid white Americans. Prior to, and during, the U.S. Civil War, pro- and antislavery interests traded in conspiracy theories designed to promote fear and hatred of those on the other side of the ever-widening gulf between North and South. Over the years and into the present day, American Catholics, Mormons, Evangelical Christians, Moslems, and Jews have all been the objects of conspiracy theories, as have homosexuals (and opponents of homosexuality), pro-lifers (and pro-choicers), liberals (and conservatives). The list goes on for far too long. In his *Empire of Conspiracy: The Culture of Paranoia in Postwar America*, Timothy Melley describes how 1950s America simultaneously entertained two opposed, yet widely accepted, conspiracy theories. One conspiracy theory, as championed by FBI Director J. Edgar Hoover (1895–1972) in his 1958 bestseller *Masters of Deceit*, concerns a combination of foreign and American-born communists actively conspiring to take control of the United States through a subtle, well-organized program of indoctrination. The competing conspiracy theory, as championed by journalist Vance Packard (1914–1996) in his 1957 bestseller *The Hidden Persuaders*, concerns a capitalist corporate plot to manipulate the entire population of the United States by means of sophisticated advertising techniques employing the latest advances in the psychological sciences.[16]

Even though conspiracy theories are nothing new, the one thing that is different in the Digital Age is the power of digital technology to spread conspiracy theories further and more quickly than at any time in the past. In the early 1980s, I was friends with an artistic, counterculture type—call him Arthur, though that is not his real name—who worked the night shift at a twenty-four-hour copy shop located less than a mile from the State Capitol Building in Boise, Idaho. Because few customers came in late at night, the biggest part of Arthur's workload was running off large batches of copies for businesses, churches, civic groups, and similar bulk-order customers. Often enough, Arthur found himself running off copies for groups that embraced extremist political, religious, and social views. Conspiracy theories were a staple of these groups' self-published literature, and Arthur would routinely make an extra copy of the most extreme content for the amusement of himself and his friends. Aside from Arthur's small circle of snickering friends, it is unlikely that anyone unaffiliated with the group that actually created the conspiracy-promoting literature ever laid eyes on those copies run off in the dead of night. All of which is a long-winded way of saying that, until recently, spreading a conspiracy theory took a lot of effort and more than a little money. In the twenty-first century, those same conspiracists would entirely skip the cost and inconvenience of the copy shop by promoting their ideas via websites and social media, potentially reaching large audiences who might, in turn, amplify their conspiracists messages by further sharing them.

The widespread availability of fast, cheap, and effective tools for spreading conspiracy theories leads to a key question for anyone living in the post-truth culture: "How many people really believe these conspiracy theories and how deep is their commitment to such ideas?" Because extreme behaviors make the best stories, there is an all-but-unavoidable tendency for reportage about conspiracy theories to focus on the most extreme examples and, possibly, overstate the extent of the problem. Documentary filmmaker Cullen Hoback, in an interview about his 2021 HBO docuseries *Q: Into the Storm*, states, "Now almost 20% of Americans believe in QAnon."[17] Hoback began following the QAnon story in 2018 and, as a result of making a four-episode documentary about QAnon, may know as much about the phenomenon as anyone, but how reliable is his—or anyone's—estimate of how many people believe conspiracy theories? Writing about the possibility of surveys overestimating support for QAnon, media scholar James Shanahan observes:

> As useful as survey data is, it is difficult to go from that to more nuanced questions, like what portion of respondents are true believers, versus which of them might act on that belief–and which of them are giving quick answers that seem to fit with their current thoughts or beliefs. As a result, surveys cannot replace the real forensic work that is needed to know how many QAnon "members" there really are.[18]

Indeed, what does it mean to be a member of essentially leaderless, decentralized groups like QAnon or Antifa, and to what extent does identifying oneself as a member of any group or political party mean acceptance of every orthodoxy (or conspiracy theory) promoted by that group? There are pro-life liberals just as there are conservative environmentalists, and plenty of members of both groups are capable of shaking their heads in disbelief over some of the words coming out of the mouths of the leaders of their own faction. On the other hand, consider what it might mean to signal agreement, whether to a survey taker or a friendly bartender, with a conspiracy theory such as:

- "Dr. Anthony Fauci funded a lab in Wuhan to develop the coronavirus."
or
- "The book/TV series *The Handmaid's Tale* is based on the secretive religious group People of Praise, to which Supreme Court Justice Amy Coney Barrett belonged."[19]

Does signaling agreement mean full acceptance of the truth of the conspiracy theory, or is it more an expression of individual's overall political or social orientation? For example, when participating in a survey of political opinions, responding that you believe the conspiracy theory about Justice Barrett becomes a convenient way to signal your political position while leaving the extent to which you truly believe, or do not believe, in that conspiracy theory ambiguous. That said, the number of potentially dangerous conspiracy theories circulating through the post-truth culture, coupled with the fact that some hard-to-quantify proportion of the population claims full or partial adherence to conspiracy theories, is a matter of concern. Increasing your knowledge of how conspiracy theories work and why people turn to them as a means of explaining real events and, in some cases, as a means of feeling some level of control over those events, is useful both for better understanding those who fall under the spell of conspiracy theories as well as for personally resisting the allure of conspiracy theories that speak to your own fears and biases.

THE TYPES OF CONSPIRACY THEORIES

Conspiracy theories may be classified in a number of ways. While no single classification scheme can be considered definitive, classification can be useful in helping to recognize conspiracy theories when they surface and to better understand their appeal. Political scientist Michael Barkun identifies three types of conspiracy theories:[20]

- *Event conspiracy theories* are based around a single incident, such as the TWA 800 disaster or the outcome of a contested election.
- *Systemic conspiracy theories* purport to expose endeavors with wide-ranging goals, such as taking over an entire country. An example would be a conspiracy theory promoting the idea that Islamic conspirators are planning to take political control over Western nations, establish Sharia law, and ultimately ban all other religions. Individual event conspiracies can constitute one part of a systematic conspiracy, as when a conspiracy theorist argues that the faking of the Apollo space missions is part of a systemic conspiracy to cover up the existence of extraterrestrial aliens.
- *Superconspiracy theories* posit the existence of complex, interconnected subconspiracies under the control of an evil overlord so secretive that those involved in subconspiracies are unaware of the puppet master's existence or that they themselves are pawns in a larger game. An example of a superconspiracy theory is the so-called Reptilian Conspiracy Theory which proposes that world events, political leaders, and governments

have been, for some unspecified time, secretly under the control of alien lizard people who intend to conquer the entire planet (assuming they have not done so already). Event and systematic conspiracies can both function as parts of a larger superconspiracy. For example:

- ○ *Event Conspiracy Theory:* The COVID-19 pandemic was a hoax perpetrated by the U.S. government.
- ○ *Systemic Conspiracy Theory:* The U.S. government is using COVID-19 vaccinations as a means of secretly microchipping American citizens.
- ○ *Superconspiracy Theory:* Once the U.S. government has microchipped a sufficient number of American citizens, the secret Zionist Occupation Government will step in to take total control of the United States.

Using a different classification scheme, Jess Walker, an author and the books editor of the libertarian magazine *Reason*, identifies five types of conspiracy theories:[21]

- *The Enemy-Outside* is a type of conspiracy theory based on the proposition that one or more persons external to a group (a community, a nation, etc.) are conspiring against those within the group. When rumors circulate that out-of-town referees conspired in advance to ensure the hated rival team would defeat the beloved home team, that is an example of an enemy-outside conspiracy.
- *The Enemy-Within* is a type of conspiracy theory based on the proposition that one or more persons internal to a group (community, nation, etc.) are conspiring against the group to which they ostensibly belong. In the 1950s, a popular enemy-within conspiracy theory was based on the idea that seemingly normal, law-abiding, and patriotic neighbors might be secret communist agents. In the post-9/11 United States, similar enemy-within conspiracies are based on the idea that Muslim Americans are terrorists in hiding.
- *The Enemy-Above* is a type of conspiracy theory based on the proposition that one or more members of a powerful elite are conspiring to gain an advantage over the less powerful. A rumor that a sports league's rich and powerful team owners decided in advance which team would win the Big Game is an example of an enemy-above conspiracy theory.
- *The Enemy-Below* is a type of conspiracy theory based on the proposition that the members of the underclass are plotting to disrupt the social order, usually through a violent revolution. Enemy-below conspiracy theories tend to surface during times of civil unrest, especially when

there are mass demonstrations or riots, and they typically play on fears that the underclass is not interested in obtaining equal rights with the overclass but, rather, in completely destroying the overclass. It is common for enemy-below conspiracy theories to include claims that the underclass is being prompted to action by evil-minded "outside agitators," the implication being that the underclass is incapable of standing up for itself without assistance from renegade members of the overclass. All four types of enemy-based conspiracy theories can make use of *windmill enemies.* Windmill enemies can be either entirely made-up enemies—*"This is clearly the work of the Venusian mole people"*—or they can be actual people whose threat is imaginary—*"The Girl Scouts are out to control the country by putting microchips in the Thin Mints."*

• *The Benevolent Conspiracy* is based on the proposition that one or more guardian protectors are secretly looking out for the good of the world and/or the benefit of deserving individuals. Benevolent conspiracy theories can involve groups or individuals who right wrongs in ways ranging from doing good deeds to carrying out acts of protective vigilantism. Benevolent conspiracy theories edge into the supernatural when the stories incorporate actual angels interfering in the lives of mortal humans.

One category of conspiracy theory not mentioned by Barkun or Walker is the *Joke Conspiracy Theory.* Claims that U.S. Senator Ted Cruz is the Zodiac Killer and that his criminal past is being covered up by powerful political forces is one current example of a joke conspiracy theory. Because Cruz was not born until two years after the Zodiac Killer's first confirmed murders, the Cruz-Zodiac Killer conspiracy theory is not one that anyone with even a small grip on reality can take seriously. Even if some claim to truly believe that Cruz is the Zodiac Killer, the whole concept is too ludicrous to be understood as anything other than a joke. As ridiculous as joke conspiracy theories may be, the distancing effect of cyberspace can make it difficult to tell when people are being serious about what they truly believe versus when they are joking. Nor is telling what is serious from what is a joke made any easier by online trolls who revel in the sport of promoting outrageous rumors and conspiracy theories (in which they do not truly believe) and then tweaking the noses of anyone who rises to their bait. In 2020 a comedian created, as a joke, two fake social media posts announcing that Antifa would be holding events in Lafayette, Louisiana; in response, the city initiated a preemptive police response to forestall any acts of violence by either pro- or anti-Antifa elements. The City of Lafayette later sued the poster of the fake announcements for the cost of the police response.[22]

The conspiracy theory about Ted Cruz actually being the Zodiac Killer is also an example of a type of conspiracy theory that can be called a *Whole-Cloth Conspiracy Theory*. Statements about real-world events, such as the following, are empirical because they are falsifiable:

- President John F. Kennedy was assassinated in Dallas, Texas, on November 22, 1963.
- TWA 800 exploded and fell into the ocean on July 17, 1996.
- The late spring and summer of 2020 was marked by protests over the death of George Floyd as he was being arrested by officers of the Minneapolis Police Department.

There are multiple conspiracy theories surrounding each of these events, and even though those conspiracy theories are not empirical, each has at least a small toehold in reality by virtue of being based on actual, verifiable events. Whole-cloth conspiracy theories do not have even that much going for them, being spun entirely from the cloth of fantasy. For example, when Barak Obama was president of the United States, a photograph circulated online with the claim that it depicted five hundred thousand disposable coffins stored at a site belonging to the Federal Emergency Management Agency (FEMA). The disposable coffins, so the claim went, were for use at secret FEMA detention centers being prepared in the event of a popular revolt against the federal government. In fact, what the photograph depicted were not five hundred thousand government-owned coffins but, instead, seventy thousand to eighty thousand burial vault liners. More to the point, the vault liners were privately owned and were being stored on private property.[23] Even if there actually were a government conspiracy to set up FEMA-controlled detention centers, the items depicted in the photograph were not coffins and had nothing to do with the government or detention centers of any sort. The FEMA coffins rumor was a whole-cloth conspiracy theory from start to finish.

CHARACTERISTICS OF CONSPIRACY THEORIES

While being able to identify the characteristics of conspiracy theories is a useful skill for sorting out conspiracy theories from more credible forms of inquiry, it is important to avoid either/or evaluations based on one or a few characteristics. The situation is similar to propaganda. Just as any persuasive argument may exhibit some characteristics of propaganda without being considered propaganda, any communication that exhibits some characteristics of a conspiracy theory does not automatically equal a conspiracy theory in the making. What is most important is to be alert to the possibility that someone is spreading a conspiracy theory (or rumor), to consider the entirety of the argument being presented and, as impartially as possible, evaluate the credibility of the supporting evidence.

Elaborate Presentations of Evidence

In the interest of appearing to be operating entirely on verifiable factual information, conspiracists will often go to extraordinary lengths to present evidence that appears to be credible—even scientific—despite the fact that what they are presenting is invented or irrelevant. Famously, proponents of the various conspiracy theories regarding the Apollo space missions have devoted tens of thousands of words to excruciatingly detailed, ostensibly scientific, analyses of every aspect of the photographs taken by Apollo 11 astronauts Neil Armstrong (1930–2012) and Buzz Aldrin (1930–) while the two walked on the Moon in July 1969. In some of the photographs taken by the Apollo 11 astronauts, the camera's crosshairs appear to be behind the object being photographed, a detail which conspiracists have cited as irrefutable evidence that the photographs are fakes. However, such claims ignore a simple fact of photography, "Although the crosshairs in a number of Apollo photographs appear to be behind objects, they occur only in bright, white parts of the photographs. This phenomenon is commonplace and happens on Earth also; therefore, it is in no way indicative of fraud."[24] Unsubstantiated nonsense dressed up in the clothing of rational, open inquiry is still unsubstantiated nonsense.

Cherry Picking Evidence

Conspiracy theorists focus exclusively on evidence that supports their chosen conspiracy theories while ignoring evidence—often a preponderance of evidence—that shows their conclusions cannot be true. In the case of TWA 800, conspiracists have made much of a handful of eyewitnesses who claim to have seen a missile streaking toward and striking the aircraft; however, these same conspiracists ignore the well-documented fact that none of the eyewitnesses interviewed in the aftermath of the event could have seen a missile strike the aircraft. The explanation for why this is so is quite simple. All the witness who claimed to have seen a missile reported they did not look skyward until after hearing the fatal explosion, the sound of which could not have reached their ears until some forty seconds after it occurred, far too late for them to have seen a missile intercept the aircraft.[25] What the eyewitnesses saw was burning jet fuel dripping downward rather than a missile streaking upward.

Rejecting Contrary Evidence

When conspiracists do happen to acknowledge the existence of evidence that contradicts their claims, the magic of circular reasoning (see previous discussion) allows them to dismiss any such evidence, no matter how credible or voluminous. The National Transportation Safety Board's 341-page-long report on TWA 800 (cited previously) documents years of painstaking work by dozens of knowledgeable experts to follow every lead, consider every possibility (including the possibilities of both terrorism and an errant U.S. Navy missile), and fully understand the cause of the explosion, yet conspiracists brush off its findings as further evidence of a well-coordinated cover up. *"Why, would the government produce such a detailed report if they weren't hiding a conspiracy—one that goes all the way to the very top?"*

Embracing the Renegade

Conspiracists often embrace and uphold a renegade—an individual who has left the camp of the enemy to alert a sleeping world to the danger it faces—as the ultimate authority on the facts surrounding any conspiracy. After all, who would know more about what is *really* going on than a former member of the Ku Klux Klan or a conscience-stricken Wall Street insider? While renegades can function as whistleblowers, and whistleblowers can be key to exposing real conspiracies, problems arise when conspiracists are too ready to accept any and all claims by a renegade without doing the basic work of verifying the validity of those claims. For example, Anatoliy Golitsyn (1926–2008), a KGB official who defected from the Soviet Union, accused British Prime Minister Harold Wilson (1916–1995) of having been a KGB operative, an accusation that critics of Wilson and his British Labour Party wove into various conspiracy theories even though there was no credible evidence to back up Golitsyn's claim.[26] In the worse cases, self-proclaimed renegades can turn out to have entirely invented their backstories. In 2018, a Canadian citizen convinced both journalists and government officials that he had served as a fighter and executioner for ISIL. He then spread the alarm that an ISIL conspiracy aimed at Western targets was in the works. As it turns out, his autobiography and warnings were all lies. The most violent act the self-proclaimed terrorist had ever performed was slicing meat and wrapping pitas at his parents' Toronto shawarma shop.[27]

Offering Simple Explanations

Ambiguity and complexity are harder to sell than straight-line stories with a single, well-defined cause leading to a specific effect. Take the example of cancer, a cluster of over one hundred diseases in which abnormal cell growth can invade the body. Although some forms of cancer are highly treatable, especially when detected early, other forms resist treatment and result in high rates of mortality. In the face of such complexity, fear, and sense of power-lessness, people are drawn to conspiracy theories that offer simple explana-tions: *"Of course they have a cure. They hide it from us because the medical establishment makes billions treating cancer."* Similarly, an antiaircraft mis-sile makes for a much simpler, and more dramatically engaging, story than the complex and boring technical details of how a short circuit in a fuel tank is capable of blowing a giant airplane out of the sky.

Simple Alternative Explanation

Conspiracists will insist that their simple alternative explanation validates a conspiracy theory by virtue of its very simplicity. *"Human beings haven't gone back to the Moon since December 1972. Why? The simple explanation is that there are aliens up there who don't want us going back."* In fact, there are a lot of explanations for why humans have not traveled to the Moon for half a century and counting: the expense, the limited value of what can be learned from additional manned missions, shifting national priorities, the novelty of the race to the Moon having lost its luster, etc. For conspiracists, the problem with multiple, nuanced explanations is that they lack the certainty and definitive sense of closure provided by a simple alternative explanation.

Antiestablishment

Most conspiracy theories are built around a narrative in which the powerful, typically secretive forces of the establishment—in such forms as govern-ments, academics (especially scientists and social scientists), the media, religions, secret societies (such as the Freemasons and the Illuminati), law enforcement, the wealthy, labor unions, big corporations—stand in conflict with the less-powerful, sorely wronged, ordinary people of the world. Con-spiracists may seek to establish their underdog, antiestablishment status by claiming that their information has been forced underground by the authori-ties and can only be shared furtively among an elite group of trusted insiders. (Such claims are made despite the fact that, most often, the same conspiracy theories can be found being openly shared via multiple sources.) The flat-tering prospect of being privy to secret, forbidden information has multiple appeals. One such appeal is the desire to count oneself among the informed insiders rather than as just another one of the mindless, misinformed *sheeple*. A second appeal is the feeling that access to information exposing the crimes of the establishment overturns the power dynamic, giving those who see themselves—possibly with justification—as having been wronged, controlled, or simply ignored a sense of agency over events that otherwise seem to be beyond the control of ordinary individuals.

Downtrodden Us versus Powerful Them

The antiestablishment narrative of conspiracy theories creates an us-versus-them scenario which requires a powerful enemy—shadowy or well-defined or (somehow) both—at whom to point the finger of blame. The Evil Empire that is the establishment always has the upper hand, wielding far more power and influence than do the good, brave, moral, chosen, and resilient underdogs who courageously speak the truth in the face of their enemy's lies. Creating a common enemy is, of course, an ancient strategy for building unity among an otherwise not-very-cohesive group. At the same time, creating an enemy becomes a way of dismissing any evidence that contradicts the conspiracist's views: *"Anybody who denies the truth we are sharing has either been brainwashed by our enemies or is actively working for them."*

Stigmatized Knowledge

For conspiracists, the establishment continually conspires to mislead the unwitting by spreading the false Gospel of *accepted knowledge*. Such as:

- Humans have traveled to and returned from the Moon.
- The Earth is a sphere.
- There is no scientifically established causal link between vaccination and autism.
- Pop singer Avril Lavigne did not die by suicide in 2003 and was not subsequently replaced by a lookalike.

As the property of the establishment, these and other examples of accepted knowledge can be dismissed out of hand as manufactured lies. *"I mean, just consider the source."* The establishment—a group whose definition varies among conspiracists—always has some nefarious reason for spreading accepted knowledge, though what that reason may be or why spreading it makes any sense is often left unclear or simply ignored. Because accepted knowledge is, by definition, false knowledge, the only logical conclusion for the conspiracist is that its counterpart, *stigmatized knowledge*, must be true:

- Procter & Gamble's former "Man in the Moon" logo is proof that the company is owned by Satanists.
- Entertainer Lady Gaga and politician Nancy Pelosi wear red to represent the blood of babies murdered by their network of co-conspirators.
- AIDS was created as a biological weapon to reduce the population of persons of color and homosexuals.
- Elvis Presley (1935–1977) faked his death in 1977 and has been seen alive many times over the years.

The acceptance of stigmatized knowledge as truth becomes, by extension, a way of demonstrating resistance against the oppressive establishment. For the conspiracist, extreme cynicism about accepted knowledge, a cynicism which members of the conspiracist in-group endorse as proof of superior wisdom, if not innate intelligence, can morph into naïve acceptance of stigmatized knowledge. As economist and journalist Tim Harford writes, "Conspiracy theorists believe strange ideas, yes. But these outlandish beliefs rest on a solid foundation of disbelief."[28] In the *X-Files* television series, the text on a UFO poster over the desk of conspiracy-obsessed FBI Special Agent Fox Mulder reads, "I WANT TO BELIEVE." What remains unsaid is that wanting to believe one thing requires disbelieving its opposite. To believe that TWA 800 was taken down by a missile, you must choose to disbelieve all the evidence that it was not. To believe that Neil Armstrong never walked on the Moon, you must choose to disbelieve all the evidence that he, in fact, did.

Monopoly on the Truth

If all accepted knowledge is false knowledge, then the truth is found only in the stigmatized knowledge advanced by conspiracists. In cyberspace, any content creator's claim along the lines of, *"This is your one source for the truth. Your go-to for the uncensored real facts that they don't want you to know,"* all but guarantees you have arrived at a gateway to conspiracy theories, rumors, and misinformation. The conspiracist's claim of having a monopoly on truth is, nonetheless, a powerful allure as well as selling point. After all, who does not want to be privy to the one Truth with a capital *T*? At the same time, a monopoly claim on truth becomes a way of discouraging followers from considering any information that may run contrary to the conspiracist's version of the truth. (And, conveniently enough, a discouragement from choosing to become a follower of some other competitor for traffic, followers, likes, and influence.)

Nothing Happens by Accident

In a world filled with powerful, secretive enemies, nothing can happen by mere accident. After all, an aircraft does not just blow up by accident—some evil person or persons must have caused that to happen. The flip side of nothing happening by accident is that everything is connected via carefully constructed secret plans that are most readily explained through the vehicle of conspiracy theories.

Nothing Is as It Seems

For the conspiracist, we live in a world that is built on lies. Rather than serving the public in rather boring and routine ways, government employees and the agencies they work for are part of a conspiracy to strip citizens of their freedom. Seemingly benign charities are fronts for criminal activities. Generous philanthropists operate with evil hidden agendas. Manufacturers produce products that are intentionally designed to sicken and kill the very customers on whom their profits depend. If you start from the proposition that nothing is as it seems, then facts become meaningless and any explanation that runs counter to the way things *seem* to be has validity, unmoored though that explanation may be from facts. If, in the post-truth culture, nothing is what it seems to be, then anything at all can be true if you want it to be.

Apocalyptic/Millenarian

Conspiracists may promote beliefs that are apocalyptic (end of the world) or millenarian (a complete transformation of society via divine intervention or secular social upheaval). Some conspiracy theories attach specific dates (e.g., the Mayan Apocalypse predicted for December 21, 2012) to either the end of all life on Earth or the downfall of the current social order. The apocalyptic and millenarian aspects of conspiracist ideation appeal to the mindsets of survivalists, militia members, cultists, and others who have retreated, or simply fantasized about retreating, from mainstream society. The apocalyptic nature of many conspiracy theories holds an appeal for some religiously minded individuals. In an article published one year after the conspiracy-haunted assassination of President John F. Kennedy, and many years before the creation of cyberspace, American historian Richard Hofstadter (1916–1970) observes that the "paranoid spokesman sees the fate of conspiracy in apocalyptic terms . . . like religious millennialists he expresses the anxiety of those who are living through the last days and he is sometimes disposed to set a date for the apocalypse."[29]

Exaggerating the Threat

In order to engage the interest and attentions of current and potential adherents, conspiracists do not hesitate to exaggerate the magnitude of the looming threat. Conspiracies are very often presented as urgent matters of life or death, total freedom or abject slavery, prosperity or destitution. According to conspiracists, things are looking very bad, the hidden enemy is about to pounce, and the countdown clock has nearly ticked down to zero. The danger dial is turned up to eleven more often than not, and the end is perilously near. All hope, however, is never lost. If there were not a chance, however slim, of the downtrodden sharers of a conspiracy theory somehow triumphing against their powerful enemies, there would be no point in sharing it. There is, after all, little entertainment value to be extracted from an entirely hopeless fight.

Propaganda Techniques

Conspiracy theories often employ one of more of the propaganda techniques discussed in chapter 5. For example, conspiracy theories are, like propaganda, deliberately and systematically designed to elicit desired responses, including such responses as financial support, political or social activism, outrage, and, in extreme cases, violence. Since the 1980s, various conspiracy theories have claimed that Procter & Gamble's Man in the Moon logo is a Satanic symbol and, more specifically, that the company's president has appeared on various daytime talk shows to speak openly about his membership in the Church of Satan. In 2017, Procter & Gamble won a lawsuit against four former Amway distributors for spreading falsehoods about Procter & Gamble's involvement in Satanism.[30] Boycotts of Procter and Gamble were one predictable, and possibly intended, response to the Satanism conspiracy theories: Procter and Gamble is, after all, a direct competitor with Amway. Another characteristic that conspiracy theories share with propaganda is that both may include appeals to history and tradition as a way to win over those they target. Conspiracy theories warning that English is being systematically replaced by other languages will often invoke the United States' history as an English-speaking country while ignoring the fact that the United States has, historically, always been home to large and varied non-English-speaking communities, both immigrant and Native American.

Repetition Makes It So

For individual conspiracy theories, but even more so for conspiracist ideation writ large, repetition makes it so. As mentioned in chapter 2, the cognitive bias known as the *availability cascade* leads people to more readily accept the credibility of a collective belief the more often it is repeated. The frequent repetition of UFO conspiracy theories—including via popular entertainment—normalizes the acceptance of those conspiracy theories as fact. Stories that the U.S. government conspires to hide aliens and alien technology in the Nevada desert's infamous Area 51 have been around since the 1950s and may be more widely believed now than they ever were in the past. Which raises an important, if obvious, point about conspiracy theories: their popularity, level of acceptance, or existence does not in any way change reality. Conspiracy theories about UFOs neither prove nor disprove the existence of UFOs. If, tomorrow morning, extraterrestrial aliens were to land a UFO in Times Square in broad daylight, walk down the ramp, and say, "Take us to your leader," it would not automatically validate every existing UFO conspiracy theory any more than the unexpected announcement of a new, nonpolluting engine that runs all day on a pint of seawater would validate every long-standing conspiracy theory claiming that Big Oil has been suppressing the invention of a practical water engine in order to line its corporate pockets.

Psychologically Manipulative

Conspiracy theories play to a wide variety of cognitive biases in addition to the availability cascade. Examples of cognitive biases often expressed by conspiracists include the following:

- *Backfire effect:* Evidenced when conspiracists adhere ever more tightly to a conspiracy theory despite being presented with evidence proving it to be a fantasy.
- *Confirmation bias:* Comes into play when conspiracists seek out only information that supports their existing beliefs while ignoring any contradictory evidence.
- *Reactance:* This cognitive bias, which drives a person to do the opposite of what others expect, is reflected in the tendency of conspiracists to position themselves as unique, free-thinking, antiestablishment iconoclasts who stand apart from the herdlike, brainwashed majority.
- *Hostile attribution bias:* Explains the conspiracist's tendency to see those who reject conspiracist ideation not merely as different, but as enemies who are either in on the conspiracy or have been brainwashed by the lies of the powerful establishment.

THE APPEAL OF CONSPIRACY THEORIES:
LIFE IS JUST . . . SO UNFAIR

For anyone able to step back from the sound and fury of conspiracy theories to see them for the fictions that they are, the universal question is, *"Why would anyone believe such utter nonsense?"* Before considering this question, it is necessary to acknowledge that even those who see themselves as above falling for a conspiracy theory may, in fact, have allowed a conspiracy theory or two to influence their worldview. After all, a stereotypical liberal who would not give the time of day to a conspiracy theory that positions environmentalists or Planned Parenthood as the enemy might not be so quick to dismiss a conspiracy theory in which the villain of the piece is a Wall Street investment bank or the National Rifle Association. Nobody is perfectly immune to the allure of conspiracy theories, though some have stronger immune systems than others. Among those who consider themselves more immune, there is a tendency to see adherents of conspiracy theories as uneducated, naïve, blinded by anger, and easily duped. This view of conspiracists is reflected in paternalistic calls to control content on social media as a means of preventing the gullible masses from being led down the path of conspiracist ideation. While gullibility and unsophisticated worldviews play a role in the allure of conspiracy theories, there is more to it than that. One appeal of conspiracy theories is that they offer escapist entertainment by functioning as a form of electronic folklore that brings some comfort, however cold, to those for whom the shifting economies and social norms of the Digital Age have brought the opposite of opportunity, ease, and sense of purpose. There are, in fact, many similarities between conspiracy theories and the kinds of folklore and urban legends in which the powerless triumph over the powerful. Just consider the narrative kinship between the folkloric story of Br'er Rabbit putting one over on Br'er Fox and the sort of modern-day conspiracy theory that makes adherents feel they have cleverly outsmarted the establishment by uncovering its dark conspiracies before they can be implemented.

Shared adherence to conspiracy theories permits alienated individuals to form digital communities in which they can share their fears, frustrations, and sense of loss with widely scattered, yet like-minded, strangers. In order to better understand what it is like to be part of a community of digital conspiracists, journalist Stuart Thompson spent three weeks as a lurker in a virtual community formed around shared adherence to a suite of QAnon conspiracy theories. Thompson's report of a tightknit, mutually supportive community held together by their shared hopes for a successful resolution to what they see as a massively unfair conspiracy to usurp American democracy provides a revealing look into the lives of conspiracists who do not conveniently fit the stereotype of *"people who believe such utter nonsense."*[31]

Digital technology may be the vector for the popular spread of conspiracy theories, but a prevailing sense of the unfairness of life—coupled with a perplexing loss of self-respect among those who find themselves on the wrong side of the widening gap between rich and poor, educated and uneducated, powerful and powerless—may be as much to blame as the technology itself.[32] Author Michael Lewis, perhaps best known for his books *Moneyball* (2003) and *The Blind Side* (2006), hosts a podcast series entitled "Against the Rules with Michael Lewis: Don't Pick Sides Unless It's My Side." The overarching theme of the first season of the series is that people in the United States no longer respect the referee, an establishment figure Lewis broadly defines as any human being whose job and/or purpose in life is to impart fairness into such aspects of ordinary life as economics, government, law, education, or sports. In considering the diminishing role of the referee in American life, Lewis' podcasts detail of a number of shockingly unfair real-life scenarios. The episode "The Magic Shoebox" exposes a technologically facilitated unfairness in the stock market.[33] The episode "The Seven Minute Rule" looks at, among other affronts to the concept of fairness, a student-loan system that operates more like organized crime than anything resembling a legitimate business operation.[34] Lewis' podcasts are both eye opening and, for anyone with a sense of fair play, disillusioning.

Although conspiracy theories are not the focus of Lewis' podcasts, the type of systemic, unrefereed unfairness he explores in "Against the Rules" helps to explain, at least in part, the appeal of conspiracy theories to that segment of the population that feels marginalized and disempowered by forces beyond their control. One function of a soul-satisfying conspiracy theory is to vindicate feelings, however vague, that the system is simply not fair. For anyone who feels victimized by systemic unfairness—and most people feel that way to one extent or another—there is a desire to be personally absolved of any blame for the failures and frustrations imposed on them by an unfeeling and unfair world. Conspiracy theories grant absolution by first removing any ambiguity about the existence of unfairness and then by removing any ambiguity about who is to blame for the unfairness. Looking at the world through the uncomplicated lens of conspiracist ideation, it becomes possible to say with absolute certainty, *"The system really is unfair. The problem lies not with me. The problem lies with . . . them."*

The problem lies, as well, with a world that is largely composed of unsatisfying shades of gray and frustratingly complex ambiguity. For example, in the podcast episode "The Magic Shoebox," Michael Lewis provides credible evidence that unscrupulous business interests profit from a technological loophole—in Lewis' words "a broken slot machine"—that allows those with wealth and influence to rake in vast sums of money from the stock market without enduring any of the risk faced by ordinary investors. Even worse, the well-connected few who have access to the broken slot machine are acquiring this money—lots and lots of money—at the expense of millions of ordinary people who have no idea there are cheaters in the house profiting off of their losses. As might be expected in a complex, shades-of-gray world, critics counter that Lewis (who has a master's of arts degree in economics and worked for a time as a broker for Solomon Brothers) does not fully understand the workings of the stock market and that what he presents as an unfair advantage offers no advantage at all and is, in fact, not only perfectly fair but beneficial to all concerned. Who are we supposed to believe? The writer Michael Lewis—who profits from telling a compelling story (one that his critics might characterize as muckraking)—or the captains of Wall Street—an elite club that profits handsomely from public confidence in the fundamental fairness of capitalist financial systems? Such messy real-world ambiguity is unsatisfying whether you see the stock market as a racket designed to help the rich get richer or as the perfectly level, self-regulating playing field of the free market.

The world as depicted in conspiracy theories, on the other hand, dispenses with complexity and ambiguity. Conspiracy theories present a sharp-focus, starkly black-and-white world in which good and evil, hero and villain, fair and unfair, right and wrong each form well-defined pairs of distinct polar opposites. Unlike ambiguous reality, conspiracy theories can serve up the type of absolute certainty we have become used to seeing in our popular entertainment. Whether you are intrigued by a juicy conspiracy theory or entertained by a gripping Hollywood action film, you don't need a PhD in media studies to follow the plot or tell the good guys from the bad.

For their narrative structure, conspiracy theories owe much to the familiar form of modern folklore that comprises the three-act structure of countless films and television shows:

- Act I: The Setup
- Act II: The Confrontation
- Act III: The Resolution

Tellingly, conspiracy theories generally provide only Act I and Act II:

Act I: The U.S. Navy accidentally shoots down a civilian airliner.
Act II: Vigilant citizens discover and expose the hidden truth to the world. And then . . . ?

A conspiracy theory rarely includes an Act III because a story that is left unresolved remains all the more engaging, much like a television soap opera that can go on for decades. Instead of a resolution, a compelling conspiracy theory provides a cliffhanger and, for many conspiracists, a call to adventure. The narrative structure of a typical conspiracy theory is very similar to the ending of *Star Wars: The Empire Strikes Back*, a film that functions as Act II of the original *Star Wars* trilogy. At the end of *The Empire Strikes Back*, Darth Vader and the forces of the Evil Empire appear to have fully triumphed over the plucky rebels; however, if Hollywood has taught us anything (and it certainly has) it is that there will be an Act III (namely, *Star Wars: Return of the Jedi*) in which the plucky rebels ultimately, unambiguously, and triumphantly resolve the conflict. As much as they borrow from the structure of film and television, the conspiracy theories that thrive in cyberspace borrow at least as much from the structure of videogames (which, themselves, borrow from film and television). Similar to a videogame, a compelling conspiracy theory sets up a situation and then launches willing conspiracists into an unresolved adventure. Both gamers and conspiracists vent their anger and disdain for their common enemy, strategize on how they will defeat the final boss, and form supportive communities based on shared knowledge and jargon of which the outside world remains largely ignorant. As with watching a film or playing a videogame, the demands made by a conspiracy theory are, typically, not very taxing in real-world terms. Rather than being asked to leave your moisture farm and travel across the galaxy to confront truly dangerous opponents, preparation for a yet-to-be-launched Act III of any conspiracy theory can be, with rare exceptions, managed without getting out of your chair. Liking a tweet, adding your two cents to a long string of like-minded comments, forwarding a post, and talking smack about all the courage you will display when the time comes for action are small prices to pay for buying into an engaging conspiracy theory that can provide as much vindication, clarity, sense of community, emotional stimulation, and straight-up pleasure as any film or videogame.

With rare exceptions, adherents to conspiracy theories remain permanently stuck at the end of Act II, impatiently, excitedly, sometimes vibrantly waiting for a call to action to be followed by a heroic, triumphant, and definitive resolution. That said, history shows that, on those occasions when conspiracists are moved to actively bring about a resolution, Act III is more often a tragedy than a happy ending—more often a witch hunt, a *Kristallnacht*, or a lynching than an event worth celebrating. The men and women who stormed the U.S. Capitol building on January 6, 2021, while wearing QAnon garb were quite publicly seeking an Act III resolution to what they saw as a wicked conspiracy to cheat their admired leader out of the presidency. Just because most conspiracy theories do not result in concrete actions does not mean that some conspiracy theories cannot spill over into the real world to produce real consequences.

CAN ANYTHING BE DONE ABOUT THE SPREAD OF CONSPIRACY THEORIES?

If you take the point of view that digital technology, especially in the form of social media, is the main vector for the spread of conspiracy theories, one solution logically lies in establishing some level of control over that vector. An example of this approach surfaced in the in the aftermath of the storming of the U.S. Capitol Building when Twitter controversially blocked the account of former U.S. President Donald Trump along with tens of thousands of other accounts tied to the spreading of conspiracy theories (most notably theories surrounding the results of the 2020 U.S. presidential election). The ban drew immediate criticism from civil libertarians and drove some Trump supporters—conspiracists or not—to alternative social media platforms that cater to their political stances. Taking a different approach from the social media companies, voting-machine manufacturers Dominion and Smartmatic filed civil lawsuits against individuals and news outlets that the companies claim defamed them by spreading conspiracy theories about their voting machines during and following the 2020 U.S. elections.[35] In addition to actions by corporations and civil lawsuits, there have been calls for government regulation to control social media.[36] For conspiracists, any attempts to control social media merely confirm beliefs that the all-powerful establishment is out to silence its underdog opponents by any means possible. The long-term effect of punitive or regulatory actions taken against conspiracists by private businesses or governments remains to be seen. Conspiracy theories may continue to spread despite corporate and regulatory attempts to control them. Alternatively, the circulation of conspiracy theories may become limited to a smaller, if significant, group of devoted adherents—a Digital Age variation on the conspiracist photocopies that once circulated mostly among those who were already committed adherents.

As with any form of noncredible information, the struggle to limit the damage caused by conspiracy theories depends as much, if not more, on the actions of individuals than on the actions of for-profit business interests and governments. Remembering that people are more sensitive to a possible threat when they believe that they (and the things they value) are in the crosshairs as opposed to when the crosshairs appear to be on someone else (and the things others value), each of us can strive to be better at recognizing conspiracy theories when we see them (even if they happen to speak to our own hopes and fears) and on not passing them along as factual information. As hard as it can be to keep oneself from falling for a conspiracy theory, convincing someone who has adopted a strongly conspiracist ideation that they have gone down a mental rabbit hole is much, much harder. When a person has committed to belief in conspiracy theories, the social and psychological forces at work can make that person's mind impervious to rational arguments as well as to even the most indisputable of facts. In extreme cases, taking on a conspiracist ideation is comparable to joining a cult, and, once joined, a cult is rarely easy to leave. Tim Harford has suggested that instead of countering conspiracists' beliefs with facts which conspiracists have a priori rejected as false, a more productive path is to challenge conspiracists' to explain the factual bases of their beliefs.[37] Mustering a defense of one's own unfounded beliefs is a much greater challenge than simply parrying every attack with the durable shield of circular reasoning. Similarly, if conspiracists ask that others be skeptical of accepted knowledge, it is not at all unfair to ask those same conspiracists to be equally skeptical of the stigmatized knowledge in which they believe and would have others believe as well. *"If I am a gullible fool to believe that destruction of TWA 800 was an accident, please explain to me why you are not a gullible fool for believing it was shot down by a missile?"*

Somewhat alarmingly, the psychological forces at work in the spread of conspiracy theories may be even stronger than the already powerful influence exerted by cognitive biases. There is growing evidence that conspiracist ideation is a reflection of a mental health crisis made worse by such pressures as economic uncertainty, substance abuse, and post-traumatic stress disorder.[38] Compounding the problem is the relentlessness and speed of technological change. While it may turn out that the best way to rein in the spread of conspiracy theories is to improve access to mental health services, that is not to argue that everyone who believes in a conspiracy theory should be written off as mentally ill. Indeed, the writing off of large groups of people on the basis of such factors as poverty, race, lack of education, lack of opportunity, or religious beliefs has likely contributed significantly to the spread of conspiracy theories in the United States and around the world. Why would anyone willingly go along with the accepted knowledge when those who present themselves as the creators and stewards of that knowledge treat you—and those like you—as something less than fully human? If anything, the struggle to rein in the spread of conspiracy theories requires more all-around patience and empathy from all concerned, not less. We could all do a much better job of not thinking the worst of those with whom we disagree, of resisting the urge to dismiss the humanity of those for whom conspiracy theories provide some sense of control in a world that often makes, to them, little sense.

NOTES

1. National Transportation Safety Board, "Aircraft Accident Report: In-Flight Breakup Over the Atlantic Ocean Trans World Airlines Flight 800 Boeing 747-131, N93119 Near East Moriches, New York, July 17, 1996" (Washington, DC: National Transportation Safety Board, August 23, 2000), xvi, https://www.ntsb.gov/investigations/AccidentReports/Reports/AAR0003.pdf.

2. Skip Hollandsworth, "The Lost Boys," *Texas Monthly*, April 2011, https://www.texasmonthly.com/articles/the-lost-boys/.

3. Timothy Melley, *Empire of Conspiracy: The Culture of Paranoia in Postwar America* (Ithaca, NY: Cornell University Press, 2000), 28.

4. Oxford University Press, "Conspiracy, n.," *OED Online*, accessed February 10, 2021, https://www.oed.com/view/Entry/39766.

5. Karl Raimund Popper, *The Open Society and Its Enemies* (Princeton: Princeton University Press, 1950), 287.

6. Popper, 287–88.

7. David Robert Grimes, "On the Viability of Conspiratorial Beliefs," *PLOS ONE* 11, no. 1 (January 26, 2016): e0147905.

8. Larry B. Stammer, "Environment Radicals Target of Probe into Lumber Mill Accident," *Los Angeles Times*, May 15, 1987, 3, 22.

9. *The Week*, "The Conspiracy Theories behind the BP Oil Spill," July 13, 2010, https://www.theweek.co.uk/13253/conspiracy-theories-behind-bp-oil-spill.

10. Sarah Hall, John Mitchell, and Brian Steinwascher, "The Evolution of Criminal Conspiracy Law and 'Flipping the Script' in United States v. Elizabeth Holmes," *The Champion*, April 2020, 42, https://www.thompsonhine.com/uploads/1137/doc/Hall-Mitchell_Steinwascher_USvHolmes_April_2020_Champion_web-10.pdf.

11. Karl R. Popper, *The Logic of Scientific Discovery* (New York: Basic Books, 1959), 41.

12. Pat Milton, "FBI Denies Newsman's Claim Navy Missile Shot Down TWA Flight 800," *AP NEWS*, November 8, 1996, https://apnews.com/article/7411e8c7cc0a61445574074924828dc8.

13. Garth S. Jowett and Victoria J. O'Donnell, *Propaganda & Persuasion*, seventh edition (Thousand Oaks: Sage Publications, 2018).

14. Thomas Milan Konda, *Conspiracies of Conspiracies: How Delusions Have Overrun America* (Chicago: University of Chicago Press, 2019), 2.

15. Patricia A. Turner, "Church's Fried Chicken and The Klan: A Rhetorical Analysis of Rumor in the Black Community," *Western Folklore* 46, no. 4 (October 1987): 294–306.

16. Melley, 1–4.

17. Meredith Blake, "QAnon HBO Docuseries Asks Who Is Q? And May Have the Answer," *Los Angeles Times*, March 28, 2021, https://www.latimes.com/entertainment-arts/tv/story/2021-03-28/qanon-docuseries-hbo-who-is-q.

18. James Shanahan, "Support for QAnon is Hard to Measure—And Polls May Overestimate It," *The Conversation*, accessed March 5, 2021, http://theconversation.com/support-for-qanon-is-hard-to-measure-and-polls-may-overestimate-it-156020.

19. Observatory on Social Media, "Tracking Public Opinion About Unsupported Narratives in the 2020 Presidential Election" (Bloomington, IN: Indiana Observatory on Social Media, 2020), 2–3, http://osome.iu.edu/research/survey/files/FinalSummary_UnsupportedNarratives_OSoMe.pdf.

20. Michael Barkun, *Culture of Conspiracy: Apocalyptic Visions in Contemporary America*, second edition (Berkeley, CA: University of California Press, 2013), 6.

21. Jesse Walker, *The United States of Paranoia: A Conspiracy Theory* (New York: Harper, 2013), 16.

22. Claire Taylor, "Judge Rules Lafayette Lawsuit over Fake Antifa Events May Proceed," *The Acadiana Advocate*, March 19, 2021, https://www.theadvocate.com/acadiana/news/article_25de7782-88f5-11eb-9608-e76b08bac4a0.html.

23. *The Florida Times-Union*, "Fact Check: The Truth about Those 'FEMA Coffins,'" February 4, 2014, https://www.jacksonville.com/article/20140204/NEWS/801258710.

24. David D. Perlmutter and Nicole Smith Dahmen, "(In)Visible Evidence: Pictorially Enhanced Disbelief in the Apollo Moon Landings," *Visual Communication* 7, no. 2 (May 1, 2008): 240.

25. National Transportation Safety Board, 248.

26. Ben Macintyre, "Operation Labour: How Soviet Spooks Infiltrated the Left; Wilson and Corbyn Are Just Two of the Leading Figures of British Socialism Who Have Struggled to Escape the Shadow of the Red Spy Network, Writes Ben Macintyre," *The Times* [London, England], February 24, 2018, 34–35.

27. Mark Mazzetti et al., "A Riveting ISIS Story, Told in a Times Podcast, Falls Apart," *The New York Times*, December 18, 2020, https://www.nytimes.com/2020/12/18/world/middleeast/caliphate-chaudhry-hoax.html.

28. Tim Harford, "What Conspiracy Theorists Don't Believe," *The Atlantic*, March 16, 2021, https://www.theatlantic.com/ideas/archive/2021/03/the-conspiracy-theorists-problem-isnt-what-they-believe/618285/.

29. Richard Hofstadter, "The Paranoid Style in American Politics," *Harper's Magazine*, November 1964, https://harpers.org/archive/1964/11/the-paranoid-style-in-american-politics/.

30. "Procter & Gamble Wins $19 Million in Satanism Suit," *The New York Times*, March 20, 2017, https://www.nytimes.com/2007/03/20/business/worldbusiness/20iht-satan.4966053.html.

31. Stuart A. Thompson, "Opinion: Three Weeks Inside a Pro-Trump QAnon Chat Room," *The New York Times*, January 26, 2021, https://www.nytimes.com/interactive/2021/01/26/opinion/trump-qanon-washington-capitol-hill.html.

32. Arie Kruglanski, "How the Quest for Significance and Respect Underlies the White Supremacist Movement, Conspiracy Theories and a Range of Other Problems," *The Conversation*, accessed March 11, 2021, http://theconversation.com/how-the-quest-for-significance-and-respect-underlies-the-white-supremacist-movement-conspiracy-theories-and-a-range-of-other-problems-156027.

33. Michael Lewis, "The Magic Shoebox," *Against the Rules with Michael Lewis*, accessed February 18, 2021, https://atrpodcast.com/episodes/the-magic-shoebox-s1!33643.

34. Michael Lewis, "The Seven Minute Rule," *Against the Rules with Michael Lewis,* accessed February 18, 2021, https://atrpodcast.com/episodes/the-seven-minute -rule-s1!1c964.

35. Grace Dean and Shamsian Jacob, "From Rudy Giuliani to Fox News, Here's Everyone Dominion and Smartmatic Are Suing over Election Conspiracy Theories so Far," *Business Insider,* March 28, 2021, https://www.businessinsider.com/everyone -dominion-smartmatic-suing-defamation-election-conspiracy-theories-2021-2.

36. Dipayan Ghosh, "Are We Entering a New Era of Social Media Regulation?" *Harvard Business Review,* January 14, 2021, https://hbr.org/2021/01/are-we-entering -a-new-era-of-social-media-regulation.

37. Harford.

38. Sophia Moskalenko, "Many QAnon Followers Report Having Mental Health Diagnoses," *The Conversation,* accessed March 26, 2021, http://theconversation.com/ many-qanon-followers-report-having-mental-health-diagnoses-157299.

BIBLIOGRAPHY

Barkun, Michael. *Culture of Conspiracy: Apocalyptic Visions in Contemporary America.* Second edition. Berkeley, CA: University of California Press, 2013.

Blake, Meredith. "QAnon HBO Docuseries Asks Who Is Q? And May Have the Answer." *Los Angeles Times,* March 28, 2021. https://www.latimes.com/ entertainment-arts/tv/story/2021-03-28/qanon-docuseries-hbo-who-is-q.

Dean, Grace, and Jacob Shamsian. "From Rudy Giuliani to Fox News, Here's Every-one Dominion and Smartmatic Are Suing over Election Conspiracy Theories so Far." *Business Insider,* March 28, 2021. https://www.businessinsider.com/every-one-dominion-smartmatic-suing-defamation-election-conspiracy-theories-2021-2.

Ghosh, Dipayan. "Are We Entering a New Era of Social Media Regulation?" *Har-vard Business Review,* January 14, 2021. https://hbr.org/2021/01/are-we-entering -a-new-era-of-social-media-regulation.

Grimes, David Robert. "On the Viability of Conspiratorial Beliefs." *PLOS ONE* 11, no. 1 (January 26, 2016): e0147905.

Hall, Sarah, John Mitchell, and Brian Steinwascher. "The Evolution of Criminal Con-spiracy Law and 'Flipping the Script' in United States v. Elizabeth Holmes." *The Champion,* April 2020, 34–44. https://www.thompsonhine.com/uploads/1137/doc/ Hall-Mitchell_Steinwascher_USvHolmes_April_2020_Champion_web-10.pdf.

Harford, Tim. "What Conspiracy Theorists Don't Believe." *The Atlantic,* March 16, 2021. https://www.theatlantic.com/ideas/archive/2021/03/the-conspiracy-theorists -problem-isnt-what-they-believe/618285/.

Hofstadter, Richard. "The Paranoid Style in American Politics." *Harper's Maga-zine,* November 1964. https://harpers.org/archive/1964/11/the-paranoid-style-in -american-politics/.

Hollandsworth, Skip. "The Lost Boys." *Texas Monthly,* April 2011. https://www .texasmonthly.com/articles/the-lost-boys/.

Jowett, Garth S., and Victoria J. O'Donnell. *Propaganda & Persuasion.* Seventh edition. Thousand Oaks: Sage Publications, 2018.

Konda, Thomas Milan. *Conspiracies of Conspiracies: How Delusions Have Overrun America.* Chicago: University of Chicago Press, 2019.

Kruglanski, Arie. "How the Quest for Significance and Respect Underlies the White Supremacist Movement, Conspiracy Theories and a Range of Other Problems." *The Conversation.* Accessed March 11, 2021, http://theconversation.com/how-the-quest-for-significance-and-respect-underlies-the-white-supremacist-movement-conspiracy-theories-and-a-range-of-other-problems-156027.

Lewis, Michael. *The Blind Side: Evolution of a Game.* New York: W. W. Norton, 2007.

Lewis, Michael. "The Magic Shoebox." *Against the Rules with Michael Lewis.* Accessed February 18, 2021, https://atrpodcast.com/episodes/the-magic-shoebox-s1!33643.

Lewis, Michael. *Moneyball: The Art of Winning an Unfair Game.* First edition. New York: W. W. Norton, 2003.

Lewis, Michael. "The Seven Minute Rule." *Against the Rules with Michael Lewis.* Accessed February 18, 2021, https://atrpodcast.com/episodes/the-seven-minute-rule-s1!1c964.

Macintyre, Ben. "Operation Labour: How Soviet Spooks Infiltrated the Left; Wilson and Corbyn Are Just Two of the Leading Figures of British Socialism Who Have Struggled to Escape the Shadow of the Red Spy Network, Writes Ben Macintyre." *The Times* [London, England], February 24, 2018.

Mazzetti, Mark, Ian Austen, Graham Bowley, and Malachy Browne. "A Riveting ISIS Story, Told in a Times Podcast, Falls Apart." *The New York Times,* December 18, 2020. https://www.nytimes.com/2020/12/18/world/middleeast/caliphate-chaudhry-hoax.html.

Melley, Timothy. *Empire of Conspiracy: The Culture of Paranoia in Postwar America.* Ithaca, NY: Cornell University Press, 2000.

Milton, Pat. "FBI Denies Newsman's Claim Navy Missile Shot Down TWA Flight 800." *AP NEWS,* November 8, 1996. https://apnews.com/article/7411e8c7cc0a61445574074924828dc8.

Moskalenko, Sophia. "Many QAnon Followers Report Having Mental Health Diagnoses." *The Conversation.* Accessed March 26, 2021, http://theconversation.com/many-qanon-followers-report-having-mental-health-diagnoses-157299.

National Transportation Safety Board. "Aircraft Accident Report: In-Flight Breakup Over the Atlantic Ocean Trans World Airlines Flight 800 Boeing 747-131, N93119 Near East Moriches, New York, July 17, 1996." Washington, DC: National Transportation Safety Board, August 23, 2000. https://www.ntsb.gov/investigations/AccidentReports/Reports/AAR0003.pdf.

Observatory on Social Media. "Tracking Public Opinion About Unsupported Narratives in the 2020 Presidential Election." Bloomington, IN: Indiana Observatory on Social Media, 2020. http://osome.iu.edu/research/survey/files/FinalSummary_UnsupportedNarratives_OSoMe.pdf.

Oxford University Press. "Conspiracy, n." *OED Online*. Accessed February 10, 2021, https://www.oed.com/view/Entry/39766.

Perlmutter, David D., and Nicole Smith Dahmen. "(In)Visible Evidence: Pictorially Enhanced Disbelief in the Apollo Moon Landings." *Visual Communication* 7, no. 2 (May 1, 2008): 229–51.

Popper, Karl Raimund. *The Open Society and Its Enemies*. Princeton: Princeton University Press, 1950.

Shanahan, James. "Support for QAnon is Hard to Measure—and Polls May Overestimate It." *The Conversation*. Accessed March 5, 2021, http://theconversation.com/support-for-qanon-is-hard-to-measure-and-polls-may-overestimate-it-156020.

Stammer, Larry B. "Environment Radicals Target of Probe into Lumber Mill Accident." *Los Angeles Times*, May 15, 1987.

Taylor, Claire. "Judge Rules Lafayette Lawsuit over Fake Antifa Events May Proceed." *The Acadiana Advocate*, March 19, 2021. https://www.theadvocate.com/acadiana/news/article_25de7782-88f5-11eb-9608-e76b08bac4a0.html.

The Florida Times-Union. "Fact Check: The Truth about Those 'FEMA Coffins.'" February 4, 2014. https://www.jacksonville.com/article/20140204/NEWS/801258710.

The New York Times. "Procter & Gamble Wins $19 Million in Satanism Suit." March 20, 2017. https://www.nytimes.com/2007/03/20/business/worldbusiness/20iht-satan.4966053.html.

The Week. "Conspiracy Theories behind the BP Oil Spill, The." *The Week*, July 13, 2010. https://www.theweek.co.uk/13253/conspiracy-theories-behind-bp-oil-spill.

Thompson, Stuart A. "Opinion: Three Weeks Inside a Pro-Trump QAnon Chat Room." *The New York Times*, January 26, 2021. https://www.nytimes.com/interactive/2021/01/26/opinion/trump-qanon-washington-capitol-hill.html.

Turner, Patricia A. "Church's Fried Chicken and The Klan: A Rhetorical Analysis of Rumor in the Black Community." *Western Folklore* 46, no. 4 (October 1987): 294–306.

Walker, Jesse. *The United States of Paranoia: A Conspiracy Theory*. New York: Harper, 2013.

8

The Powerful Influence of Popular Culture— Amplified by Digital Technology— On the Post-Truth Culture

Chapter 2 of this book considers Amos Tversky and Daniel Kahneman's concept of heuristics and their finding that people are attracted to heuristics because they provide uncomplicated strategies for quick decision making that do not result in cognitive overload (i.e., too much thinking) and do not require consideration of all the available evidence. Tversky and Kahneman are highly mathematical in their approach, focusing on how people who either do not understand statistics or cannot be bothered to "do the math" employ heuristics as shortcuts for numerical decisions making. For example, people use heuristics to make financial decisions that, in most cases, should be made on the basis of a thorough mathematical analysis rather than on the mere approximation possible with a heuristic. The purpose of this chapter is to consider how nonmathematical social and cultural approximations—in the form of heuristics transmitted via popular culture—shape thinking and decision making in the post-truth culture. While the popular culture heuristics swarming the post-truth culture can be helpful, even necessary, in that they can approximate what would be known if a person took the time to consider more than just a few key facts and points of evidence and to think through what all the available information adds up to, popular culture heuristics provide, at best, only approximations of reality. At their worst, these heuristics are far off the mark and contribute to the kind of extreme and unrealistic thinking that has come to characterize the excesses of the post-truth culture.

LIONS, DONKEYS, AND MR. CHAMBERLAIN

If you set out to study the history of the First World War at anything more than a superficial level, the phrase "lions led by donkeys" will come to your attention soon enough. The idea conveyed by this phrase can be summarized as follows: The British General Staff of the First World War, "the Donkeys," was composed of rigidly unimaginative men from the stuffy upper classes. Harboring a callous disregard for the lives of the troops serving under them and operating under the delusion that endlessly repeating the woefully out-dated strategies and tactics of nineteenth-century warfare would ultimately prevail on battlefields dominated by sophisticated twentieth-century weap-ons, the Donkeys futilely dispatched wave after wave of unimaginably brave foot soldiers, "the Lions," to be cut down by entrenched machine guns or blown to pieces by long-range artillery.

While the phrase "lions led by donkeys" predates the First World War and regularly turns up in the years following the war, its popularity as a framing device for the history of the First World War really took hold with the 1961 publication of *The Donkeys*, a work of revisionist history by British author Alan Clark (1928–1999).[1] Thanks to the commercial success of *The Donkeys* (as of 2021, the book remains in print), a succession of popular culture books, articles, films, and television programs have gone on to embrace, expand, and mythologize the theory. The 1969 British film *Oh! What a Lovely War*, which incorporates period songs as it criticizes the horrors of the First World War, employs lions-led-by-donkeys as a recurring theme. Twenty years later, the British television series *Blackadder Goes Forth* (1989) similarly relied on lions-led-by-donkeys as the source for much of its dark humor.

I remember enjoying *Oh! What a Lovely War*, and I later became (and remain) a fan of *Blackadder Goes Forth*. For much of my adult life, my understanding of the history of the First World War conformed to the lions-led-by-donkeys theory. Eventually, however, my understanding of the war underwent a change. Somewhere along the line I read *The Guns of August*, an essential scholarly book on the outbreak of the First World War written by historian Barbara W. Tuckman (1912–1989).[2] Tuckman's book inspired me to read other scholarly histories of the war. To my surprise, I discovered that serious historians regard the lions-led-by-donkeys trope as a superficial, grossly exaggerated oversimplification. While essentially all serious histori-ans agree that British military leaders, as well as their counterparts from the other warring nations, made some monumentally costly blunders—especially early in the war—the scholarly consensus is that the senior British generals learned from their mistakes and, despite their culturally entrenched biases in favor of outdated horse cavalry tactics, came to embrace innovation and adopt new tactics, strategies, and weapons, including the entirely new technological innovations of the tank and airplane.

As is the case with the First World War, the Second World War offers examples of popular culture theories that have become fixtures in the popular mind despite straying quite far from the known historical facts. One such example is the popular assessment of British Prime Minster Neville Chamberlain (1869–1940), which can be summed up as follows: Desperately seeking to avoid war at any cost, in September 1938 Prime Minister Chamberlain signed the Munich Agreement, a pact giving Germany free reign to march into and take control of the German-speaking parts of Northern Czechoslovakia. Emboldened by Chamberlain's show of weakness, German Chancellor Adolf Hitler (1889–1945) went on to undertake ever-more ambitious conquests that eventually resulted in the deaths of millions. If only Chamberlain had shown some backbone by flexing Britain's military muscle instead of resorting to appeasement through diplomacy, Hitler could have been, at minimum, stopped sooner; in the best case, the Second World War might have been avoided entirely.

Following the Second World War, the blame-Chamberlain theory came to be popularly regarded as historical gospel. Even today, politicians and pundits seeking to justify the use of military force will invoke Chamberlain's name as a shorthand way of branding as a naïve coward any politician who stands in opposition to the use of force.[3] The blame-Chamberlain theory is on display in the Academy-Award-winning 2017 film *Darkest Hour*, a worshipful, significantly fictionalized, biography of Winston Churchill. Predictably, in lionizing Churchill the creators of *Darkest Hour* take considerable historical liberties, including inaccurately portraying Chamberlain as seeking a negotiated peace long after the declaration of war against Germany—a declaration initially called for, if arguably too late, by Chamberlain himself.

As with the lions-led-by-donkeys interpretation of the First World War, there is more to the story than the blame-Chamberlain theory would have it. Hitler *might* have backed down if only Chamberlain had manned up and threatened war, but it is equally possible that Hitler would have marched down the path of conquest regardless of any threats. The blame-Chamberlain theory also overlooks the fact that Chamberlain was more aware than most of his critics (especially his latter-day critics) that the economically depressed Britain of 1938 needed time to rebuild its military if it were to have a chance succeeding against the much larger and better equipped German military.[4] As Chamberlain biographer Robert C. Self describes it: "In retrospect, Chamberlain's optimism about Hitler's good intentions in the wake of Munich appears to be facile and naïve. But in fairness, it is important to emphasize this never precluded support for what he considered to be necessary defensive rearmament."[5] While nobody would give Chamberlain an A+ for his handling of Hitler, his grade is much closer to a B–/C+ than the hard F his critics (most of them influenced by the facile conclusions reached by the blame-Chamberlain theory) universally assign to his performance.

How is it possible that conclusions reached via overly simplified theo-ries—heuristic shortcuts—about complex historical events have the power to shape thinking to the point that, decades after the fact, these theories remain capable of influencing real-world decisions? For just as hawks still invoke Chamberlain's appeasement of Hitler to advocate for war, doves still invoke a lions-led-by-donkeys scenario to advocate for peace. One reason that overly simplified interpretations of history have such long lives is that there is sig-nificant money to be made from popular culture's "History Lite" industry. Year after year, Hollywood manages to turn out a handful of based-on-actual-events historical entertainments—some more loosely based on the known facts than others—that sell tickets and win awards. Similarly, books that cherry-pick facts to offer up easily digested popular culture theories of what the past can tell us about the present sell well. For an example of relevance to the blame-Chamberlain theory, British Prime Minister Boris Johnson's hagi-ographic biography of Winston Churchill, *The Churchill Factor: How One Man Made History*, was a popular culture bestseller in the United Kingdom as well as abroad.[6] Television is part of the History Lite industry, with the parent company of History (formerly The History Channel) and its stable of cable television and social media spin-offs enjoying earnings of $694.46 million for the fiscal year ending in 2020.[7] History Lite is a profitable industry due to its heuristic approach, which features easily digestible conclusions and the avoidance of the messy ambiguity that comes with serious historical inquiry.

History Lite also appeals to its audience through its tendency to confirm existing biases, a trait it has in common with conspiracy theories. For any-one holding a class-warfare grudge against hereditary wealth and privilege, the lions-led-by-donkeys theory confirms that bias quite nicely. For anyone who sees life as an endless series of conflicts in which only the strong sur-vive, the blame-Chamberlain theory strongly confirms that bias. In addition to appealing to confirmation biases, History Lite also invokes the cognitive bias of the availability cascade by endlessly repeating facile conclusions until they seem perfectly credible. If you hear enough times that *"The lives of the slaves on plantations weren't that bad"* or *"Officials at Ellis Island randomly changed immigrants' last names to sound more American,"* then these and other History Lite sound bites can become established truths even without having actual historical evidence to back them up. Even the topics favored by History Lite—with its focus on war, crime, disasters, and celebrity—are chosen because they lend themselves to easy simplification, effortless com-prehension, straight-line causes and effects, and clearly distinguished heroes and villains. History Lite generally avoids the more complex, less sensational areas of historical inquiry, such as cultural history, economic history, intellec-tual history, and social history. If you are looking to profit by selling history as popular culture entertainment, sensational treatments of the Battle of the Bulge or the crimes of Ted Bundy (1946–1989) are always going to be safer bets than, say, a thorough examination of the social and economic impacts of U.S. Federal Housing Administration loan practices from the New Deal to the end of the Clinton administration.

History Lite is not the only output of popular culture filling the post-truth culture with heuristics. It is common to encounter facile approximations touching on not only history, but also politics, ideology, religion, science, education culture, love, sex, economics, language, entertainment, race, class—pretty much the gamut of human activities and interests. Tweets and memes are prefect examples of heuristic communications, being both approximate and low in cognitive load. Rule 34 is long-standing internet axiom that says something to the effect of, *"If it exists, there is online pornography about it."* If there is not yet such an axiom, there should be one that says something to the effect of, *"If it exists in human society, there are heuristics about it."* The omnipresence and popularity of heuristics does not mean that present-day people are more gullible or more intellectually lazy than people who came before. Heuristics are at least as old as the first stereotypes about that noisy band of humanoids from the other side of the ravine. The difference today is that technology allows so much information to be thrown at us from so many quarters that the approximations and convenient mental shortcuts offered up by heuristics have become the most practical, albeit imperfect, way to manage information overload and attain some measure of control over the cognitive dissonance induced by all the voices staking conflicting claims to truth and authority. Even though heuristics may offer some respite from the noise of the post-truth culture, it is important to be aware that the approximations they offer up are more the cause of the post-truth retreat from facts, truth, and reality than they are a solution to the problem to too much information moving too quickly.

HEURISTICS AND PROPAGANDA: A REMARKABLE RESEMBLANCE

As someone who, for many years, glibly accepted lions-led-by-donkeys as factually sound historical interpretation, I know how easy it is to not recognize a heuristic for the approximation that it is. As someone who writes about information and its impact on people, I worry that I am not only a sometimes-unaware consumer of heuristics, but also a potential purveyor of approximations dressed up as sound conclusions. I certainly encourage every reader to question the validity of any and all of my conclusions, including my thesis regarding the role of heuristics in the creation of the post-truth culture. One reason it is so easy for anyone, including me, to not recognize a heuristic when presented with one is that heuristics have become so numerous and widespread in the Digital Age as to become invisible to the naked eye, a circumstance that calls to mind a parable related in the opening paragraphs of "This Is Water" by American author David Foster Wallace (1962–2008):

> There are these two young fish swimming along and they happen to meet an older fish swimming the other way, who nods at them and says, "Morning, boys. How's the water?" And the two young fish swim on for a bit, and then eventually one of them looks over at the other and goes, "What the hell is water?"[8]

By being everywhere yet invisible, heuristics resemble the type of propaganda that is able to exert tremendous influence due to the fact that its prevalence allows it to hide in plain sight, undetectable as propaganda. This is not the only similarity heuristics shares with propaganda. Both propaganda and heuristics have the potential to exert a powerful influence, yet their influence is neither guaranteed nor absolute. To paraphrase the old cliché, propaganda and heuristics may influence some of the people all of the time or all of the people some of time, but never all of the people all of the time. It is also true that propaganda and heuristics share the characteristic of not being the exclusive property of any individual or group. Just as during the Cold War the world was subjected to both pro- and anti-Soviet propaganda, so too today it is common to encounter competing heuristics leading to contradictory conclusions. One clever meme can heuristically lead to the conclusion that there is nothing more important than reducing your carbon footprint, while a clever countermeme can lead to the conclusion that climate change is an unscientific conspiracy cooked up by enemies of the free market. And just as there can be beneficial propaganda, there are beneficial heuristics that, despite being mere approximations, nonetheless inspire individuals and societies to make better decisions than they otherwise would. There is, however, one crucial difference between propaganda and heuristics. While the powerful influence of propaganda is routinely discussed and loudly denounced (at times, by those who are themselves nothing more than propagandists), the equally powerful influence of heuristics is less well known, rarely discussed, and almost never denounced.

POPULAR CULTURE HEURISTICS

Popular culture is a complicated phenomenon to pin down. One common definition holds that popular culture is simply anything that happens to be popular. If enough people like something, then whatever it is they like is, by definition, popular culture. Under such a definition, the phrase *mass culture* may be used interchangeably with *popular culture*. A different, somewhat out-of-fashion definition of popular culture casts it as an expression of *low culture* that stands in contrast to an implicitly superior *high culture*. Under this definition, a television reality show would be considered low/popular culture, whereas productions of Shakespeare's *Macbeth* or *A Winter's Tale* would be considered high culture, the defining (and totally subjective) differ-ence being that high culture is seen as obtaining a level of artistic achieve-ment to which no work of low/popular culture could possibly aspire. Yet another interpretation of popular culture casts it as a corporate/elitist tool for distracting the masses and keeping them in line as obedient consumers. The view of popular culture as a force for oppression is reflected in the words of distinguish linguist and outspoken media critic Noam Chomsky who, when asked if television shows such as *Roseanne* (the original series that ran from 1988 to 1997) or *The Simpsons* could function as subversions of consumer culture, replied, "This isn't real popular culture, the real art of the people. This is just stuff which is served up to them to rot their minds. Real popular culture is folk art—coalminers' songs and so forth."[9] However it is defined or interpreted, popular culture is an area of research of serious interest to scholars representing such wide-ranging fields as media studies, sociology, psychology, musicology, literature, and political science. If the exact defini-tion of popular culture is a subject of debate, so too is what falls or does not fall under the heading of popular culture. For example, should film and televi-sion versions of Jane Austen's *Emma* or *Pride and Prejudice* be counted as examples of high culture by virtue of being based on eighteenth-century nov-els recognized as canonical works of British literature, or should all films and television shows be considered works of popular culture simply on the basis of the medium in which they appear? Is the 1996 film *Emma*, which is heavily based on the novel *Emma*, arguably a work of popular culture? Is the 1995 film *Clueless*, which is very loosely based on the novel *Emma*, *definitively* a work a popular culture? Even if there is room for debate about what is or is not popular culture, there is general agreement that popular culture, however defined, casts a powerful influence on present-day thought and behavior.

Before the existence of anything remotely resembling popular culture as it is understood in the present day, there was folk culture (what Chomsky identifies as authentic "real popular culture"). Folk culture existed, and still exists, in many traditional, usually localized forms, including songs, tales, dances, jokes, visual art, drama, foodways, clothing, and material goods. Forms of popular culture emerged from folk culture around the same time that capitalism, with its demands for commercial viability, was taking hold in Renaissance Europe. For example, though the plays of William Shakespeare

(1564–1616) reflect the influence of a folk culture that was still very much alive in Elizabethan England, they differ from folk plays by virtue of having been written, staged, and performed with the goal of earning a profit, something that would not have been true of, say, a medieval mystery play performed by amateurs for the religious edification of the local villagers. And even though I just referenced two Shakespeare plays as examples of high culture, for roughly a century and a half after they were first written and performed Shakespeare's plays were considered low (i.e., popular) culture. As pointed out in chapter 4, the first edition of Shakespeare's poetry (at the time considered high-culture art) was published with his name on the title page while his play *Romeo and Juliet* (at the time considered low-culture entertainment) was on its fourth printing before the author's name appeared on the title page. The fact is that Shakespeare's plays were not elevated to the status of literary art until they were taken up by high-culture champions in the second half of the eighteenth century.[10] The framing of popular culture as low culture persisted well into the twentieth century. For the average American or European in 1920, a popular jazz song would have been seen as work of low-culture entertainment having little or no artistic merit, while an aria from a Verdi opera would have been considered a work of high culture and therefore worthy of being called *art*. That the low/high divide is artificial is demonstrated by the fact that works of popular culture can be as authentic and artistic as any work deemed to be high culture. All but the snootiest of culture snobs will admit there are popular culture films, television programs, songs, and books that stand out as great works of art. Certainly, it would be hard to make the case that *Macbeth* or *A Winter's Tale* are not art because at one time they had been considered to be nothing more than low-culture entertainments. Even in the case of artificially manufactured popular culture phenomena such as the 1960s TV-friendly Beatles knockoff the Monkees or any of the current crop of "industry-plant" bands routinely called out on social media as examples of corporate cultural appropriation, there is always the possibility that some of the work produced by these manufactured acts is as authentic and as worthy of being called art as anything produced by artists whose career trajectories were not engineered by data analysts working out of corporate high-rises.

The low/high distinction may seem quaint today because it began fading away around the middle of the twentieth century, a time when the power of popular culture's social and economic influence was expanding far beyond previous boundaries. There were many forces behind the mid-twentieth-century growth of popular culture's power and influence, including increased leisure time, a rising middle class, and the spread of television into millions of homes around the world. Yet another force hastening the transformation of popular culture was what has been called the "invention of the teenager."[11] While the word *teenager* had not entered the language in its current sense until the 1940s, by the 1950s such social changes as post-war economic prosperity, smaller families, and the transference of most teenagers from the full-time workforce into high schools and colleges had created not only a teenage culture distinct from adult culture, but also a new economic force to be reckoned with and marketed to in ways, and to an extent, which would have been unimaginable only a single generation before.[12] That the concept of the teenager took root in the United States and then spread elsewhere reflects the fact that the post-war boom in popular culture was led by the United States, a nation which continues to be a major exporter of popular culture.

To employ a personal illustration of how the invention of teenagers contributed to the growth of popular culture, I found among a collection of letters from my mother to her sisters one that my mother wrote shortly after Elvis Presley's first appearance on the *Ed Sullivan Show* on September 9, 1956. In that letter, my mother comments on Presley's performance, writing that she did not think much of it, being neither scandalized nor particularly entertained. At the time she wrote that letter, my mother was a thirty-eight-year-old Army veteran of the Second World War, married, lower-middle-class, and the mother of two daughters, ages eight and ten. It was very likely that she knew about Elvis only because of television, and it is certain that she would never have seen him perform if not for his television appearances. Typical of most adults at that time, my mother would have never dreamed of paying money for an Elvis Presley recording and probably would not have walked across the street to see him perform for free, much less have plunked down money for a ticket. To most adults of that era, Elvis and rock and roll were popular culture kids' stuff, a concept that seems foreign in a present day where it is not at all unusual for adults to be ardent, informed, and opinionated fans of the latest trends in popular music and entertainment, not to mention it being completely acceptable for professional media critics and academic scholars to write about popular culture phenomena ranging from comic books to Beyoncé with all the attentive seriousness of an academic in the 1930s writing about the works Marcel Proust (1871–1922) or Wolfgang Amadeus Mozart (1756–1791). The late-twentieth and early twenty-first centuries' reevaluation of the importance of works of popular culture is best explained by the real driving force behind every aspect of popular culture: money. Each of Elvis' three appearances on the *Ed Sullivan Show*—two in fall of 1956 and one in January 1957—captured at least 80 percent of the total viewing audience, a lucrative ratings triumph that no advertiser could afford to ignore.[13] By way of comparison, the Super Bowl game played on February 1, 2015 (as of 2021, the most watched broadcast in the history of U.S. television) drew 71 percent of the total viewing audience.[14] Economically, what is most significant about Elvis' early and successful television appearances is that, at the time they occurred, a survey conducted on behalf of *Scholastic* magazine found there were thirteen million teenagers in the United States with a combined income (much of it discretionary) of seven billion dollars per year.[15] While translating what a dollar was worth in the past to its value in the present is far from an exact science, seven billion dollars in 1956 would approach something like $475 billion in 2021.

To state the obvious, the raw economic value of popular culture has only grown since the end of the Second World War. In 2019, the worldwide value of the entertainment and media market was $2.1 trillion, with that value estimated to grow to $2.5 trillion by 2024.[16] A handful of illustrative examples of the economic value of popular culture include:

- *Harry Potter* creator J.K. Rowling's total wealth in 2020 was estimated to be between $650 million and $1.2 billion.[17]
- Celebrity entrepreneur Kylie Jenner topped *Forbes*' list of the one hundred celebrities who earned the most money in 2020. In that year, Jenner earned $590 million, well ahead of her closest competitor (and former husband of her half-sister), musician and entrepreneur Kanye West, who earned a respectable $170 million.[18]
- In 2020, Facebook posted a net income of $29.15 billion for the year.[19]
- Despite 2019 being a "disappointing" year for signing up new subscribers, Netflix streaming service brought in around $4.9 billion in revenue for the year.[20]
- In 2020, the world's twenty-five most valuable sports teams were worth a combined ninety-three billion dollars.[21]

When Vannevar Bush was writing "As We May Think" in the closing months of the Second World War, his visionary scientific mind was able to imagine a future containing something very close to what would become the internet. It was entirely unlikely, however, that Bush could have imagined a popular-culture-dominated future in which being famous for being famous could earn one person over half a billion dollars in a single year or in which such low-culture (in the eyes of Bush's generation) comic-book characters as Captain America and Wonder Woman, both of whom debuted in 1941, would remain popular enough to serve as the foundations of film franchises enjoyed by a massive worldwide audience. Nor could Bush have imagined that the future's real-life version of the memex, his hypothetical tool for scientific and scholarly communication, would eventually serve as a platform for millions of would-be social media celebrities posting smartphone photographs and videos in the faint hope of reaping online wealth and celebrity (two concepts that are effectively inseparable in the currency of popular culture). The fact that a few of these dreamers actually manage to hit the wealth/ celebrity jackpot might very well make Bush's first-class brain explode like an overloaded starship computer in a popular culture space opera. Over the second half of the twentieth century, popular culture became far too profitable to be dismissed as a collection of inconsequential, low-culture amusements for children and the poor. The money to be made and the power to be wrung from popular culture, in all its forms, ensured not only its growth, but also its all-encompassing presence in, and influence on, daily life.

Popular culture exerts a powerful influence on the post-truth culture because it is the primary source of the heuristics consumed by millions of people around the world. Many of these heuristics, which might just as well be called "popular culture heuristics," originate from sources of popular culture entertainment, notably film and television, though other sources of popular culture heuristics include the written word (in fiction and nonfiction formats), visual art, music, theater, traditional media, social media, and politics (in all of its forms, including electoral politics, law, economic systems, and identity politics). Regardless of its source of origin, millions of people harbor beliefs and exhibit behaviors absorbed through exposure to the heuristics of popular culture.

ENTERTAINMENT AS A SOURCE OF POPULAR CULTURE HEURISTICS

A concept that turns up frequently in discussions of popular culture entertainment is the *trope*. The administrators of the TV Tropes wiki define a trope as "a narrative device or convention used in storytelling or production of a creative work."[22] While not exactly identical to a heuristic, tropes often behave in ways that are very similar to heuristics, acting as shortcuts that impose little or no cognitive load and deliver simplified messages that approximate reality. Because tropes are most commonly associated with popular culture entertainment, their main purpose is to influence decision making related to fictional works. When films and television shows present the initial meeting between two attractive characters as resulting in immediate dislike, often punctuating the scene with an exchange of insults, media-savvy viewers knows that they are seeing the trope known as "the meet cute" and will expect the characters to end up in a romance. Though harmless enough as storytelling conventions, popular culture tropes have a way finding their way into real life and influencing decisions that have actual consequences. After the 1993 film *Menace*

II Society featured characters firing semiautomatic pistols using a side grip, some real-world shooters began adopting the style.[23] While it may look cool and intimidating and serve as a shortcut way of identifying the shooter as an outlaw, the consensus of trained firearms experts is that holding a pistol sideways is a terrible idea for shooters who intend to hit what they are aiming at and not hit what they are not aiming at. The sideways pistol grip is just one example of a trope that, having made the leap from fiction into real life, turns out to be impractical if not dangerous.

As a visit to the exhaustive TV Tropes website will demonstrate, there are thousands of popular culture tropes, more than a few of which exert considerable influence in the real world. For example, influential tropes associated with the genre of the western in all its popular culture forms—including films, television, books, comic books, fashion, art, and music—would fill a good-sized volume. Anyone who has had more than a bit of exposure to popular culture is likely to be familiar with such western tropes as the white-hatted hero, the showdown at high noon, or the saloon in which a fight will almost without fail break out. The tropes of the western are so familiar that they often become the subject of parody, perhaps most notably in Mel Brooks' *Blazing Saddles* (1974), a film in which most of the humor arises from the audience's familiarity with all the standard tropes of the western. Evidence that the tropes of the western genre have extended their reach into the real world is all around. Food businesses like steakhouses and barbecue restaurants often adopt western themes to associate themselves with popular culture notions of cattle ranching and honest, no-nonsense American cooking. Sports teams such as the Dallas Cowboys, Texas Rangers, San Francisco 49ers, and Denver Broncos employ western tropes as part of their team names and images, while the public image of the entire sport of rodeo is deeply rooted in western tropes. The recreational activities of cowboy action shooting and mountain-man reenactments are both based on western tropes, including some tropes which have, at best, a tenuous relationship to historical facts. In 2019, still reeling after a series of corporate scandals, Well Fargo released an updated logo featuring a stagecoach in an obvious attempt to repair its tarnished image by reconnecting the company with its Old West origins.[24] Many country music performers adopt western clothing as part of their public image, and the wardrobe of U.S. President Ronald Regan famously included western-inspired fashions—cowboy hats, jeans, western-style shirts—as a way of associating his identity with such popular culture cowboy virtues as hard work, courage, and old-fashioned American values. There was at one time, and may still be, a popular bumper sticker displaying the song lyrics, "My heroes have always been cowboys" alongside an illustration of Reagan.

Another example of a popular culture entertainment genre that is a major source of tropes is the police procedural, in both its fictional and true crime formats. Popular culture tropes about police are so pervasive as to have taken on a semblance of reality for many. Millions of people who have never been arrested in their lives, including some people who have never set foot in the United States, can recite the Miranda warning as well as sworn police officers thanks to films and television shows about American police. Similarly, the notion that police in the United States are required to Mirandize all suspects immediately upon arrest has been widely spread by popular culture entertainments despite being fundamentally untrue. Police are required to issue a Miranda warning only if, as part of a criminal investigation, they "hope to or desire to use your statements as evidence against you."[25] Many other police-related tropes are widely accepted as facts in the popular imagination. Police and courtroom dramas often depict police lineups and courtroom finger pointing as moments of high drama even though, as discussed in chapter 2, real-life eyewitness testimony is far from reliable when it comes to identifying suspects. And despite popular culture depictions of fingerprint evidence as slam-dunk proof of guilt, a recent study involving 125 fingerprinting agencies found "false-positive error rates of 15.9% and 28.1% on two fingerprint [close non-matches]. This error rate is inconsistent with the popular notion that fingerprint evidence is nearly infallible."[26] Perhaps most disturbing of all is that a confession to a crime—a frequently depicted trope in popular culture police dramas and true crime entertainments—is not necessarily proof of guilt. In recent years, evidence has surfaced documenting the fact that an alarming number of seemingly voluntary confessions were actually false "police-induced confessions."[27] All of which leads to some unsettling questions: *"If you were on trial for a crime you did not commit, how comfortable would you be with the possibility that some of the people who have your fate in their hands—including police officers, attorneys, jury members, and even the trial judge—have been influenced by popular culture tropes relating to crime and criminal justice? How comfortable would you be with the knowledge that their decision making may be based as much on simplistic approximations gleaned from popular-culture heuristics as on the actual facts of the case?"*

SELF-AWARENESS IN POPULAR CULTURE

Befitting a skeptical philosophy that does not recognize the validity of fixed truths or assumed certainties, postmodernism all but demands an attitude of ironic self-awareness. While not all popular culture can be tagged with the postmodernist label, it is not hard to find examples of popular culture that make fun of themselves with a self-deprecating postmodernist wink. Self-referential, self-deprecating advertisements provide one example of postmodern irony at work in popular culture. In article published in the *International Journal of Advertising*, marketing theorist Paulie Boutlis writes, "Postmodernism sanctifies anything 'low,' done in 'bad taste' and thought unworthy of 'serious analysis.' In this sense, it is an invaluable (if underused) ally to advertising."[28] Boutlis then goes on to reference ironic "postmodernist" advertisements from such brands as Volkswagen, Sprite, Benneton, Coke, and Calvin Kline. An early example of ironic, self-deprecating advertising campaigns was the famous "We Try Harder" campaign, in which the Avis rental car company made a virtue of the fact that it was far smaller than Hertz, the nation's largest car rental company. The highly successful, entirely counterintuitive campaign was created and launched in 1962 by Paula Green (one possible inspiration for the character of Peggy Olson of AMC's *Mad Men*) and included slogans like, "When you're only No. 2, you try harder. Or else."[29] The appeal of the "We Try Harder" campaign and similar ironic, self-deprecating advertisements is their ability to bring jaded, media-savvy consumers in on the joke, assuring such consumers that, being too smart to fall for phony, self-important sales pitches, they are therefore capable of enjoying a bit of fun at the expense of stuffed-shirt traditionalists. All the while, of course, never forgetting to nudge those jaded, media-savvy consumers to buy whatever is being oh-so-ironically advertised.

Films and television shows can also display ironic self-awareness when they choose to make fun of their power to influence thinking, behavior, and personal identity. The television series *Barry* provides an excellent recent example of this. The main character of *Barry* is Barry Berkman, a reluctant professional hitman who, in an attempt to get out of the business of killing people for a living, enrolls in acting classes. In the episode "The Show Must Go On, Probably?" (2019), Barry's fellow acting students decide to dramatize what they interpret as the most traumatic event in Barry's life—the first time he took the life of another human being while serving as a Marine in Afghanistan. The class's improvised version of Barry's experience is completely over the top, with the student actor playing the part of Barry tearfully throwing himself to the ground after firing the fatal shot and the student actors playing Barry's fellow Marines going into histrionics as they comfort their emotionally devasted comrade. The irony of their dramatic interpretation is revealed when the scene immediately switches to Barry's memory of the event, in which he takes careful aim at a far distant, entirely oblivious Afghani who is quite possibly a noncombatant. Instead of breaking into tears after firing the fatal long-range shot, Barry grins as his fellow Marines high-five him and chant his name as if he just scored the game-winning touchdown. By basing their interpretation of Barry's combat experience on inauthentic popular culture heuristics gleaned from melodramatic films and television shows, the acting students demonstrate that even though they may believe they have an authentic understanding of the psychological toll of combat, their understanding does not even reach the level of approximation. In a subsequent episode, "Past = Present x Future Over Yesterday" (2019), a nervous Barry, desperate to avoid owning up to a (different) war crime he committed while in Afghanistan, himself employs a popular culture heuristic, reciting the "They will never take our freedom speech" from the film *Braveheart* (1995) with the intention of leading others to believe he actually spoke those words in the heat of battle. Barry's naïve coopting of a popular culture heuristic backfires, as his media-savvy acting teacher instantly identifies the speech as being from *Braveheart* and calls Barry out on it—as much for Barry's inept delivery of the lines as for Barry's pretense. While the foolishness of allowing popular culture heuristics to shape one's understanding of reality is played for laughs in *Barry*, the consequences can be more serious in real life. For example, popular culture's fascination with violent crime has contributed to the impression that crime in the United States is much worse than the actual data indicate, resulting in fearfulness, suspicion of others, and the misallocation of resources to combat "rising" violent criminal activity even though, according to all the data, violent crime has been declining nationwide for many years. Even when confronted with the facts, people will still insist that violent crime is getting worse because popular culture has convinced them not only to feel that it is getting worse, but also to prioritize their feelings over facts.[30]

ADVERTISING AS A POPULAR CULTURE MEDIUM

Narrated in the first-person voice of an incarcerated teenage boy trapped on the bottom rungs of Britain's social and economic ladders, Alan Sillitoe's celebrated 1959 short story "The Loneliness of the Long-Distance Runner" includes the following passage about the powerful influence of advertising on the narrator's impoverished, highly dysfunctional family as they view "adverts" on their very first television, a prized possession acquired through the dubious windfall of a five hundred British pound life insurance payout upon the death of the narrator's father from throat cancer:

> Because it's surprising how quick you can get used to a different life. To begin with, the adverts on the telly had shown us how much more there was in the world to buy than we'd ever dreamed of when we'd looked into shop windows but hadn't seen all there was to see because we didn't have the money to buy

it with anyway. And the telly made all these things seem twenty times better than we'd ever thought they were. Even adverts at the cinema were cool and tame, because now we were seeing them in private at home. We used to cock our noses up at things in shops that didn't move, but suddenly we saw their real value because they jumped and glittered around the screen and had some pasty-faced tart going head over heels to get her nail-polished grabbers on to them or her lipstick lips over them, not like the crumby adverts you saw on posters or in newspapers as dead as doornails; these were flickering around loose, half-open packets and tins, making you think that all you had to do was finish opening them before they were yours.[31]

Of all the flotsam and jetsam gathered under the banner of popular culture, advertising may have the most righteous claim to the spot at the top of the pile. Like popular culture as a whole, advertising has a worldwide influence and omnipresence that is almost impossible to avoid. If an individual were to try to entirely eliminate from their life all exposure to advertising, it would mean no television, radio, films (due to product placements), newspapers, or magazines, not to mention no going online. Because advertising will be on display at most in-person events, attending concerts or sports competitions would be off limits. Unless a person lives in an extraordinarily remote location, merely stepping outside would mean exposure to display advertising on billboards, buildings, and bus stops. Traveling any distance would demand a blindfold, as both commercial and private vehicles of all sorts routinely sport decals, bumper stickers, and body wraps promoting everything from carpet cleaning services to energy drinks to the driver's favorite brand of fishing rods. And good luck finding any place where people are not openly displaying brands and logos on their clothing. In addition to it inescapable omnipresence, advertising deserves to be seen as an expression of popular culture for being, like popular culture as a whole, so purely about making a profit. Lots of profit. In 2019 media owners took in $613.9 billion in advertising revenues worldwide, and though that number dipped by about 5.8 percent in the pandemic year of 2020, it is predicted to rise to $762.76 billion by 2024.[32]

Advertising takes many forms, but if any one form can be thought of as archetypal, it is the sort of old-school, completely unironic advertisement intentionally designed to get the recipient of the message to buy (in the broadest sense of the word) whatever the advertiser is selling. Media scholar Jib Fowles (1940–2020) categorizes such advertisements, in which all the content is focused on whatever is being sold, as *simple advertisements*.[33] Simple advertisements are used to sell (in the broadest sense of the word) anything from vehicles to bottles of soda to smartphones to the promises of a candidate for political office, typically by making a convincing case for the desirability of whatever is being sold. For anyone with more than a bit of media savvy, managing simple advertisements is, well, pretty simple. *"I am/am not going to buy that brand of frozen dinner." "I am/am not going to vote for that ballot proposition." "I do/do not believe the claims about the effectiveness of that diet supplement."*

Fowles contrasts simple advertisements with the type of advertisement he classifies as *compound advertisements*:

> where, besides the commodity information, there exists noncommodity material (the symbolic elements that constitute the appeal). . . . The task of the advertisement is to get consumers to transfer the positive associations of the noncommodity material onto the commodity, so that freedom and ruggedness equal Marlboro cigarettes, and friendship equals Bud Light.[34]

Compound advertisements work by appealing to who we believe we are and, even more importantly, to who we believe we could be if only we are able to acquire whatever it is that will allow us to live fulfilled and authentic lives. As mentioned in chapter 6, the brilliantly successful "Prouder, Stronger, Better" (aka "Morning in America") advertising campaign that helped reelect Ronald Reagan in 1984 relied on compound advertisements invoking symbols of what Americans in the mid-1980s wanted to believe about themselves and their country and then neatly transferred those "symbolic elements" to what was actually being sold (i.e., "Vote for Ronald Reagan"). Similarly, while advertisements for SUVs showing a vehicle splashing through a pristine running stream in the middle of nowhere are most certainly about selling a Ford or a Jeep or a Land Rover, they are also about transferring symbols of independence, self-reliance, courage, freedom, and uniqueness to ownership of a commodity.[35] *"If I buy that vehicle, I will possess not just an SUV, but also some or all of those desirable traits."*

The advertisements described in the "The Loneliness of the Long-Distance Runner" function as simple advertisements in that they cause the story's narrator to desperately want the items being sold on the family's new "twenty-one-inch telly." But the televised images the narrator describes also function like complex advertisements as demonstrated by the narrator's naïve observations that they "had shown us how much more there was in the world to buy than we'd ever dreamed of" and how they "made all these things seem twenty times better than we'd ever thought they were." In the process of showing off material goods, the advertisements offer up symbols of an imagined life for which the narrator finds himself yearning. Yearning all the more because the advertisements make that life seem normal and expected despite being unattainable in the narrator's reality. "Because it's surprising," as the narrator observes, "how quick you can get used to a different life." That is true even when the different life is based on approximations that fall quite short of reality.

A striking example the way in which compound advertisements work by transferring symbol to product occurs in an advertisement that played during an episode of Tim Harford's *Cautionary Tales* podcast series.[36] The advertisement begins with singer-songwriter Gwen Stefani asserting, "Confidence is pretty much everything for a performer. You know, even if you have to fake it. It's everything." This is followed by women making such statements as "People can feel your confidence from a mile away" and the assurance that the beauty product company being advertised, Allergan Aesthetics, "empowers confidence" and is "inspiring a culture of confidence."

To be clear, Harford does not pick the advertisements that run on his podcasts nor is there anything inherently wrong with feeling confident. Confidence is certainly preferable to feeling either underconfident or overconfident, and for anyone who is, or has ever been, successful, some measure of confidence was likely part of the formula. But besides striking an off note in juxtaposition to the frequent lessons *Cautionary Tales* teaches about the dangers of unwarranted confidence—such as the episode "The Deadly Airship Race,"[37] which relates the story of how unwarranted confidence in a badly designed, poorly built, and recklessly overloaded airship led to a catastrophic crash—the advertisement for Allergan Aesthetics is a textbook example of attempting to sell a product by associating it with a highly abstract, if desirable, symbolic element. The advertisement talks of "inspiring a culture of confidence," but is that phrase really anything more than a bit of popular culture word salad disinviting the hearer from taking the pains to think through what, if anything, "a culture of confidence" actually signifies? And even though Gwen Stefani may claim that "Confidence is pretty much everything for a performer," it is impossible to believe that talent, practice, hard work, and possibly some degree of luck are not more important to Stefani's success than whatever amount of confidence she may very well possess. People bursting with confidence audition for reality television talent competitions all the time only to be laughed off the stage after being publicly humiliated by a meanspirited reality show judge (a stock popular culture character that has become its own trope). Regardless of its true importance to success, confidence is not something you can buy any more than you can buy any of the other ephemeral symbolic elements so dear to the heart of advertisers: freedom, sexiness, respect, attitude, swagger, uniqueness. When you stop to think about it, the idea that you can acquire a quality like uniqueness—or its near neighbor, distinction—by purchasing a product that is sold to thousands, if not millions, of other human beings is absurd. Taken to its extreme, attempting to establish a unique identity by acquiring mass-produced goods becomes a lot like saying, *"I want a tattoo that's popular with people who want to be different."*

In the confidence advertisement, the target audience is obviously women, but the same techniques are used to sell products that appeal to men. The website of the firearms manufacturer Bushmaster at one time promoted its military-style rifles via print advertisements that proclaimed "Consider Your Man Card Reissued" while also offering a related online promotion where visitors could obtain a Man Card if they "prove they're a man by answering a series of manhood questions."[38] If the idea that confidence is all a woman needs to find success and happiness is absurd, it is no more absurd than the idea that manliness is something that can be symbolized by a card issued via the website of a for-profit business. Any association between manliness and firearms ownership is, of course, popular culture fantasy. To actually purchase a firearm there is no requirement to pass any sort of manliness test, and, rather than a Man Card, the crucial card for purchasing firearms is a credit card. For anyone who may be interested in doing so, it is no longer possible to go online and obtain a Man Card from Bushmaster. The company eventually ended its print Man Card advertisements and deleted all traces of the promotion from its website, in part because of the negative publicity generated when, eleven days before Christmas 2012, a deeply disturbed young man used *his mother's* Bushmaster rifle to murder six adult staff and twenty students—ages ranging from six to seven—at an elementary school.

One effect, in some cases an intended effect, of the association of products with abstract symbols is to promote brand loyalty by creating brand rivalries among customers. Ford versus Chevy is a long-standing brand rivalry, as is Coke versus Pepsi. The technology world features a rivalry between iPhone and Android users as well as one between PC and Mac users. Sport fans can be so loyal to a favorite team that their rivalries at times turn violent. In some cases, the source of a rivalry can be not only what you consume, but where you purchase the things you consume. In 2021 there was an attempt on social media to create a rivalry among do-it-yourselfers by painting consumers who shop at Home Depot as more real and down to earth (with an unspoken suggestion of also being more politically conservative) than consumers who shop at Lowe's. For anyone not familiar with Home Depot and Lowe's, both are big-box home improvement stores that employ identical warehouse-style layouts to sell similar, if not identical, products. Setting aside the fact that many people shop at both Home Depot and Lowe's, the idea that those who shop at one are somehow fundamentally different from those who shop at the other is yet another popular culture absurdity on the same level as the idea that confidence or manliness is something that can be purchased.

A related effect of associating brand loyalty with personal identity is to transform ownership of certain iconic products into assumptions about personal identity. When you learn that someone owns a Tesla automobile, what

assumptions do you make about that person? What about the person who
owns a Bushmaster rifle? Has had cosmetic Botox injections? A degree from
an Ivy League university? A taste for $150 Fuente Fuente Opus X cigars?
What about the individual who sports a wardrobe entirely comprised of vintage clothes picked up while thrifting? Or someone whose upper arms are
covered with Maori-inspired tattoos? Along with the assumptions observers
make about the identity of owners of iconic products, individuals who own
such products may find ownership shaping their identities. A person may start
out merely purchasing a motorcycle only to eventually end up assuming—
quite possibly without initially intending to do so—the identity of a *biker*
with all the accessories, beliefs, and behaviors popular culture associates with
the biker persona. Stephen King's 1978 horror novel *Christine* tells the story
of a young man who, after purchasing a used Plymouth Fury, has his entire
identity transformed into a popular culture stereotype of the kind of person
who owns a muscle car. Stephen King being Stephen King, the impetus for
the transformation is demonic in nature, but the world is full of similar, if
not quite so dramatic, transformations in which the impetus behind changes
in personal identity are popular culture associations with the ownership of
iconic products rather than supernatural forces. The old saying is, "You are
what you eat." In a popular culture world heavily influenced by compound
advertisements, it may be more correct to say, "You are what you own."

IS IT POSSIBLE TO LIVE AUTHENTICALLY IN A POPULAR CULTURE WORLD?

"Whicker's World," an episode from the third series of the *Monty Python
Flying Circus* television series, includes a skit entitled, "Mrs. Premise and
Mrs. Conclusion Visit Jean-Paul Sartre."[39] In the skit Mrs. Premise, played
by John Cleese (1939–), and Mrs. Conclusion, played by Graham Chapman
(1941–1989) get into a philosophical debate while visiting a laundromat and
conclude the only way to settle their dispute is to make a phone call to the
home French existentialist philosopher Jean-Paul Sartre. Learning that Jean-
Paul is not available at the moment, Mrs. Premise inquires of Madame Sartre,
"When will he be free?" Her question sets up a punchline in the form of an
aside to Mrs. Conclusion, who, like the viewer, can hear only one side of the
call: "She says he's spent the last sixty years trying to work that one out."
 The opening chapter of this book describes the existentialist concept of
authenticity, the goal of which is to make choices in life that are true to one's
genuine self as opposed to a living a life of *bad faith* that follows a path laid
out for you by others. For an existentialist like Sartre, freedom is essential,

as authenticity cannot exist without freedom. Even if you do not embrace existentialism as a philosophy (and many people do not), there are at least two fundamental principles for living an authentic life that, regardless of philosophy or creed, are close to universal. The first of these is the principle that individuals have some level of free will to make choices, while the second is the principle that individuals may be held to some extent accountable for the choices they make. For anyone who wants to live authentically, the question is, *"How do I live an authentic life while emersed in the inescapable, ever-deepening waters of popular culture?"*

Being able to recognize popular culture heuristics when you see them is one way to live more authentically. This means understanding that heuristics can come from both entertainment and nonentertainment outlets of popular culture, often exerting their influence on how we think without our being aware of it. For example, the popular culture of the United States is especially obsessed with the concept of freedom, though the national obsession does not necessarily translate into the level of thoughtfulness about the nature of freedom exhibited by, say, a French existentialist philosopher. American politicians love to go on and on about freedom, usually focusing on the ways they are in favor of it while their opponents are not. Lyrics about freedom turn up in popular culture songs ranging from Civil Rights anthems to country songs advocating flag-waving patriotism to straight-up love songs. In popular culture storytelling, fighting for freedom is frequently used as an iron-clad justification for violence on the part of the story's protagonists. *"It's okay for Luke to kill everyone on the Death Star because, you know, freedom."* Taking a cue from popular culture, the politically sensitive code name for the 2003 U.S. invasion of Iraqi was "Operation Iraqi Freedom," while the fighting in Afghanistan was code named "Operation Enduring Freedom." The aforementioned historical epic *Braveheart*, winner of an Academy Award for Best Picture of the Year, depicts William Wallace (circa 1270–1305) lecturing the Scottish army about freedom and ends with him bellowing a drawn-out cry of "Freeeeeeeee-dom" in his death scene. While *Braveheart* may offer up some memorable moments of drama, it is unlikely a thirteenth-century Scottish nobleman would have had anything to say about the concept of freedom that would resonate at any level with freedom as understood by the sort of present-day individual who considers *Braveheart* to be an outstanding example of inspirational filmmaking.

The point is that, even though popular culture makes a lot of noise about freedom, it has little of substance to say on the subject. Advertisers frequently associate possessing the thing being advertised with being free, or even imply that the act of purchasing it serves as tangible proof that the purchaser is free, but owning a product no more bestows freedom than being exposed to symbols associated with freedom bestows freedom. Everywhere yet imperceptible ("This Is Water"), the mass of popular culture heuristics pointing in the approximate direction of freedom function as a kind of cultural chaff, making it nearly impossible for individuals to distinguish genuine freedom from the kind of false freedom cooked up to sell cars, clothing, and candidates. While it is true that humans have always struggled over questions of freedom and the challenges of living an authentic life, the task has been made more difficult by a relentless popular culture industry amplified by the power of digital technology to the point of being all but inescapable.

Ironically enough, even while heuristics undermine the individual's pursuit of an authentic identity and authentic freedom, popular culture repeatedly stresses the importance of being true to your authentic identity. Think about how frequently you encounter inspirational popular culture messages along the lines of: *"Most of all, be true to yourself." "Don't live your life according to the expectations of others." "Follow your heart." "Live your best life."* While being true to yourself is pretty much the definition of living an authentic life, it is important to remember that poster-worthy popular culture aphorisms are among the shallowest and most inauthentic of the entirety of popular culture's massed-produced output. Inspirational popular culture reminders about being true to yourself serve only to further confuse anyone attempting to actually live an authentic life; in the end, these messages are not all that different from a beer advertisement that, after doing its best to convince you to drink beer and lots of it, takes a final two seconds to remind you to "drink responsibly."

THE LIMITS OF POPULAR CULTURE'S INFLUENCE

Popular culture exerts a powerful influence, but it is not as if all members of humanity are total slaves to popular culture any more than they are total slaves to propaganda. Just as human beings are capable, at least some of the time, of identifying propaganda when they see it, they are, at least some of the time, capable of recognizing the difference between popular culture fantasy and fact-based reality. Though the power of popular culture to influence individual decisions and shape identity is strong, its influence is in competition with many other forces, including family dynamics, economics circumstance, social pressures, and—perhaps most of all—genetics. Just consider the genetically determined human tendency to be either righthanded or lefthanded, a trait humans share with no other species, including our closest primate relatives. About 90 percent of humans are righthanded, a statistic that holds true for humans regardless of all other factors, including race, culture, and historical time period. About the only exceptions to strongly favoring one hand over the other are the relatively small number of individuals genetically disposed to be ambidextrous and the even smaller number of people who successfully train themselves to favor their nondominant hand, as seen in the uncommon example of major league baseball player Pablo Sandoval, a natural lefthander who taught himself how to throw equally well with his right hand.[40] Despite strong pressures favoring righthandedness—including taboos against left-handedness imposed by some cultures and the fact that most tools, equipment, furniture, sporting gear, and musical instruments are designed for righthanded users—few people are able to switch from left- to righthandedness.[41] The genetics of handedness are just too strong to be overcome by other influences, including that of popular culture.

MEET THE LINDA LINDAS

Imagine the following scenario. In early 1963, a music-loving teenaged American military dependent is living with her family at R.A.F. Sculthorpe in Norfolk, United Kingdom. As a special treat for her seventeenth birthday, this teenager's father drives his daughter and her two closest school friends the one hundred miles to Mansfield in Nottinghamshire so the girls can attend the February 23, 1963, performance of the Helen Shapiro Tour. The fourth-billed act on the Helen Shapiro Tour is the Beatles, a rock and roll band from Liverpool that is becoming popular among young people in the United Kingdom. While her two friends enjoy the performance well enough, the birthday girl is completely swept away by the music and charisma of the Beatles. A typical teenager, she is just dying to let *everybody* know about this amazing new band. She tells other American friends back at Sculthorpe about the Beatles. She writes letters to a few friends back in the States, but she has only so many friends to write to and, besides, there is no way to share the sights and sounds of a Beatles performance in a letter. She would love to make a phone call to her favorite cousin back in the States and tell her all about the Beatles. Maybe play for that cousin her newly purchased "Love Me Do" forty-five. But overseas long-distance phone calls are just too expensive to allow such extravagances. She has the desire, but lacks the means, to spread the word about the Beatles.

For Beatlemania to explode on the U.S. scene, it was going to take a lot more than their being stumbled upon by the odd young American living abroad. It was going to take time and money. The Beatles had first started to become known after establishing a local Liverpool fanbase that eventually spread around the United Kingdom and even made its way into parts of Continental Europe following the band's club appearances in Hamburg, West Germany. The Beatles soon became popular enough to sign on with an entrepreneurial young manager named Brian Epstein (1934–1967), which led to a recording contract with EMI Records, which in turn led to the band being teamed up with a genius recording engineer named George Martin (1926–2016). Thanks to their growing popularity in the United Kingdom and Europe, by the end of 1963 the Beatles were able to acquire the financial backing necessary to test the potentially lucrative waters of the United States, a country where the Beatles were not well known prior to their arrival there on February 7, 1964. The first mention of the Beatles in the *New York Times* did not appear until November 4, 1963, and many of the early reports on the Beatles were not flattering, as reflected in a *New York Times* headline dated December 26, 1963: "Liverpool Cellar Clubs Rock to Beat Groups: Long-Haired Youths with Guitars Take Charge as Cult."[42] The Beatles did manage to get some American radio airplay in advance of the official U.S. release of their recordings, which had been initially scheduled for early 1964. Using a British recording hand carried from the United Kingdom by a flight attendant, a Washington, DC, disc jockey named Carroll James generated a groundswell of local interest in the Beatles after playing "I Want to Hold Your Hand" during a broadcast on December 17, 1963.[43] As word of mouth was slowly spreading in the United States, the Beatles' American label, Capitol Records, took affirmative steps to ensure the Beatles would come to the attention of the broader American public, signing the band to appearances on the influential *Ed Sullivan Show* while investing a record fifty thousand dollars (equivalent to about $440,000 in 2021) into aggressively promoting the Beatles before most Americans had heard so much as one note from George Harrison's gently weeping guitar.[44] Capitol Record's advertising dollars proved to be well spent. Several thousand enthusiastic fans were on hand when the band landed at John F. Kennedy Airport, and the Beatles' appearances on the *Ed Sullivan Show* turned out to be screaming successes on par with Elvis Presley's appearances seven years earlier. In a span of a just few weeks, all of America was aware that John, Paul, George, and Ringo had arrived and were staking out a very large claim on the popular culture map.

That was how it worked in the time before social media became the most important engine for the spread of popular culture. It hardly needs to be said that things have changed since the 1960s. On May 4, 2021, an all-girl punk rock band called the Linda Lindas performed a set at the Los Angeles Public Library.[45] After the library posted a video of the Linda Lindas' performance, the band's song "Racist, Sexist Boy" went viral. Less than three weeks later, the Linda Lindas had a contract with Epitaph Records even though the band members, whose ages at the time ranged from ten to sixteen, were too young to sign a legal contract on their own behalf. By June 2021, a Google search of "Linda Lindas" (with quotation marks) returned about 2,850,000 results. While the Linda Lindas' performance at the Los Angeles Public Library was their big viral break, it was not as if the band had materialized entirely out of nowhere. Before playing the L.A. Public Library, the Linda Lindas had opened for the punk band Bikini Kill, written and performed their song "The Claudia Kishi Club" for a Netflix documentary of the same name, and recorded songs for the comedy film *MOXiE!* Even so, the lift required to propel the Linda Lindas to fame in 2021 was much, much less than what was required to transform the Beatles from a local club band into international superstars. Nobody had to fly the Linda Lindas across an ocean or invest over four hundred thousand dollars in a promotional campaign in order to make millions of people in the United States and abroad suddenly aware of their existence. In a world with social media, it is not possible for any phenomenon with any potential for popular culture success to remain undiscovered for long. It does not matter if that phenomenon is taking place in a dark club in Liverpool. A brightly lit public library in Los Angeles. A subway station in Seoul. A leased art space in Oakland, California . . . or Oakland, Nova Scotia. Or, quite possibly, at a remote compound full of angry armed men. Not everything that becomes a popular culture success is as benign as a quartet of young people armed with nothing more dangerous than two guitars, a bass, and a drum set.

By the time you read these words, the Linda Lindas may be as forgotten as the Deadbeats or the Spitfire Boys. Or more popular than the Beatles, who themselves were, according to John Lennon (1940–1980), "More Popular Than Jesus." Though Lennon's infamous remark is remembered for setting off a massive cancel culture reaction in the United States, it is illustrative to point out that a reaction that would have taken minutes to catch fire in the era of social media took much longer to manifest in that earlier time. Lennon's remark was first published in the *London Evening Standard* on March 4, 1966, but it was not until July 1966 that expressions of outrage were given voice by American Christians triggered by Lennon's sacrilegious comparison.[46] If a twenty-first-century celebrity such as Lady Gaga or Post Malone were to say anything nearly as controversial as what Lennon said in 1966, the popular reaction would be instantaneous. In a world equipped with a global, always on, real-time feedback loop, there is no delaying either popular approval or popular approbation.

Prior to social media, there were always buffers delaying the feedback loop between the creators and distributors of popular culture and those who consume it. An Elizabethan audience might cheer or boo a new play at the Globe Theatre, but it took time for word of mouth to spread the audience reaction beyond the perimeter of the playhouse. Even after the advent of large-circulation newspapers and electronic communications such as the telegraph, telephone, radio, and television, such buffers as professional reviewers, publishers, record companies, and broadcasters stood between the creators and distributors of popular culture and the voices that comprise the popular culture feedback loop. In 1960, if a new western-themed television series laid an egg, it took time for Nielsen rating numbers and published reviews to make it clear that the series was unpopular with fans and critics. Compare that to what happened on May 12, 2019, the night "The Bells," the penultimate episode of *Game of Thrones*, premiered. There was no need to wait for the reviews of professional television critics to know that the episode had laid a giant dragon's egg with most viewers. Before Kings Landing had gone up in flames, thousands of *Game of Thrones* fans were roasting the episode on social media, as were a number of professional critics. The flattening of the feedback loop to real time, or close to it, has done more than give a voice to millions who were once voiceless. It has coopted all those instantly sounded, unbuffered, and largely unfiltered voices and turned them into an essential part of the popular culture money-making machine. The instant public feedback loop has become a source of online entertainment (and profits) in the much same way that the adolescent girls who screamed as the Fab Four played the *Ed Sullivan Show* and Shea Stadium were part of the entertainment (and profits) to be extracted from Beatlemaina. For *Game of Thrones* fans, part of the fun of watching the premier of "The Bells" was not only watching the episode, but also following the real-time social media responses and contributing their own voices to the social media conversation, often in the hope that their contributions would elicit responses from others. The trolls, stans, influencers, snarkers, comedians, and haters are all part of the online spectacle, creating fresh, traffic-boosting content at no cost to the social media platforms themselves. No wonder the owners of social media are so reluctant to censor any of the voices, no matter how extreme or untruthful. Those voices are bitcoin in the bank.

POPULAR CULTURE AND THE CREATION
OF THE POST-TRUTH CULTURE

Not everything that is part of the post-truth culture is entirely new. Lying, propaganda, advertising, and other ways of misusing information to manipulate people have been around since long before there was a cyberspace. There are, however, two new and notable manifestations of a digitally amplified popular culture exerting powerful influences on the post-truth culture.

The first manifestation takes the form of popular culture heuristics—their unprecedented numbers; the speed at which they are created, delivered, and endlessly repeated; and the appeal their approximations of reality hold for a world beset with more information that anyone can process at anything more than a superficial level. The facile approximations of popular culture heuristics fall very much in line with the concept of the Gutenberg Parenthesis in which a post-literal culture is "moving from the rationality accompanied by the printed book to an altogether different way of processing, characterized by interactivity and much faster pace."[47]

The second manifestation is the flattening of the feedback loop to near real time. The harnessing of feedback to the speed and power of digital data analysis has become a boon to marketers of everything from automobiles to entertainment to political messages, allowing the fine-tuning of advertisements at a speed and with a personally targeted accuracy previously unimaginable. The flattened feedback loop has already been misused to manipulate perceptions of public opinion, as when a mob of haters review-bombs Rotten Tomatoes to downvote a film most of the mob has not seen; even more concerning is the truly frightening potential of machine learning and artificial intelligence to influence genuine public opinion through the creation of waves of manufactured, inauthentic public opinion: *"If so many people think that way, then maybe it is not such a bad idea after all?"*

Imagine popular culture as a prism in the shape of an equilateral triangle. The three equal sides of the prism are made up of the three basic elements of popular culture: power, profit, and celebrity. These three elements, as judged by the standards of popular culture, are not only equivalent, but also as inseparable as the sides of a physical prism. This prism serves as an ideal medium through which the post-truth culture is projected because it is a medium in which truth is filtered out unless, by sheer coincidence, truth happens to contribute to the attainment of power, profit, or celebrity. Donald Trump's performative tweets figured into his *power* as president of the United States, but whether the content of those tweets was true or not true did not matter as long as they touched a popular nerve and, in so doing, generated a large popular response. It did not matter if that response was positive or negative just as long as it was large enough to demonstrate that the person sending those tweets, Donald Trump, was in possession of power. Similarly, in the context of *profit*, truth plays no indispensable role. Profit, in the digital world, is driven by advertising. "Senator, we run ads."[48] Truth factors into advertising only as it impacts the effectiveness of an advertisement, with the ultimate measure of effectiveness being profit (or, for noncommercial advertisements, profit's popular culture equivalents of fame and power). If a product advertisement can generate profit by convincing women that confidence is everything or by convincing men that owning a rifle makes them masters of manliness, whether those symbolic associations are true or not true matters not at all. The third side of the prism, *celebrity*, shares with the other two sides a, at best, tangential relationship with truth. The list of celebrities whose backstories are all or in part fictional is long. When the Beatles were being promoted in the United States, the truth that John Lennon was both married and a father was kept under wraps out of fear that the truth would lessen Lennon's appeal to young female fans and damage the Beatles popular culture image. For a similar present-day example, the true origins of industry-plant musical acts are covered up to make them appear to have arisen organically, to seem authentically indie rather than inauthentically industrial. There are cases in which the revelation of the truth turns celebrity to infamy, but infamy does not always equal disgrace and failure in the post-truth culture. There are far more examples of individuals and groups who thrive despite, or even because of, infamy than those whose careers are actually taken down by accusations (truthful of not) of wrongdoing. In the post-truth culture, when the reputation of a celebrity comes under attack it has become common for the celebrity to lay claim to being a put upon victim of a cancel culture vendetta, a strategy that can actually serve to boost the celebrity's popularity in the eyes of fans who see such attacks as both a badge of honor and a validation of the celebrity's iconoclastic authenticity. The career of publicly disgraced comedian Louis C.K. was declared "tanked" when information about his sexual misconduct surfaced in 2018, but by 2020 he was again filling theaters, gleefully and defiantly making jokes about his sexual misconduct and the impact of being called out for it.[49]

Truth and facts do not matter, or at least matter less, in the post-truth culture because the post-truth culture is the creation of an ever-more powerful, digitally amplified popular culture in which truth is not a factor in the pursuit of popular culture's three-in-one brass ring of profit/power/celebrity. By the standards of popular culture, grabbing the ring without the benefit of truth is absolutely the same, and equally as good, as grabbing it with the benefit of truth. This conclusion, if true, leaves open the question of how to evolve beyond a post-truth culture to a new cultural orientation in which truth and facts matter, or at least matter more. Technology itself may offer a way out via the creation of better tools for managing information overload and making sense of what information is credible and what is not. The problems with turning to technology for a solution are that (1) such technology will come to exist only if there is money to be made from it and (2) history shows that any technology that can be used for good can be used for evil. If artificial intelligence can be used to free humanity from the quagmire of the post-truth culture, it can also be turned against humanity to keep us in darkness, quite possibly without anyone fully realizing that a smooth technological trick has been played. There is always the danger that the fundamental social changes wrought by digital technology will ultimately, and possibly already have, become as imperceptible to humans as water is to fish. Another possible pathway out of a world in which truth and facts have been rendered largely toothless is for popular culture to lose much of its current influence and, as it collapses on itself, take down the post-truth culture with it. This will happen only if popular culture were to become much less profitable than it currently is, a circumstance that, while possible, is hard to imagine in light of decades of incredible growth for the popular culture industry.

The most hopeful view of the situation is to remember that popular culture is a human creation over which humans, ultimately, exert complete control. Popular culture is powerful, but it is not an uncontrollable force of nature, not a volcanic caldera waiting to explode or a giant meteor streaking straight toward the planet. Ultimately, it lies in the hands of human beings to decide what limits, if any, there are on the influence of popular culture. If humanity is able to survive the next few decades of technological change and, in particular, to not be taken down by either some unintended or unforeseen consequence of artificial intelligence or by the deliberate weaponization of information, the people of the world may be able to get a better handle than they currently have on digital technology and the social and cognitive disruptions brought on by unprecedented change.

NOTES

1. Alan Clark, *The Donkeys* (New York: Morrow, 1962).

2. Barbara W. Tuchman, *The Guns of August* (New York: Macmillan, 1962).

3. Fredrik Logevall and Kenneth Osgood, "The Ghost of Munich: America's Appeasement Complex," *World Affairs* 173, no. 2 (August 2010): 13–26.

4. Robert C. Self, *Neville Chamberlain: A Biography* (Aldershot, England: Ashgate Publishing, Ltd., 2006), 270.

5. Self, 332–33.

6. Boris Johnson, *The Churchill Factor: How One Man Made History* (New York: Riverhead Books, 2014).

7. "A&E Television Networks: Company Report" (Dun & Bradstreet, 2020), https://www.dnb.com/business-directory/company-profiles.ae_television_networks_llc.d0b74af0b7dc556be2f4041e8860a58e.html.

8. David Foster Wallace, "This Is Water," *Farnam Street*, April 28, 2012.

9. Noam Chomsky, "Let's Stay Chummy, Chomsky," interview by Pat Kane, June 27, 1997, https://www.independent.co.uk/news/media/let-s-stay-chummy -chomsky-1257575.html.

10. Stuart Gillespie and Neil Rhodes, eds., *Shakespeare and Elizabethan Popular Culture* (London: Arden Shakespeare, 2006), 2–3.

11. Thomas Hine, *The Rise and Fall of the American Teenager* (New York: Bard, 1999), 4-5.

12. Frank A Fasick, "On the 'Invention' of Adolescence," *The Journal of Early Adolescence* 14, no. 1 (1994): 10–18.

13. Gary R. Edgerton, *The Columbia History of American Television* (New York: Columbia University Press, 2007), 188.

14. Maury Brown, "Record 114.4 Million Watch Super Bowl XLIX, Making It Most-Watched TV Program In U.S. History," *Forbes*, February 2, 2015, https://www.forbes.com/sites/maurybrown/2015/02/02/record-114-4-million-watched-patriots-seahawks-in-super-bowl-xlix-smash-last-years-by-2-2-million/.

15. Edgerton, 188.

16. Statista, "Entertainment and Media Industry Market Size," *Statista*, accessed April 12, 2021, https://www.statista.com/statistics/237749/value-of-the-global-entertainment-and-media-market/.

17. Hillary Hoffower, "What Is J.K. Rowling's Net Worth? Here's How She Spends Her Fortune," *Business Insider*, June 18, 2020, https://www.businessinsider.com/jk-rowling-net-worth-spending-harry-potter-2020-6.

18. Zack O'Malley Greenburg and Rob LaFranco, "The Celebrity 100: The World's Highest-Paid Celebrities 2020," *Forbes*, accessed April 25, 2021, https://www.forbes.com/celebrities/.

19. Facebook Investor Relations, "Facebook Reports Fourth Quarter and Full Year 2020 Results," *Facebook Investor Relations*, January 27, 2021, https://investor.fb.com/investor-news/press-release-details/2021/Facebook-Reports-Fourth-Quarter-and-Full-Year-2020-Results/default.aspx.

20. Laura Forman, "Netflix's Black Mirror; While the Latest Season of 'Stranger Things' Commanded a Captive Audience, Netflix's Latest Earnings Release Was Largely Disenchanting," *Wall Street Journal (Online)*, July 18, 2019.

21. Kurt Badenhausen, "The World's Most Valuable Sports Teams 2020," *Forbes*, accessed April 17, 2021, https://www.forbes.com/sites/kurtbadenhausen/2020/07/31/the-worlds-most-valuable-sports-teams-2020/.

22. TV Tropes, "Welcome to TV Tropes! / Administrivia," *TV Tropes*, accessed May 12, 2021, https://tvtropes.org/pmwiki/pmwiki.php/Administrivia/WelcomeToTVTropes.

23. Brian Palmer, "Why Do Rappers Hold Their Guns Sideways?" *Slate Magazine*, December 14, 2009, https://slate.com/news-and-politics/2009/12/why-do-rappers-hold-their-guns-sideways.html.

24. Steve Cocheo and Bill Streeter, "Wells Fargo Unveils New Logo to Rebuild Its Battered Brand," *The Financial Brand*, February 4, 2019, https://thefinancialbrand.com/80290/wells-fargo-logo-rebrand/.

25. MirandaWarning.org, "Are Police Required to Read Miranda Rights?" *MirandaWarning.org*, 2021, http://www.mirandawarning.org/arepolicerequiredtoreadmirandarights.html.

26. Jonathan J. Koehler and Shiquan Liu, "Fingerprint Error Rate on Close Non-Matches," *Journal of Forensic Sciences* 66, no. 1 (2021): 132.

27. Saul M. Kassin et al., "Police-Induced Confessions: Risk Factors and Recommendations," *Law and Human Behavior* 34, no. 1 (February 2010): 4–5.

28. Paulie Boutlis, "A Theory of Postmodern Advertising," *International Journal of Advertising* 19, no. 1 (January 2000): 3–23.

29. Seth Stevenson, "Was 'We Try Harder' the Most Brilliant Ad Slogan of the 20th Century?" *Slate Magazine*, August 12, 2013, https://slate.com/business/2013/08/hertz-vs-avis-advertising-wars-how-an-ad-firm-made-a-virtue-out-of-second-place.html.

30. Ethan Siegel, "Newt Gingrich Exemplifies Just How Unscientific America Is," *Forbes*, August 5, 2016, https://www.forbes.com/sites/startswithabang/2016/08/05/newt-gingrich-exemplifies-just-how-unscientific-america-is/.

31. Alan Sillitoe, "The Loneliness of the Long-Distance Runner," in *The Loneliness of the Long-Distance Runner* (London: W.H. Allen, 1959), 21–22.

32. A. Guttman, "Global Advertising Spending 2019," *Statista*, accessed May 6, 2021, https://www.statista.com/statistics/236943/global-advertising-spending/.

33. Jib Fowles, *Advertising and Popular Culture* (Thousand Oaks, CA: Sage Publications, 1996), 11.

34. Fowles, 11.

35. In terms of both environmental damage and potential damage to an expensive piece of machinery, there is almost nothing worse you can do with a vehicle than drive it through a running stream, pristine or not.

36. Tim Harford, "The Rogue Dressed as a Captain," *Cautionary Tales*, accessed March 7, 2021, https://timharford.com/2019/11/cautionary-tales-ep-2-the-rogue-dressed-as-a-captain/.

37. Tim Harford, "The Deadly Airship Race," *Cautionary Tales*, accessed May 28, 2021, https://timharford.com/2019/11/cautionary-tales-ep-4-the-deadly-airship-race/.

38. Douglas Kellner, "The Sandy Hook Slaughter and Copy Cat Killers in a Media Celebrity Society: Analyses and Plans for Action," *Logos* 12, no. 1 (2013).

39. Ian MacNaughton, "Mrs. Premise and Mrs. Conclusion Visit Jean-Paul Sartre," *Monty Python's Flying Circus* (London, England: BBC, October 19, 1972).

40. Matt Monagan, "Pablo Sandoval Pitched a Perfect Inning, but Even More Shocking, He Could've Done the Same Thing Left-Handed," *MLB.com*, April 30, 2019, https://www.mlb.com/cut4/pablo-sandoval-can-pitch-left-handed-c274571398.

41. V. S. Ramachandran, "V. Cultural and Environmental Influences on Handedness," in *Encyclopedia of the Human Brain* (Elsevier Science and Technology, 2002).

42. "Liverpool Cellar Clubs Rock to Beat Groups: Long-Haired Youths with Guitars Take Charge as Cult," *New York Times*, December 26, 1963, 34.

43. Claudia Levy, "Deejay Carroll James Dies; First to Play Beatles in U.S.," *The Washington Post*, March 28, 1997, B, 4:1.

44. Ian Inglis, "'The Beatles Are Coming!' Conjecture and Conviction in the Myth of Kennedy, America, and the Beatles," *Popular Music and Society* 24, no. 2 (June 2000): 103.

45. Los Angeles Public Library, *TEENtastic Tuesdays: AAPI Heritage Month Kick-off with The Linda Lindas*, 2021, https://www.youtube.com/watch?v=3msSlr4PkDE.

46. Mark Sullivan, "'More Popular Than Jesus': The Beatles and the Religious Far Right," *Popular Music* 6, no. 3 (October 1987): 313–26.

47. Lars Ole Sauerberg, "The Gutenberg Parenthesis—Print, Book and Cognition," *Orbis Litterarum* 64, no. 2 (April 2009): 79.

48. Facebook, Social Media Privacy, and the Use and Abuse of Data, § Senate Hearing 115-683, Committee on Commerce, Science, and Transportation United States Senate and the Committee on the Judiciary United States Senate (2018), 21, https://www.govinfo.gov/content/pkg/CHRG-115shrg37801/html/CHRG-115shrg37801.htm.

49. Elahe Izadi, "Louis C.K.'s Sexual Misconduct Tanked His Career. Now He's Selling out Theaters," *Washington Post*, March 11, 2020, https://www.washingtonpost.com/arts-entertainment/2020/03/11/louis-ck-new-standup/.

BIBLIOGRAPHY

"A&E Television Networks: Company Report." Dun & Bradstreet, 2020. https://www.dnb.com/business-directory/company-profiles.ae_television_networks_llc.d0b74af0b7dc556be2f4041e8860a58e.html.

Badenhausen, Kurt. "The World's Most Valuable Sports Teams 2020." *Forbes.* Accessed April 17, 2021, https://www.forbes.com/sites/kurtbadenhausen/2020/07/31/the-worlds-most-valuable-sports-teams-2020/.

Brown, Maury. "Record 114.4 Million Watch Super Bowl XLIX, Making It Most-Watched TV Program in U.S. History." *Forbes*, February 2, 2015. https://www.forbes.com/sites/maurybrown/2015/02/02/record-114-4-million-watched-patriots-seahawks-in-super-bowl-xlix-smash-last-years-by-2-2-million/.

Boutlis, Paulie. "A Theory of Postmodern Advertising." *International Journal of Advertising* 19, no. 1 (January 2000): 3–23.

Chomsky, Noam. "Let's Stay Chummy, Chomsky." Interview by Pat Kane, June 27, 1997. https://www.independent.co.uk/news/media/let-s-stay-chummy-chomsky-1257575.html.

Clark, Alan. *The Donkeys*. New York: Morrow, 1962.

Clinch, Matt. "Around Half the World's Population Tuned in to This Year's Soccer World Cup." *CNBC*, December 21, 2018. https://www.cnbc.com/2018/12/21/world-cup-2018-half-the-worlds-population-tuned-in-to-this-years-soccer-tournament.html.

Cocheo, Steve, and Bill Streeter. "Wells Fargo Unveils New Logo to Rebuild Its Battered Brand." *The Financial Brand*, February 4, 2019. https://thefinancialbrand.com/80290/wells-fargo-logo-rebrand/.

Edgerton, Gary R. *The Columbia History of American Television*. New York: Columbia University Press, 2007.

Facebook Investor Relations. "Facebook Reports Fourth Quarter and Full Year 2020 Results." *Facebook Investor Relations*, January 27, 2021. https://investor.fb.com/

investor-news/press-release-details/2021/Facebook-Reports-Fourth-Quarter-and
-Full-Year-2020-Results/default.aspx.

Facebook, Social Media Privacy, and the Use and Abuse of Data, Pub. L. No. Senate Hearing 115-683, § Committee on Commerce, Science, and Transportation United States Senate and the Committee on the Judiciary United States Senate (2018). https://www.govinfo.gov/content/pkg/CHRG-115shrg37801/html/CHRG-115shrg37801.htm.

Fasick, Frank A. "On the 'Invention' of Adolescence." *The Journal of Early Adolescence* 14, no. 1 (1994): 6–23.

Forman, Laura. "Netflix's Black Mirror; While the Latest Season of 'Stranger Things' Commanded a Captive Audience, Netflix's Latest Earnings Release Was Largely Disenchanting." *Wall Street Journal (Online)*. July 18, 2019.

Fowles, Jib. *Advertising and Popular Culture*. Thousand Oaks, CA: Sage Publications, 1996.

Gillespie, Stuart, and Neil Rhodes, eds. *Shakespeare and Elizabethan Popular Culture*. London: Arden Shakespeare, 2006.

Guttman, A. "Global Advertising Spending 2019." *Statista*. Accessed May 6, 2021, https://www.statista.com/statistics/236943/global-advertising-spending/.

Harford, Tim. "The Deadly Airship Race." *Cautionary Tales*. Accessed May 28, 2021, https://timharford.com/2019/11/cautionary-tales-ep-4-the-deadly-airship-race/.

Harford, Tim. "The Rogue Dressed as a Captain." *Cautionary Tales*. Accessed March 7, 2021, https://timharford.com/2019/11/cautionary-tales-ep-2-the-rogue-dressed-as-a-captain/.

Hine, Thomas. *The Rise and Fall of the American Teenager*. New York: Bard, 1999.

Hoffower, Hillary. "What Is J.K. Rowling's Net Worth? Here's How She Spends Her Fortune." *Business Insider*, June 18, 2020. https://www.businessinsider.com/jk-rowling-net-worth-spending-harry-potter-2020-6.

Inglis, Ian. "'The Beatles Are Coming!' Conjecture and Conviction in the Myth of Kennedy, America, and the Beatles." *Popular Music and Society* 24, no. 2 (June 2000): 93–108.

Izadi, Elahe. "Louis C.K.'s Sexual Misconduct Tanked His Career. Now He's Selling out Theaters." *Washington Post*, March 11, 2020. https://www.washingtonpost.com/arts-entertainment/2020/03/11/louis-ck-new-standup/.

Johnson, Boris. *The Churchill Factor: How One Man Made History*. New York: Riverhead Books, 2014.

Kassin, Saul M., Steven A. Drizin, Thomas Grisso, Gisli H. Gudjonsson, Richard A. Leo, and Allison D. Redlich. "Police-Induced Confessions: Risk Factors and Recommendations." *Law and Human Behavior* 34, no. 1 (February 2010): 3–38.

Kellner, Douglas. "The Sandy Hook Slaughter and Copy Cat Killers in a Media Celebrity Society: Analyses and Plans for Action." *Logos* 12, no. 1 (2013).

Koehler, Jonathan J., and Shiquan Liu. "Fingerprint Error Rate on Close Non-Matches." *Journal of Forensic Sciences* 66, no. 1 (2021): 129–34.

Levy, Claudia. "Deejay Carroll James Dies; First to Play Beatles in U.S." *The Washington Post*. March 28, 1997.

"Liverpool Cellar Clubs Rock to Beat Groups: Long-Haired Youths with Guitars Take Charge as Cult." *New York Times*, December 26, 1963.

Logevall, Fredrik, and Kenneth Osgood. "The Ghost of Munich: America's Appeasement Complex." *World Affairs* 173, no. 2 (August 2010): 13–26.

Los Angeles Public Library. *TEENtastic Tuesdays: AAPI Heritage Month Kick-off with The Linda Lindas*, 2021. https://www.youtube.com/watch?v=3msSlr4PkDE.

MacNaughton, Ian. "Mrs. Premise and Mrs. Conclusion Visit Jean-Paul Sartre." *Monty Python's Flying Circus*. London, England: BBC, October 19, 1972.

MirandaWarning.org. "Are Police Required to Read Miranda Rights?" *MirandaWarning.org*, 2021. http://www.mirandawarning.org/arepolicerequiredtoread-mirandarights.html.

Monagan, Matt. "Pablo Sandoval Pitched a Perfect Inning, but Even More Shocking, He Could've Done the Same Thing Left-Handed." *MLB.com*, April 30, 2019. https://www.mlb.com/cut4/pablo-sandoval-can-pitch-left-handed-c274571398.

O'Malley Greenburg, Zack, and Rob LaFranco. "The Celebrity 100: The World's Highest-Paid Celebrities 2020." *Forbes*. Accessed April 25, 2021, https://www.forbes.com/celebrities/.

Palmer, Brian. "Why Do Rappers Hold Their Guns Sideways?" *Slate Magazine*, December 14, 2009. https://slate.com/news-and-politics/2009/12/why-do-rappers-hold-their-guns-sideways.html.

Ramachandran, V. S. "V. Cultural and Environmental Influences on Handedness." In *Encyclopedia of the Human Brain*. Elsevier Science and Technology, 2002.

Sauerberg, Lars Ole. "The Gutenberg Parenthesis—Print, Book and Cognition." *Orbis Litterarum* 64, no. 2 (April 2009): 79–80.

Self, Robert C. *Neville Chamberlain: A Biography*. Aldershot, England: Ashgate Publishing, Ltd., 2006.

Siegel, Ethan. "Newt Gingrich Exemplifies Just How Unscientific America Is." *Forbes*, August 5, 2016. https://www.forbes.com/sites/startswithabang/2016/08/05/newt-gingrich-exemplifies-just-how-unscientific-america-is/.

Sillitoe, Alan. "The Loneliness of the Long-Distance Runner." In *The Loneliness of the Long-Distance Runner*, 7–54. London: W.H. Allen, 1959.

Statista. "Entertainment and Media Industry Market Size." *Statista*. Accessed April 12, 2021, https://www.statista.com/statistics/237749/value-of-the-global-entertainment-and-media-market/.

Stevenson, Seth. "Was 'We Try Harder' the Most Brilliant Ad Slogan of the 20th Century?" *Slate Magazine*, August 12, 2013. https://slate.com/business/2013/08/hertz-vs-avis-advertising-wars-how-an-ad-firm-made-a-virtue-out-of-second-place.html.

Sullivan, Mark. "'More Popular Than Jesus': The Beatles and the Religious Far Right." *Popular Music* 6, no. 3 (October 1987): 313–26.

Tuchman, Barbara W. *The Guns of August*. New York: Macmillan, 1962.

TV Tropes. "Welcome to TV Tropes! / Administrivia." *TV Tropes*. Accessed May 12, 2021, https://tvtropes.org/pmwiki/pmwiki.php/Administrivia/WelcomeToTVTropes.

Wallace, David Foster. "This Is Water." *Farnam Street*, April 28, 2012. https://fs.blog/2012/04/david-foster-wallace-this-is-water/.

Index

About the Author

Donald A. Barclay has worked as an academic librarian since 1990, holding positions at New Mexico State University, the University of Houston, the Texas Medical Center, and the University of California, Merced. He has been at UC Merced since 2002 and currently holds the position of Deputy University Librarian. He has authored numerous articles and books over the course of his career on topics ranging from the literature of the American West, to children's literature, to library and information science. His book *Fake News, Propaganda, and Plain Old Lies: How to Find Trustworthy Information in the Digital Age*, was published by Rowman & Littlefield in June 2018.

He earned his bachelor's degree from Boise State University and holds masters' degrees in both English and Library and Information Science from the University of California, Berkeley. Prior to working as a librarian, he spent ten seasons working as a wildland fire fighter, most of that time as a member of a U.S. Forest Service Hotshot Crew.

He lives in Merced, California with his wife Caroline and three daughters—Mary Tess, Emily, and Alexandra.